IN SUNSHINE
AND IN SHADOW

IN SUNSHINE
AND IN SHADOW

Geoff Cope and Yorkshire cricket

Stephen Chalke

FAIRFIELD BOOKS

Fairfield Books
17 George's Road, Bath BA1 6EY
Tel 01225-335813

First published 2017

ISBN 978 0 9568511 9 2

Printed and bound in Great Britain by
CPI Antony Rowe, Bumpers Way, Chippenham SN14 6LH

Contents

Geoff bowling at Lord's, July 1970

Introduction

There has probably never been a more genial or better-liked player ever to come into the dressing room than Geoff Cope, and he absolutely loved playing cricket. This was infectious and made him popular amongst a very wide section of our followers. It always seemed to me that, if there were 20,000 watching us, 19,500 were personal friends of G. Cope.

John Hampshire

This is the story of a boy, born in the aftermath of war in Leeds, who dreamed of playing cricket for Yorkshire and fulfilled his dream. In the long, hot summer of 1976 he was the leading wicket-taker in the country. He was selected for two overseas tours and played three Tests for England. Then in later life, after a successful career in the paper trade, he joined the committee of Yorkshire County Cricket Club and was a pivotal figure in rescuing the club from impending bankruptcy. On the field and off it, his has been a life of great achievement.

That has been the sunshine, but there has also been shadow. Geoff's life has been one in which he has had to deal with more than his share of adversity. Twice, during his playing career, his bowling action was deemed to be illegal and, without clear guidance where the fault lay, he underwent months of reconstructive work away from the county game he loved. Then, after his playing days, he was diagnosed with retinitis pigmentosa, a condition that in time cost him his job and is gradually, year by year, reducing his field of vision till one day he will be completely blind.

These are setbacks that would test the most resilient of us, and there was a spell after he lost his job that Geoff fell into the dark pit of depression. Helped by family and friends, he emerged in time to be a crucial part of Yorkshire cricket's revival. He was a founder member of the four-man board that saved the county from going into administration; and even now, along with his guide dog, he can be found on every match day, entertaining the visitors in the Hawke Suite.

Entertaining visitors, providing hospitality – it is a perfect job for Geoff. Warm and convivial, full of banter, he is at his happiest when surrounded by people, and his fund of stories is seemingly endless. I have been there on match days, and I have seen it at first hand. When he tells a tale, he has that rare gift that he can bring it alive, make the listeners feel that they are there where it is happening, that they know the characters.

The idea for this book came from Scyld Berry of the *Daily Telegraph*. A session with Geoff, hearing his tales of Wilfred Rhodes and Johnny Wardle, convinced him that here was testimony that had to be preserved. He rang me with the idea, and I had no hesitation in saying yes. "I'd love to work with him," I said.

The book has been created from long hours with Geoff, when he has taken me through his life – all the ups and downs, the characters he has known, the special moments that have stayed in the memory. There has been plenty of laughter and, occasionally, some tears. We have had some wonderful days.

At all these sessions we have been joined by Ron Deaton, whose knowledge of Yorkshire cricket past and present has helped to ensure that the book has stayed faithful to known facts. Ron's enthusiastic involvement in the project, as with his role in my book with Bob Appleyard, has helped me greatly.

We have received important support from Geoff's friend David Warner, who for many years was cricket correspondent of the *Bradford Telegraph and Argus* and now edits the county's yearbook. He has provided invaluable insights into the events both of Geoff's playing days and of his time on the committee and the board. I am also grateful to Geoff's friend John Helm for reading the manuscript and making helpful suggestions.

Above all, I thank June for looking after me so well on my visits to their house. Geoff has been lucky in his marriage, and undoubtedly that has been a factor in his getting through the hard times in his life.

Two of my visits have coincided with evening football matches at Halifax Town, where Geoff and his guide dog Lester are the joint Vice Presidents, and I must thank the directors for making me so welcome. It is a club with a great sense of community, and that suits Geoff well. He knows everybody, from the players to the gatemen, and he talks to them all, spreading good cheer.

He could be sorry for himself about his near-blindness; he could be bitter about his two suspensions from bowling. He knows that. But he is determined not to be. To date, he has raised more than £200,000 for the Guide Dogs for the Blind Association. And he has told me the story of his life as honestly as he can.

Geoff is a gifted story-teller. He has a good memory, he reads people and situations well, and he can bring characters alive, spicing his stories with atmospheric dialogue. He is not frightened of emotion, he has a lovely sense of humour and, above all, he has an enduring love of the game of cricket at all its levels. So I have tried throughout the book to reproduce his voice as he speaks – not, as in ghosted autobiographies, to invent words for him. In the laying out of the text I have made clear where he is speaking and where I am providing the linking passages.

Geoff Cope may not be a household name in the same league as Fred Trueman and Geoffrey Boycott, but he has a story worth telling – and he tells it well. I hope you enjoy reading it as much as I have enjoyed writing it.

Stephen Chalke
Bath, June 2017

1

Yorkshire may well be looking towards this lad

1957

It was the biggest day yet in the ten-year-old Geoffrey Cope's sporting life. The final of the Sheldon Trophy for junior schools in Leeds: Manston Church of England School against Upper Wortley. On Saturday 20 July 1957. At the Arthur Thornton Sports Ground off the Dewsbury Road in south Leeds.

Sixty years on, Geoff can still recall the build-up to the day.

> There had been a lot of rain, and matches kept getting postponed. It finished up that we had to play the quarter, the semi and the final on the Thursday, Friday and Saturday, with the last day of the school term on the Friday. Then we had one more match in the league to play on the following Monday.

These were not 20-over matches with a soft ball, with every fielder bowling two overs. They were 'proper' cricket, and the details survive in the exercise book in which his Manston teacher, Ken Fletcher, kept the score – an exercise book that remains among Geoff's most prized possessions.

Thursday 18 July at Parkside
Middleton 39 (Cope 4-6 in 7.2 overs) Manston 40-8 (Cope 15)

Friday 19 July at the Leeds Police ground
Headingley 74 (Cope 2-19 in 8 overs) Manston 76-7 (Cope 35*)

Geoff was not yet in the top year of junior school, but long evenings of cricket and football in the park gave him plenty of stamina for these games. He batted at number three, and he bowled his off-spin first change.

> They were four o'clock starts, after school, and in the Headingley game there were 59 overs. The game on Saturday was a two o'clock start, but two of our key players were away, starting their family holidays, so I finished up opening the bowling.

Geoff was an only child, and among the spectators were his parents. His father, John Lister Cope, was a little man who had been nicknamed 'Tiny Tim' during his wartime service in the RAF.

> I used to laugh that he drove a mini by looking through the steering wheel. But he'd been a good footballer before the war, an old-fashioned inside forward in a local team that won everything and broke all the

records. He had the opportunity to go down to Arsenal, to see if he could make it as a professional, but he thought it was too much of a gamble. So he joined his uncle's French polishing business.

He was an excellent pianist. He loved his piano; he spent a lot of time at home on it. And he was always being asked to play when we visited friends. He was the deputy organist at Harehills Lane Methodist Chapel for 47 years. They had organists now and then, but invariably they didn't stay too long, so it was always down to Dad as the deputy. He tended to swing the hymns; he was a bit of a rebel. I'd often go down with him when he practised. "I'm just going to have a play on the organ. Do you want to come?" And off we went. He would rattle out Eddie Calvert's *Oh Mein Papa* and all sorts. We used to have a good laugh.

He had a fabulous sense of humour. Often the chapel would do a pantomime or a show, and Dad would always be one of the leads: an Ugly Sister, that sort of role. He would get them all cracking to learn their lines, yet he never learned his own. He just came on and did it. When I was about seven, I was sat in the front row and he was doing Widow Twankey, and they brought on the old wringing machine. It was in the script that somebody would push him and his hands would go through the wringer. Well, of course, he started crying, and I shot out of my seat, round the back and onto the stage, shouting: "Stop, that's my dad."

In those days your entertainment was basically your own doing.

Our house had a brick wall and, when I was small, I used to sit on the wall waiting for Dad to come round the corner. I'd go greet him and not give him a chance hardly to take his coat off before we had to be playing football or cricket. One of my old friends there said, "We used to play down the drive, but Copey used half the road as well because that's where 22 yards measured out." Where the kerb was, you could see where I'd gone through the tarmacadam with my footmarks. Dad would say, "Come on then, we'll play twenty minutes before tea. And you've got to give your all. No messing about, we're going to do it properly. I'm not letting you bat unless you get me out. And you're not going to let me bat if you're batting." If he felt I was starting to act a bit – trying out a legger or something – he'd say, "What's that for? Come on. Properly." He was very good that way.

He'd never taken the risk himself with his football or his music so he spent his time encouraging me. He did once say to me, "Look, I've gone through life, saying IF. It's the wrong way to go. But I've made my bed, and I'm going to make it work."

Born on 1 January 1911, he married Geoff's mother Marjorie shortly before the outbreak of war in 1939. Geoff did not arrive till 23 February 1947 but, though he was an only child, their semi-detached redbrick house in Manston Crescent was always crowded:

> After six months of their marriage, Dad's Dad came to live with them. Grandad Cope had a cholostomy amongst other things, and they gave him two years to live. And he died at 90. So Mum and Dad's life, from Mum saying "He can stay with us", was spent all that time looking after him. Also, when I was young, Mum's Mum, Grandma Morris, was burgled by a next-door neighbour. By the time we got down to York Road, near Harehills, all I can remember is Grandma sitting there in her coat, with her hat on, a suitcase packed. She said to my Dad, "You've looked after your father all these years, you can look after me."
>
> Through my growing-up years Mum and Dad had the front bedroom, Grandad had the back bedroom, I had the box room, and the lounge downstairs was converted to Grandma's bedroom. So if I was bringing home friends and I took them in the front room, Grandma's bed was there.
>
> Grandad was very deaf. And, if you had friends, after five minutes the door would open. "There's no rush but, if you tell me what time you're thinking of going, I'll make sure you don't miss your buses." Grandma was a mini-Peggy Mount. She was noisy, she would say what she felt. "Don't speak to me like that because you don't speak to your father like that." And likewise Mum would catch it. Mum and Dad would say, "I know it's hard for you, Geoffrey, but you shouldn't interfere."
>
> It was not an easy childhood. But it was a childhood where Mum and Dad gave their lives looking after their parents and looking after me. I never suffered – because of the love that they gave to me.

Geoff's mother had none of the interest in sport that his father had, but she came with him to the matches. And on that day at the Arthur Thornton Ground, she was there, knitting away as Geoff took the field.

> Mum was taller than Dad. She enjoyed her dancing very much. From the pictures I have she was very thin when she was younger, but she became a bigger lady, well-made, not fat but solid and strong.
>
> She did her own baking. There were times when life was financially a major struggle, but Mum and Dad never wanted that to be known; they always went out with a smile. And they got on with what was necessary. I'm not saying we were on the breadline, we weren't poor and in rags, but we didn't have luxuries.

Every time I went out to play cricket, I played in clean gear, I played in smart gear. When I came home from football, she immediately washed everything. She insisted on Friday night that I dried and polished my boots; she even went as far as washing the laces. If I'd left a pair of shorts in my bag, and I brought them out all creased for the Saturday match, she'd say, "Where did you have those? Why didn't you pull them out? You'll never do that again."

She was a magic lady. She was loving, she was caring, everything you want a mum to be.

John and Marjorie Cope on their wedding day, 1939

Manston School, half a mile from Geoff's house, took its sport seriously. The headmaster, Ernest Smelt, had played top club cricket in the county of Durham, and nothing was ever too much trouble for Ken Fletcher, the master in charge of the football and cricket teams.

It was always going to be sport for me. I loved it. When I was nine, I started going to Manston Park with the older boys, playing football and cricket. Then when I got to ten we used to spend four nights a week there with Mr Fletcher, Monday to Thursday. Then on Friday night you got your kit ready for Saturday.

In winter we would literally run from school to the park and we'd get half an hour's football in. Then, when it got too dark, Mr Fletcher used to walk us round as a unit, dropping each child off at his home.

In summer we went down to the cricket pitch, and we played till six o'clock, by which time parents were coming to collect. If they didn't, Mr Fletcher made sure that we got home all right.

I'd dash home, gulp my tea down and run straight back to the park. Mum and Dad would say, "We want you back at eight." But that's when the mischief came in because there were two gates and we'd station one lad on each, on parent guard. So, if Dad was seen coming to the top gate, they'd come and shout "Geoff" and you'd shoot out of the bottom gate, run home and be in bed before he got back. We were all in it. Just the mischief of the time. I think Mum and Dad were happy. There were quite a few times when they said, "Come on, we mean it", but I think equally they were glad that they knew where I was and they knew who I was with.

The area of grass in the corner was the best pitch we could find. We used to look after that. When it was a bit damp, we used to turn the stumps on their side and roll them with our feet, on the area where we were going to bat. It was our place, where we belonged.

We knew the chap who looked after the park, and he knew us all by our Christian names. We helped him and his two assistants when there were things going on. There were a lot of bushes, a lot of flowering areas. They took it in turns to sit in a little office and take the bookings for bowls and tennis. You felt secure. You were in a place where you knew everybody and they knew you.

There was a chap called Mr Shaw, in his 70s, who lived round the corner from the park. Every time we went to practise, he came and watched. When we got to the final of the cricket, we took him on the bus with us. He got so much pleasure being a part of it.

13

It was Ken Fletcher who inspired them, but he was not a technical coach, not one who demonstrated to them how to bat and bowl.

> He was always making sure that everybody got a chance. I remember batting in the park one day, and he said to me, "You know, I've never seen anybody at your age play through the off-side so often." I suppose very early on there was a correctness about trying to bat properly, but I have no recollection of him ever saying to me "Do this" or "Do that".
>
> At football he was this guy on the touchline bellowing away. His motivational skills were superb. We conceded a goal against Coldcotes once, and I got a bit of a knock, a knee that was starting to bleed. So I was sat there in the mud, and he came over. "Do you want them to think you're soft? You're my centre-half, come on." Right, I thought, and I picked myself up. He'd shout and bawl: "Get stuck in." All this carry-on. He was kicking every ball that was played for the whole of the twenty minutes each way. His half-time talks were absolutely inspirational.
>
> "He's a good man," Dad said. "He's doing you good."
>
> We had playing with us a couple of lads, Chris and Peter Holley. They were the sons of Tom Holley, the old centre-half who played for Leeds United for years, and Big Tom used to stand in the park and watch us. We all knew he'd played for Leeds so we were looking to catch on every word he said. I remember him once saying, "Geoff, you do remind me a lot of me. You get stuck in. But you listen to Mr Fletcher. If I'd ever had a manager like him, I'd have been a good player." And suddenly, because he said that, Mr Fletcher went up yet another notch.

For Geoff, Manston was a family school, and never was that more evident than that Saturday afternoon of the Sheldon Trophy final. There among the spectators was Mr Smelt the headmaster, with his kindly discipline:

> He prided himself of knowing within a fortnight every child by his Christian name. People would call me Geoff, and he would say, "His name is Geoffrey. That's how his mother had him christened, that's what we should call him."

There was Mr Fletcher, brimming with excitement. There were Geoff's Mum and Dad and all the parents. And Mr Shaw from Manston Park. They watched as Geoff opened the bowling against Upper Wortley. The ball-by-ball record of what followed is recorded neatly in Mr Fletcher's exercise book:

Upper Wortley 53 all out
Cope 16.1 overs, 2 maidens, 26 runs, 10 wickets

Mr Fletcher came dashing on with a tear down his cheek. My Dad with his little legs was a bit behind and he was full of it, giving me hugs and doing all sorts, and he said, "Come and see your mother." And he took me over to my mum who, like many of the ladies, was watching the match from a deck chair, doing her knit one, purl one.

"What's all this fuss about?" she said.

"Don't you realise? He's just taken all ten wickets."

Mum never dropped a stitch, never batted an eyelid. She just looked up and said, "But what about number eleven?"

That typified Mum. She never quite grasped what it was all about. But she never, never dropped the standards that she set. And those standards were very, very high. She made sure that, as far as she was concerned, I looked the best person on the pitch. That love was there.

At this stage Geoff had seen little first-class cricket. Yorkshire played only three county matches each summer in Leeds, and the matches rarely occurred when he was free. But he does recall his first trip to Headingley, when he was taken by a neighbour one Saturday in the summer of 1955. Though he did not know it, it would turn out to be Len Hutton's last appearance on the ground, only a fortnight before chronic lumbago forced the great man's retirement.

The only thing I can remember of that day and of Len Hutton is that they used to have a little, white fence that was about a foot high that went all around the ground, about two yards behind the boundary rope, and we were allowed to sit on the grass up to this fence. And Len Hutton fielded in front of me. He was, I imagine, deep square leg. As the ball came to him, he stopped it with his foot, held his back and threw it to the fielder who had run towards him. I went home, thinking, "They're saying all this about this fellow Hutton, and he can't even bend."

Geoff may have seen little first-class cricket, but he was a Yorkshire boy and he already knew what he wanted from his life.

Since I realised I could think a bit, I wanted to play for Yorkshire. Even in that schools final, Ron Yeomans wrote a little piece in the *Yorkshire Post*: LEEDS BOY, 10, TAKES ALL 10. The last sentence was, "Who knows? Some time in the future Yorkshire may well be looking towards this lad." It was a sentence that stayed with me.

The afternoon's triumph did not end with his ten wickets, though:

Manston 55 for five (Cope 36*)

The cup itself was huge. It was such a size that Micky Miller, our little wicket-keeper, could sit in it. We'd had all this cricket for three days, a lot of overs bowled in terms of nine-, ten-, eleven-year-olds. And all I can remember at the end of bowling 16 overs and batting almost the whole innings was running round the pitch to our mums and dads as if we were at Wembley, carrying this cup around with little Micky chasing after us. We were all just laughing. There was no thought of tiredness.

I look at the modern game now and I think, "Are they still on soft ball at this age?" More importantly they're restricted to three or four overs. At the end of it, it didn't do me any harm. You were young, you were fit, you wanted to do it.

July 1957. The rationing of Geoff's early years was over, and life in Britain was moving on. Half of all households now owned television sets, the first motorway – a bypass around Preston – was under construction, while British European Airways were advertising direct flights to 'the unspoiled coast of the little-known Costa Blanca'.

Late in the afternoon of that July Saturday, as Geoff and his team-mates were celebrating victory, the Prime Minister Harold Macmillan was speaking of his concern about the pace at which life was changing. "Let us be frank about it," he said. "Most of our people have never had it so good. Go around the country, go to the industrial towns, go to the farms, and you will see a state of prosperity such as we have never had in my lifetime – nor indeed ever in the history of this country. What is beginning to worry some of us is, is it too good to be true? – or perhaps I should say, is it too good to last?"

Manston played again on Monday afternoon, against Halton Moor. Once more Geoff hit the top score, with 36, as they clinched the league-and-cup double.

There was only one year in 25 when Manston didn't win anything at football or cricket, and on numerous occasions they did the 'double double': league and cup, football and cricket. For years I went back to the school on a regular basis because I loved seeing the people. I'd go to Ken Fletcher in September, and I'd say to him, "What have we got for this season?"

"I don't know, Geoff, it won't be as good as last year. Do you remember that tall lad who could catch a bit? Well, I'll have him as my goalkeeper. And you know so-and-so, he's a daft lad, isn't he? He's big enough, he can be my centre-half. So-and-so is a bit quick, he'll be my centre-forward. As for the rest, I don't know what I've got." They'd end up Played 12, Won 11, Drawn 1. And in the final. And it was the same with the cricket. "I haven't got this, and I haven't got that." And they'd still come away with something.

Twenty-five years of success. John Morgan in the *Evening Post* had got together with Rothmans, and he had this monthly award for sporting achievement. I rang him and I said, "Does Ken Fletcher qualify?" "Qualify?" he said. "He wins it."

By the corner of the park was a pub, and we arranged with the landlord to make the presentation there. Ken knew nothing about it. I got the word around, and we ended up with people from Inverness, from Devon, from Norfolk, from you name it, all pupils who'd played under Mr Fletcher. That was the easy bit. The harder task was getting Mr Fletcher to the pub because he never drank. He had a wife and four children, he only lived over the road, and somehow we got them to bring him across. As he approached, we heard him saying, "What are we doing? I've never been in here in my life."

He came through the door, and he just stood there. It was the most wonderful sight of all because he wasn't in his own environment, yet he looked round and he knew everybody. He knew every name: "What are you doing here, Tom? I thought you lived down in so-and-so." He had no idea why we were there. And finally John Morgan and the Rothmans team came in. They presented him with this lovely silver salver, and he celebrated – he had an orange juice. It was just so worthy of somebody who had given so much to so many.

He's dead now. He was in a wheelchair, in his 93rd year, and we got him to Headingley. His daughter Margaret and son Frank brought him. We took him up in the lift to the Long Room. He was looking down – and he took hold of me and he said, "It's a long way from Manston Park, isn't it?" There was a tear coming down his cheek.

Margaret said, "Thanks, Geoff, you've got through."

"It isn't a question of getting through," I said. "It should have happened years ago."

The great eye-opener for Geoff came when he was in his late teens, starting out on his career as a Yorkshire cricketer.

Dad got out this photograph of the football team he'd played in when he was young. They'd played 42 games, won something like 37 and drawn five, and the goals they'd scored were frightening.

Dad was sitting to the left of the captain, and standing on one side of the team was a chap in an overcoat, a scarf and a pair of wellies, holding a book. And it was Mr Fletcher. Dad said, "He had not an ounce of co-ordination in him. He couldn't stand on one leg and kick with the other. Yet you believed in every word he said. And he inspired you to where you've got today."

Manston School Cricket team, 1957
left to right (standing); Mr Ernest Smelt, Mr Ken Fletcher
back room: Hirst, Atkinson, Burrows, Butler, Baines, Littlewood, Martin
front row: Richardson, Miller, Carr (captain), Cope, Bartle, Halstead

Pride of his side

MAY I respectfully draw the attention of Yorkshire cricket selectors to the remarkable feat achieved by 10-year-old Geoffrey Cope, of Cross Gates, Leeds, on Saturday? Our county team of the future may be glad of him.

Playing for Manston Church of England School team he took all 10 wickets for 26 runs against Upper Wortley County Primary School and then went on to knock up 36 not out in Manston's winning total of 55 runs for five wickets.

The victory gave Manston the Sheldon Trophy, awarded for the first time in a knock-out competition open to all junior school teams in Leeds.

Leeds boy (10) takes all 10 wickets for 26

GEOFFREY COPE, a 10-year-old pupil of Manston Church of England School, performed the feat of taking all 10 wickets in a school's final.

Playing for Manston against Upper Wortley in the final of the Sheldon Trophy competition at the Arthur Thornton ground Geoffrey took 10 wickets for 26 runs in 16 overs, and then scored 33 not out for his side. Manston made 55 for five wickets and won by five wickets.

A master at the school said today that Geoffrey bowled off-spinners which considering his age, where remarkably well controlled.

Manston v Upper Wortley

1	C. Richardson 21	caught	b Marshall	3
2	A. Baines 14 11	bowled	Hall	7
3	G. Cope 41412122114 1114221		no	36
4	B. Bartle 1	caught	b Marshall	1
5	S. Carr	b	Jones	0
6	M. Miller	b	Baldridge	0
7	K. Butler 1		no	1
8	D. Halstead			
9	D. Jack			
10	R. Burrow			
11	D. Littlewood			

Byes 2 11
N ball 11   for 5 wkts 55

Wkts	1	2	3	4	5	6	7	8	9	10
Runs	2	12	31	43	44					

Catches Bart
Stumping 11,

		R
Holmes		16
Marshall	W	21
Jones		8
Baldridge		3

Byes 2 111
N Ball 1

Halstead   11-5-10-0
Cope
Burrow   10-6-8-0
Carr   2-1-1-0
Cope   16-1-2-26-10
Leg Byes 2
Byes 114

Wkts	1	2		4	5	6	7	8	9	10
Runs	0	18	18	36	40	43	49	53	53	

Mr Fletcher's notebook
Opening batsman Alan Baines' son Nick is a member of the Kaiser Chiefs

A BIG THRILL for three schoolboys at Manston Church of England School, Cross Gates, Leeds, came when England cricket captain, Mr. Peter May, visited them during his day in Leeds.

The boys are the three remaining members of last year's school cricket team which won the Sheldon Trophy (shown in picture) for the Leeds junior school teams knock-out competition and also their district league competition.

The boys are (left to right): David Halstead (11), Manston Grove; Keith Butler (10), Sandiford Terrace; and Geoffrey Cope (10), Manston Crescent. Also in the picture is Mr. Ernest Smelt, the headmaster, who is a keen cricketer with the Leeds Zingari Club in the Yorkshire Council.

2

THE Headingley?

1958-1963

It was the summer of 1958 when Geoff played his first game of adult cricket. Eleven years old, he had just left Manston School when late one Saturday morning the headmaster Ernest Smelt parked his car outside their house.

> "Mrs Cope," he said. "Is Geoffrey busy? I wonder if you'd allow him to come and play cricket this afternoon." She said, "I thought school had finished." "School has finished," he said. "This is with my men's team." "But, Mr Smelt, he's only eleven." "Mrs Cope, you brought him to me at four and a half, and I've looked after him ever since. And I will continue to do so." She said, "I'm not sure."
>
> "Oh, Mum, let me, let me," I pleaded. And Dad said, "He's in good hands." There was a discussion, and I was allowed to go.

Geoff climbed into Mr Smelt's Morris Minor estate, and off they went to the James Ives Sports Ground in Yeadon. The James Ives Woollen Mill has long closed, the sports field is now housing, but the memories of that afternoon remain with Geoff.

> It was a tie at 102 runs each. I had to sit next to Mr Smelt when we were batting, and he talked to me all the time about the game.
>
> I went in at number seven. They got me kitted up. I took my first few strides, and they said, "Geoffrey, Geoffrey, just a minute. Have you got a box?" "What's a box?" "Here, you'd better have one." It was a tense match, but they told me just to go out and play. I batted for a while, then I got out, but I can't tell you what I did or I didn't do. I was just part of it. Part of a team.
>
> It was three years before I realised they went for a drink afterwards – because Mr Smelt would pick me up in the morning in his Morris shooting-brake, then run me home straight after the match.

The team was the second eleven of Leeds Zingari, a club created in the early 1930s as a wandering side playing friendly cricket. By this time it was running two Saturday league sides, the first team in the Yorkshire Council League, the second in the Dales Council League. Ernest Smelt was the leading run-scorer in the club's history, but he was now in his late 40s, a stalwart of the second eleven alongside Norman England, a lecturer at Leeds Polytechnic, and the sons of the club President Jack Walkington, the former Hunslet and Great Britain rugby player. Geoff played with them every Saturday for the rest of that summer.

Mr England was the wicket-keeper. He used to come as a family with his wife Maureen and their lovely daughter Judith who was our scorer, and they adopted me. When I was bowling, he would come up to me, take a glove off, put his hand in his pocket and say, "I've got some Polo mints here. If you spin one this over, Geoffrey, I'll give you one." Well, I used to rip my fingers off.

If anything needed saying, it was always left to Mr Smelt. If I lapsed in the field Norman England would say, "I think we'd better just have a word here" – and Mr Smelt would come over: "Look, I know it's a long afternoon, Geoffrey, but you've got to concentrate."

"Come on, have a bowl," Mr Smelt said to me. "I'll set a field for you. You just bowl as if you're at school, only at the other end is somebody a bit bigger. If you bowl it as far up as you do to a boy, it will be a lot nearer to him so you've got to pull it back that little bit. Make him come forward and try to drive you." He put men out. If I went for four, he'd just come up to me, "Come on, we're all right, we're doing well."

I played for them when I was 12 and 13, and I started playing in the Yorkshire Council team sometimes. They were a happy lot, a good crew to be with. A chap called Arthur Swallow was the captain, and another guy called Ted Brooks. They were the two elder statesmen of the side. "When you go in to bat, Geoff," they'd say, "you just play as you play." There was no question of pushing me to speed things up; the rest of them looked after that. And I wasn't there to make up the fielding. I was given a chance to bowl and to bat.

I played one game at Arthington, and I bowled 19 overs, one for 73. And I thought I'd been hit for a thousand. But they clapped me off, saying, "That was a wonderful piece of bowling." I said, "But why?" "Why, Geoff? Because they haven't scored at four an over off you, and what have they scored off the rest of us? You've done well."

All I got, the whole time I played with Leeds Zingari, was encouragement. Nothing else.

Geoff's football also advanced, to the point where he was playing as a half-back for Leeds City Boys, but his progress was blighted by the headmaster at his grammar school, Temple Moor. It was a new school, only two years old when the eleven-year-old Geoff arrived, and he was not happy there. Cricket was not as important as it had been at Manston. The square was not yet fit for use, nobody offered any coaching and the games lessons in summer concentrated more on athletics. Worse, the winter terms were split between rugby and soccer, and the headmaster's preference was clear.

He said we were a grammar school, we should be playing rugby, not going off playing soccer, so he stopped me playing for City Boys. The education officer from Leeds went up, my dad went up, but this fellow wouldn't budge. I said, if that's the case, I don't want to do rugby, I'll do cross-country. So they made me do cross-country. If the run on Saturday was in the morning, I'd finish in the first three or four and get off to a football game. But if it was in the afternoon, I just took my time going round. It was the wrong attitude, I know, but it was an attitude created by a headmaster who would go against the wishes of Leeds Education Authority. School became an unhappy place.

With little cricket at school, he tried to join the Under-18 section of the Whitkirk Club, down the road from his school, but the man in charge, Ralph Pritchard, was not impressed by what he saw of Geoff's ability.

He suggested that I should go down to Crossgates and join them. I said, "But they're not as good as you up here." He said, "I think you'll have more chance there." "So you don't want me to come back?" "No." I cried all down the hill from Whitkirk, all the way home, because I'd been rejected.

When I went to Crossgates Cricket Club, Mr Smelt said I was to ask for Albert Hirst, the local cobbler. "You're only young," Mr Hirst said. "This is the men's team. Who's sent you?" "Mr Smelt from Manston." "Put your shoes on. You'll bowl in that net then. If Mr Smelt said you were to come, that's good enough for me." So I was allowed to practise at Crossgates.

A few years later, when Geoff was playing for the Yorkshire second eleven, he returned to Whitkirk, playing against them in a Sunday friendly. The home team fielded several juniors and, when they came in to bat, Geoff continued to bowl as competitively as he could, sending the boys back to the pavilion in quick succession and ending the game early. Ralph Pritchard, who was umpiring, was not impressed.

"I'm disappointed, Geoff," he said. "I thought you'd have given the youngsters a chance."

"I've given them the chance you gave me," I said. "By doing what you did, you hardened me up, and it made me even more determined to succeed."

Geoff's great step up the ladder came when his father took him to buy a new bat at the sports shop run by Billy Sutcliffe, who had captained Yorkshire for two years in the 1950s.

Geoff, aged about 14, in the back garden

I was feeling this bat and he said, "What are you looking for?"

I told him about the bat I'd used at junior school, the Herbert Sutcliffe Three Rose. I got all my runs with it, it was a belter. The weight was lovely.

He said, "Come on, let's talk about bats." And he was brilliant. He got me the perfect bat. And then he said, "Where do you play your cricket?"

I said, "Leeds Zingari. We don't do an awful lot at school."

"Go up to Headingley," he said.

"Where?"

"The cricket ground at Headingley."

"*THE* Headingley?"

"Yes. And there'll be a little man with a flat cap and a mac on, called Gerry McConniff. Say to him that I sent you, and I want to encourage you to play for the juniors."

Sure enough, I went up there, and I started playing for the juniors. I played Under-18 cricket at Headingley during the week, and at the weekend I played for Leeds Zingari.

At that time, with Yorkshire playing so little at Headingley, the ground was the home of Leeds Cricket Club, with a secretary Bill Carter who was also secretary of the rugby league club. The following summer, when Geoff's performances for the junior side were being noticed, he got a phone call from the secretary, asking him to play on Saturday for the Leeds 'Freelance' side, the second eleven. He was due to play for the Leeds Zingari first team, but Bill Carter pressed his case, telling him that the Freelance side were playing a higher standard of cricket. It was time for him to move on up. Not knowing what to do, Geoff rang Mr Smelt.

"I've been waiting for this phone call for a while," he said. "We'll go up to Headingley tomorrow and meet Mr Carter."

He took me up, and he spoke to Bill Carter. I'll never forget it.

"This young man," he said, "was a talented cricketer at my junior school, and we've looked after him in senior cricket. There's no doubt that he's going to play at a good level, and there's no doubt that he's got to play at a standard above Leeds Zingari. But you need my consent to say he can leave Leeds Zingari. I won't give that unless I know three things. One, that he's not playing in a one-off game because you're short this week. Two, that there's someone there of an age that can look after him, encourage him. And three, that he gets an opportunity to bat and bowl; he's not just making up the numbers. If you're happy to give me your word on those three things, then I think it's right that he should play for Leeds. But if you break any promises, I'll be on you like a ton of bricks."

Bill looked at him, and he said, "I take it you were his headmaster, Mr Smelt."

"I was."

"If you'll allow me to make a couple of phone calls, you can sit with me here and hear what's being said." So Bill made the phone calls, and sure enough the answer came back: "We will guarantee Geoff cricket till the end of the season. Don Forsyth, the Freelance captain, has promised to look after him." Then he passed on a message from Johnny Schofield, the team's slow bowler, saying, "I'll teach him everything I know" – which was lovely, because Scholey never spun a ball in his life.

So suddenly I was in among another decent set of lads. And I was playing at Headingley.

The Leeds club's professional was Johnny Lawrence, the former Somerset all-rounder who ran a cricket school in a specially built shed in his garden. Geoff had been there with Leeds Zingari, and he started to go more often.

It was three bus rides: into Leeds, out to Rothwell, then a little bus down a dark country lane. The shed had two nets and a changing facility at the back. He'd say, "What are you doing on Tuesday? Well, if you want to come and bowl for the afternoon, I've got one or two lads." He'd be having a private session, and he'd want somebody to bowl. Then, when he'd got me there to bowl for him, he went and charged me half price!

I liked Johnny. He'd got a lovely smile. He was a bit of a one-off. I sat the MCC Coaching Award there when I was 17.

Then there was the schools representative cricket: Leeds, Yorkshire, both of which he captained, the North of England and in August 1962, when he was 15 years old, a two-day game at Hastings for England Schools against G.H. Doggart's XI, a team drawn from the public schools.

The public school side included two future Test cricketers, Graham Roope and Roger Tolchard, as well as John Hutton, Len's younger son. In the England Schools team were Pat Pocock (later of Surrey and England), Graham Johnson (Kent) and three from Yorkshire: the Sheffielder Andy Burgin, who went on to play football for Halifax Town, and – despite not being much of a cricket school – two from Temple Moor, David Bradbury and Geoff.

Every county sent a representative to watch except Yorkshire; the expenses were probably a bit high so they didn't see it fit to go.

David Bradbury
(left) and Geoff

Afterwards I had several approaches from counties who wanted to take me for trials – but in those days they had to get permission first from Yorkshire. These letters came in, and there were quite a few. It woke Yorkshire up to think, "We'd better have a look at him."

I was excited, Yorkshire were showing an interest, but the nets did not start till after Christmas. I was coming up to 16 years old, still at school, and that winter of 62/3 was a terrible one. I had to catch a tram from Crossgates into the centre of Leeds, then a bus up to Headingley. I was carrying a cricket bag, and there was several inches of snow on the ground. I could see everybody looking at me, thinking "You must be mad."

The winter of 1962/3 was the harshest of the century. Snow fell on Boxing Day, and it did not melt till March. The third round of the FA Cup was scheduled for Saturday 5 January, yet it was not till the evening of Wednesday 6 March, nearly nine weeks later, that Leeds United got to play their home tie against Stoke City. The pitch was a quagmire, Stoke chose not to play the 48-year-old Stanley Matthews, and Leeds won 3-1.

The winter of 1962/3. The British and French agreed to start work on a supersonic aircraft, the BBC announced plans to create a second channel, and surgeons at Leeds General Infirmary presented to the world a Sheffield businessman, Peter Lucas, who two months earlier had received a kidney from a dead man and was now taking regular walks around the city. In so much of life there was a sense of newness, a spirit of hope.

Geoff was filled with hope and with excitement as he arrived for his first net with Yorkshire County Cricket Club. It was his first encounter with the club's two 60-year-old coaches: Arthur Booth, the slow-left-arm bowler who had topped the national averages at the age of 43 in 1946, and the no-nonsense Arthur 'Ticker' Mitchell, a leading batsman in the great Yorkshire side of the 1930s, Head Coach since 1945.

> At about six o'clock we went into the Cricket School, the Shed, by the old bowling green where the current East Stand is. We were there for an hour and a half, an hour and three-quarters, on the coldest of nights, and there was no heating, no nothing.
>
> There were these two old chaps: 'Ticker' Mitchell, with heavy-creped cotton Oxford shoes, immaculate whites, three sweaters on, a silk scarf round his neck, the county horse-blanket blazer, his county cap – and his walking stick. And at the side of him was Arthur Booth, a little man, also in whites, with his county sweaters and blazer on.
>
> By about half past seven a lad had got so cold his hands had gone blue, and he'd had them in his pockets for a few minutes. Ticker came walking along, and all of a sudden with one quick flick the walking stick rapped the lad's knuckles in his pockets. And out they shot – "oooh" – and he was wringing them. Ticker just looked at him, touched his cap and said, "Tha's had long enough to find thee 'anky, lad."
>
> And that was the end of it. "Come on, look smart, this is Yorkshire." Nobody put their hands in their pockets again.
>
> You were suddenly in amongst all this. Early doors I was shouted at quite a lot by Ticker. It didn't matter if I was in his net or in Arthur Booth's. He'd always have his words, to the point where I thought "He's picking on me." Dad by this time had met Tony Nicholson, and I'd come home saying, "He's always having a go at me." So Dad had a word with Nick, and Nick's words were: "Just tell Geoff to see those he isn't shouting at. 'Cos they won't be there next year."
>
> Arthur Mitchell used to tell me later on in life that he'd probably go through 250 lads in the Winter Shed, and if he found one out of 250 he'd done well. He was happy to find one every two years.

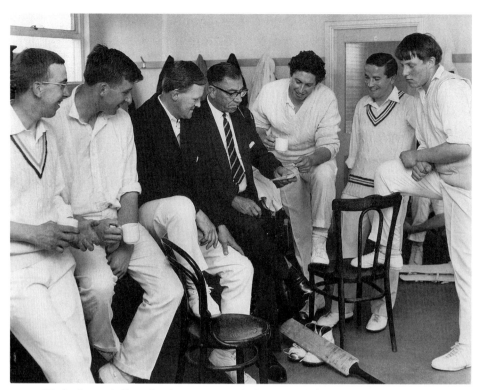

'Ticker' Mitchell in the dressing room before a Yorkshire 2nd XI game, 1966
left to right: Geoff, Peter Stringer, Derek Blackburn, 'Ticker' Mitchell,
David Middlewood, Bob Crossley, Neil Smith

In the following years, in the Winter Shed and in the pre-season nets, Geoff saw much of the two Arthurs, and he came to understand their approaches.

> Ticker's way of thinking was, "If you play for Yorkshire, you'll come up against people who want to sort you out, and you've got to be strong enough to stand up and be counted. If you can get by me, you can get by anybody." He was hard, was Ticker.
>
> Arthur Booth was the opposite. He'd encourage in a light way. "Come on, I've seen you before. You can do better than this, I know you can. So you show me. Come on." You listened, and you tried for him – whereas with Ticker you thought, "I'd better do it right or I might not be here." At the end of the session, Arthur would put his arm on your shoulder and sum it up. He always took it upon himself that he was very much the second coach, but he'd still an awful lot to offer. An awful lot. And Ticker knew that. He respected him.

Arthur talked to you about spin and about different paces of bowling, different pitches you bowl on, and it was always done in a quiet, dignified way. He'd sometimes take you out of the net. "Just sit down a minute," he'd say. Ticker would be shouting: "Come on out here, I want you to bowl." And Arthur would call back, "He'll be with you in a few minutes."

When Geoff was on the Yorkshire staff a few winters later, there were occasional sessions in the indoor nets at Park Avenue, Bradford.

The netting was so low there that, when you bowled, quite a few balls finished on top of the net. Ticker would start shouting and bawling at you. "For Christ's sake, you've got to learn to bowl in it." All this carry-on. Then afterwards he'd come up and say, "Right, I've given you a bollocking. But you are going to run me home, aren't you?" And when he got in the car, he was a different guy. He'd talk about the past, he'd talk about the future. Whatever you brought up, he'd open it up.

Arthur Booth in the Bradford Park Avenue nets, 1966
Among those standing are (first on left) David Ash, (second) Geoff, (sixth) Ian McGeechan, the Scottish rugby international, and (seventh) Chris Clifford

But those sessions at Park Avenue lay in the future. In that winter of 1962/3 Geoff was a youngster with his life in front of him, just turning 16. There was so much of life that was beyond his experience.

In 1962 Granada, in a 'Play of the Week' called *You In Your Small Corner*, broadcast television's first inter-racial kiss. Growing up in the Crossgates district of Leeds, Geoff knew little of such matters. He admits that, if he ever encountered a dark-skinned man in the street, he would feel a little afraid. But, in the summer of 1963, fresh from taking his 'O' levels, he had an awakening about 'black and white' that he has never forgotten.

> I was one of three lads chosen by Leeds Cricket Club to look after the two teams at the Headingley Test. Our role was to whiten the boots, clean the pads, do the errands. We had a little room at the end of the corridor in the old pavilion.
>
> On the first morning we knocked on the door of the England dressing room. Dexter was captain. We stood there and said, "We're here to do jobs for you." He didn't want to know. "Do we have to have you all in this dressing room?" he said. "Come back after we've gone." Fred spoke up: "You leave my little lads alone." But we left rather sheepishly. We were frightened to go back when they were there.
>
> Then we had to knock on the West Indies door. We were really nervous by then: shall we or shan't we? We knocked, and the manager answered. We were explaining who we were, and suddenly Frank Worrell put his head round the door: "Boys, please come in." In this soft-spoken voice. "Stand in front of me. Now, tell me what you're going to do." "Well, it's not what we're going to do," we said. "It's what you want us to do." "Right, the first thing you need to know is who you're dealing with. Conrad." He called Conrad Hunte over. "Conrad, take the boys round and introduce them to all the lads." We went round – Garry Sobers, Lance Gibbs, Basil Butcher, they all greeted us – then we came back to Worrell. "Right," he said. "Provided you behave yourselves, you can stay with us as long as you wish." And we were in that dressing room for four days.
>
> Big Wes Hall would pick up a paper, turn to the racing results and he'd be mimicking Peter O'Sullevan, commentating. "And Lester Piggott on Bally Royal is coming up on the stand side, there's a furlong to go, and he's almost up with Horatius. It's neck and neck now."
>
> Big Charlie Griffith was there, of course. "Charlie, it's time to work," Wes would say. And they'd go across to little Deryck Murray, pick him up under the armpits till he was about two foot off the ground,

and they'd walk him out of the dressing room, down the corridor, onto the field of the Test match. We looked at this and we thought, "Gee, don't they enjoy life!"

On the first day Kanhai got out when he was on 92. He came in the dressing room, turned round the corner, Frank Worrell was sat there, and he sank to his knees. He put his head on Frank Worrell's knees and he said, "I'm sorry, I failed you." And Frank Worrell said, "You will learn by this, and you will go on and make many more hundreds." This guy was so calm, honest, loving. The players absolutely idolised him. If he spoke, they listened.

We were privileged to be in that dressing room. We never went back in the England dressing room, not during the day. But with the West Indies we ran errands, got them snacks and things.

It was the first time in my life when I realised that it doesn't matter what colour you are, it's what's underneath that counts. And Frank Worrell was the man who did it. He really brought home to me what you can gain in life through friendship.

Frank Worrell

3

You're on that ladder, lad, well done

1963-1966

In the summer of 1963 the 16-year-old Geoff was developing his game with the Leeds club at Headingley. He had established himself in the Freelance side, playing against such teams as Grimethorpe, Sowerby Bridge and Thorne Colliery, at a time when the National Coal Board maintained sports grounds with outstanding facilities. The next step for him would be to play in the first team where the away fixtures would take him to grounds where the county played: Sheffield, Harrogate, Hull and Scarborough.

> At Headingley there were nets twice a week, on fabulous pitches that George Cawthray had prepared – with lads who really took the nets seriously. And you did fielding sessions. It became a more absorbing game because everybody wanted to improve.

Leeds Freelance side, 1963
standing: H Wilkinson, G Cope, M Mortimer, R Hainsworth, J Wilson, K Jones
sitting: I Frobisher, C Huby, D Forsyth (capt), J Barber, B Wood

George Cawthray would turn up, he'd bowl his little seamers and bat at three with a left-handed fluency and he'd be as proud as anything in his Yorkshire 2s sweater and cap. You had people like him who'd seen it all, and you had youngsters coming through who wanted to see what he'd seen. It was a major step up for me from Leeds Zingari. It wasn't going up one league; it was going up several.

You didn't miss nets because you were frightened you wouldn't be picked on the Saturday. And all the time there were people who were watching you. Robin Feather, the captain, would come in, and he'd set his stall out to have a go at me. He tried to sweep me, he tried to slog me, to do all sorts. I thought, "This guy's not exactly playing in the proper manner." It was only later I realised that he was testing me, finding out how easy it was to knock me off my length. Finally he got confidence in me, and I started playing in the first team in the Yorkshire League, coming up against old Yorkshire players in all the sides.

There was one game – was it that summer? – when Geoff was twelfth man at Bramall Lane in Sheffield, and a call came through from Billy Sutcliffe

Leeds Yorkshire League side, 1964
standing: W Kippax, C Huby, R Feather (capt), S Metcalfe, G Cawthray, J Brennan
kneeling: M Crawford, J Wooldridge, J Wilson, D Middlewood, G Cope

to say he would be late; his relief had not yet turned up at the shop. Eight years earlier Sutcliffe had been a rising star of Yorkshire cricket, hitting more than 1,200 runs in the summer and being selected for an England 'A' tour of Pakistan. But he suffered from constant comparison with his father Herbert, and his two-year reign as captain was accompanied by much grumbling from the supporters. Nowhere was the discontent louder than at Sheffield.

> As soon as he arrived at Bramall Lane, he got changed, put his pads on and went in next. And he smashed a hundred in the most fabulous innings. In those days you used to get quite a few watching and, as he was coming back to the dressing room, they all stood up and clapped. Bill looked at them: "And are you the same lot that got rid of me?" And walked in.
> His name should never have been Sutcliffe. If he'd have been Jackson or Johnson, he'd have been a good player for Yorkshire for many years.

There was a view among many that the Bradford League was the strongest in the county. There was more money about to pay players, the grounds were generally smaller, and the pitches a challenge to bat on, all of which gave the games a fiercely competitive edge. But for Geoff, as a young off-spinner, the larger grounds and flatter pitches of the Yorkshire League were a much better preparation for what lay ahead.

> The pitches in the Bradford League gave the bowler much more help. The ball would turn and bounce. So you had a yard to bowl on where in the Yorkshire League you only had a foot. If you dropped it at all short in the Yorkshire League, you got cut and pulled. You had to be very accurate.

Geoff's life plan was to play for Yorkshire. That was his single ambition, and he played all the cricket he could, even spending weeks of his summer holiday with the Bridlington club.

> I'd gone there for a Sunday game with the Yorkshire Owls when I was fourteen. Afterwards I couldn't go in the bar so I had to sit outside with an orange juice. Jim Wood, who was a headmaster, was captain of Bridlington, and he came out and talked to me. He took an interest in my cricket.
> The next year my mum and dad came over with me. Bridlington played a lot of touring teams in the summer holidays, and he asked them if they would like me to go over and stay with his family from Monday to Friday and play the games – as a learning curve for my cricket. So I stayed several times during the summers at his house.

Geoff's school work took second place, as became clear when his 'O' level results arrived, with more failures than passes.

> I went into the sixth form, redoing some 'O' levels and taking Geography 'A' level. I'd been in a General Science class for three years, and the school had put me in for separate Biology, Physics and Chemistry 'O' levels. On the Chemistry paper I wrote, 'Gone to Headingley.'

Any expectation Geoff had that he could freewheel at school while he pursued his sporting dreams was soon shattered – and his first setback came on the football field.

Leeds United were a Second Division side, but they had an ambitious manager in Don Revie, and they were assembling a group of young players who would soon make the club a power in the land. Geoff was playing sometimes in their junior side under the watchful eye of Syd Owen, who had captained Luton Town in the 1959 Cup Final.

> I trained with Sprake, Reaney, Cooper, Bremner, Charlton, Hunter. Peter Lorimer was the same age as me. I saw him come down from Scotland as a 15-year-old. Our minister, John Jackson, was the chaplain at Elland Road, and he used to sort lodgings out – and Peter was next door to where he was. I used to spend quite a bit of time with him.
> Syd Owen had hopes for me. "I think we can do something with you," he said. But I was never in their league.

Even if he had had the talent to play for the Leeds first team, that chance ended abruptly in a bizarre sequence of events that Geoff still cannot start to explain.

> Dad had to see George Stephens, the optician at Halton, and I went along with him. Dad was sitting in the chair, struggling with the chart, and jokingly I said to him, "You're hopeless, you. This is what it says." And I read right to the bottom line. George said, "Come on, get out the way. There's nothing wrong with you."
> A week or two later I was playing for Leeds United Juniors on a Saturday morning. The ball was on the right wing, I knew it was coming over and I picked where I wanted to lay it off. And all of a sudden I was peering for it. By the time I'd got it in focus, it was on me and, instead of making the movement to bring the ball under control, somebody was whacking me. I was starting to get whacked quite a bit, and Syd Owen had a go at me: "Come on, come on, quicken up." I said to Syd, "I can't see it."
> I used to sit near the back at school, and the following week I was peering at the board. Before I knew it I was sitting at the front, and I

was still peering. At home I was sitting in the chair next to the telly. Dad said, "What are you doing there? You'll ruin your eyes if you're sat so close."

We went across to Halton to see George. "Geoff says he can't see." "What? … Read me that board." He said, "Had I not seen you a fortnight ago, I'd have said you needed glasses a long time ago." He sent me to the hospital for tests. "Well, I'm amazed," he said. "They find nothing, I find nothing. I can't understand what or why." He prescribed some glasses, the old glass-bottle types, and they frightened me.

It took me a while to adjust to the shock. I don't think I was ever going to make it at football, but I had been in with an opportunity and straightaway that was dead. I went and played with friends for the Manston School senior side that they ran from the church, scored a stack-full of goals and enjoyed myself. But serious football was over. Now I had to concentrate on cricket.

By this time Geoff's father had left French polishing and was working in the office at Barnbow, the arms factory in Crossgates. French polishing, a thriving business a few years earlier, was now in serious decline.

It was an art. You would take a piece of furniture, strip it down by hand, sandpaper it hard, get it all smooth, then you'd have cloths that you folded into doves that you'd dab into the polish and apply. Everything was done by hand. In the 1950s Dad's customer base was banks, where the counters were French-polished, the Town Hall in Leeds, and all the courts. They would close a court down for three weeks while they redid the polish. Then spray polish came in, and that broke Dad's back. It was considerably cheaper and quicker, but Dad was an artist, he couldn't live with the spray.

He decided to wind down the firm, but there were two lads who had been with him for quite a while and he didn't want to see them out of work. So Dad came out of it, and he kept the business going for these two. I would pop in at various times, collect the mail, pay the cheques in, and we'd do all the bookwork at home.

In the end the lads came to us and said, "It's getting hard. We're quoting for jobs, we're trying to explain to people it's an art, but they just look at the cost."

Finally the two of them found other work, and it came to an end. But the closing stages, when his father kept it going for the sake of the men, put a strain on the household finances. Geoff's mother, on top of looking after them all at home, was working part-time in a local shop and, in the New Year of 1964, she sat Geoff down. He was coming up to his 17th birthday, looking forward to returning to the nets at Headingley, and her words upset him greatly.

"Look, I'm not going to be popular," Mum said. "You're getting excited about this game of cricket, but I want you to go out and find a job. If your cricket comes good, all well and good. If it doesn't, you've something to fall back on."

"Are you stopping me playing cricket?"

"No, I'm not, but I want you to have something behind you in case cricket doesn't work."

Those were the worst words my mum could say to me at 16. Dad had gone through life saying "if" with Arsenal, and it was as if I was going to follow by saying "if" with Yorkshire.

Dad said, "She's saying what she feels, Geoff. You'll probably understand later in life. I know it's hard to take at this moment, but you've got to do both. You've got to find a job, you've got to get yourself on the ladder, but equally you're still to work at your cricket."

It was the best advice I could be given, but I didn't think so at the time – not for some time afterwards. I took it badly, and I blamed my mum for it.

Geoff applied for and got a job with the paper merchants Wiggins Teape – on the strength of his handwriting.

During the interview Mr Loftus, the boss, said he noticed there was a lot of cricket on my application form. "What happens if Yorkshire want you to play for them?" he asked. My answer, which people still remember, was, "What's your wildest dream?"

Geoff learned about the paper trade, studied at evening classes and brought home much-needed money. In the summer he made further progress at Leeds Cricket Club. Then came the day that changed everything: Wednesday 6 January 1965.

Grandma, Grandad, everybody was still living at home. Mum was 51, a reasonably sized lady, and she was on tablets for blood pressure.

She and Dad lived life as one; they went everywhere together. They'd palled up with my friend Keith Butler's mum and dad – I called them 'Uncle' Gerald and 'Auntie' Marjorie – and they'd taken to going out as a fourball.

On this particular night they were planning to go to a Bond film – *Goldfinger*, I think – and Auntie Marjorie had rung to say she had to go to the doctors to pick something up. Mum wanted to go down there as well so she said to Dad, "Why don't you and Uncle Gerald go and watch the film?" Dad said, "No, we always go together." But she convinced him to go. So Dad and Uncle Gerald set off to the pictures at Harehills and Mum went down to the doctors at Crossgates.

I'd got home from work, and my pal Mike Wheatley turned up. He'd passed his test by this time and was driving. He said, "Night school's cancelled. The boiler's burst, and there's no heating." So we drove down to the doctors to pick Mum up.

Mum had been all right when she left the surgery but, when we got down there, she was sitting on the wall. She wasn't looking at all well, and they didn't let her back in. So we drove her home, we put her on Grandma's bed in the front room, and we rang the ambulance. Mike said, "Where's Dad?" I said, "He's down the picture house at Harehills." He said, "Come on, we're going to find him."

We shot off – quarter of an hour there, quarter of an hour back – and they were very good, they stopped the film and Dad came out.

As we drove round the corner at the top of the road, the doors of the ambulance were open. "Good," Dad said. "If they take her in, she'll be able to get some rest." Those were his words. By this time Grandma was 85, Grandad going on 90, and she'd been under so much pressure – pressure that had always been kept away from me.

We parked up. Dad got out and went towards the house, and he was met at the front door by the two ambulancemen. He turned back to me and he said, "It's too late." And I ran off down the street, crying. A neighbour ran after me, caught me up and walked me back.

Before Mike and I had gone for Dad, we'd got Mum settled. I said, "Are you all right, Mum?" She said, "Yes, I'm all right." She held my hand and she said, "Geoffrey." She always called me Geoffrey, it was never Geoff. "Geoffrey," she said, "I know I said something that you didn't like, and I hope you'll forgive me. I was only trying to look after you. I love you dearly, and I hope one day you'll bring home a Yorkshire cap for your dad." And those were the last words she said to me.

When I told Dad what she'd said, he spent some time explaining that she hadn't meant any harm, she was thinking of my best interests, how important it was to have a job. He said, "If I'd have gone to Arsenal, and I'd have broken my leg after a year, where would I have been? If you go to Yorkshire and for some reason it doesn't work, what are you going to do?" And I started to understand. I hadn't realised till then that she'd been totally supportive of my playing cricket; she was just trying to look after me.

When I was allowed to go in and see her, the first time I'd seen anybody passed away, she was the woman I knew. There was a smile, there was a warmth, there was ... just my mum. And she left me with the biggest task of all: to bring home a Yorkshire cap for my dad.

That summer of 1965 Geoff's cricket moved forward in leaps and bounds. He was a regular in the Leeds first team, taking 8-26 including a hat-trick against Rotherham Town, 12 wickets in the two games against Hull and winning the club's Lord Hawke Trophy as the outstanding bowler of the season. In all matches, playing whenever and for whoever he could, he took 121 wickets – and, most significantly of all, he was selected in June to play for the Yorkshire second eleven in a two-day Minor Counties Championship match against Cumberland at the Edenside ground in Carlisle. It was a big step, but he had the comfort of knowing that his captain would be his captain at Leeds, Robin Feather.

By this time his grandfather had been taken into hospital, and Geoff called on him on the Tuesday evening before leaving for the game.

He was sat bolt upright in his bed: six foot tall, with a fine body. He had been a shoemaker by trade; he still did some at home for us. I told him I was playing for Yorkshire 2s, and he said, "Right, you do well, and I'll be here to hear how you got on."

Carlisle? It was like going to Australia for me. Somebody took me by car, then a man met me at the hotel: "Can I carry your bag?" I thought, "What's he on about here?" "No, I'll carry me own, thank you." It was a different world. I'd been taken out of my everyday cricket. It was my first chance to live my dream. Robin tried his best to tell me, "Just be yourself. Bowl as you're bowling for Leeds."

Next day the rules were set out. The principle of discipline was there from day one, preparing you for the first team. The blazer was a thick horse-blanket, and you had to wear it at lunch. If it was 80 degrees, you could ask if it was possible to take it off. Woe betide you if you turned up with kit that wasn't clean.

I couldn't go to see Grandad the night I got back, but I went the following night. "Come on, sit on this bed, tell me all about the game," he said.

On a pitch that took some turn Cumberland had been all out for 148, Yorkshire replied with 168, then rain washed away the game. Talking loudly to overcome the old man's deafness, Geoff told him proudly that he had bowled 17 overs and taken four wickets for 29 runs.

"You went for how many? How did they get all those runs off you?"

Then he said to me, "So you've enjoyed it. You're on that ladder, lad, well done."

He spoke to Dad. Then, when we were leaving, he called me back. And don't ask me why or how, he just said, "You might not see me again, lad. But I wish you well. Work hard." And he died that night. As far as the hospital was concerned, he was doing well.

Geoff played five times for the second eleven that summer, using up the majority of his fifteen days of annual leave at Wiggins Teape. Playing alongside John Hampshire, Chris Balderstone, Richard Hutton and Barry Wood, he took 15 wickets at 13.46 runs each, and he ended the season at the top of the team's bowling averages.

At home, however, he had to deal with a third death, one that was deeply unpleasant.

Grandma was diagnosed with cancer, and she was taken into Leeds St James's, into an old people's ward. We went to see her, and it was not a good place to be; the aroma was awful.

Next thing I got a call at work from our next-door neighbour. "We need your dad here quick. Your grandma's come home." She'd convinced them that there was somebody at home to look after her.

It was terrible. Because her wounds were open, she'd spread so much mess everywhere – all over the downstairs carpet, her bed, the furniture in the front room. The doctor said it was a disease that couldn't be cleaned up: "All this will have to be burned." She went back to hospital, and she died soon afterwards. So in a short space of time I'd lost three, and this last one – and what we had to do to clear up the mess – finished me.

The worst thing was that Mum had gone first. My Mum and Dad had never had a life together at all. That probably hurt me more than anything.

I was left with work, I was left with Dad, and the best way out of it all was we went back to basics. We were there, the two of us. Whoever went to the launderette, the other one did the ironing. Cooking. It was all a new world. But Dad was strong, he made me strong, and we started laughing together which was hard to do after what had gone on. Dad and I were always close, but from that day we were rarely apart. People used to call us Morecambe and Wise.

Geoff was still playing football with the Manston team, but his father was anxious that he would pick up an injury that would set back his cricket.

"I'll be all right, Dad," I said. "I'll look after myself." But he was right. It ended up, he bought some season tickets for Leeds United, and we watched a lot.

Then one day Mike Wheatley took me on one side and said, "Look, I might hurt you, pal, but I'm going to say something that I think should be said ... At the moment you and your dad are inseparable. If your dad says, 'There's a cowboy on, are you going to watch it with me?', you just turn around and say, 'Yes, of course I am.' And I'd say the same. But you've a life to lead, and he's a life to lead. And we're not seeing as much of you as we did."

When he spoke with Dad about it, Dad was shocked because he didn't realise how it was seen from the outside. I didn't want it to change because we were both happy. But Mike was very wise. I had another life to lead.

For the summer of 1966 the captaincy of the Yorkshire second eleven passed from Robin Feather to Derek Blackburn, another amateur cricketer, an insurance broker. Immediately he put Geoff on the spot by arriving at his house one day before the season started, asking the young off-spinner if he would come and play his cricket with him at the Bradford club.

Fear was in my conversation. Everything was right for me at Leeds, and here was the new second eleven captain wanting me to play at Bradford. He talked to me about the competitiveness of the Bradford League, and he asked why I'd chosen the Yorkshire League when money was available in the Bradford League. I told him because of the people around me and because of the pitches – more of them were of county standard. And at the end of the conversation I said, "I'm very worried because you're the new second eleven captain and if I say no to you here, will that affect me?"

"Geoff," he said, "you're playing at Leeds which is a very good club with excellent facilities. Everything that you've talked to me about is cricket sense. I wanted you as a player because you'd fit into my team, but it will not affect anything to do with Yorkshire 2s." And he was straight to his word.

The city of Leeds was looking to the future. The first phase of an Inner Ring Road, part of a £25 million scheme to create a 'Motorway City of the Seventies', had seen the demolition of 365 homes; an ambitious International Pool, an Olympic-sized swimming bath, was under construction in Westgate; and a newly opened office block, the 20-storey Royal Exchange House on City Square, became Leeds' tallest building.

The Yorkshire first team began the summer of 1966, as was their wont, with a week down south: playing MCC at Lord's, then one of the universities – this year Oxford. It was a chance for some match practice, ahead of the all-important championship programme, and, with half an eye on the future, the county invited the 19-year-old Geoff Cope to join them.

Geoff Boycott picked me up in his Victor 101 estate car. We stayed at the Clarendon Court Hotel, where I roomed with Phil Sharpe. The dream was coming true; they were going to play me at Oxford.

City of Leeds Education Committee

MANSTON CHURCH SCHOOL   SCHOOL
CROSS GATES, LEEDS.   LEEDS

20 / 4 / 1966

Dear Geoff,
Congratulations from all at Manston on being chosen for Yorkshire. We'll keep our fingers crossed for you and hope that they'll have the good sense to play you in both matches.

Best wishes,

Ernest Smith

4

Tha best's not good enough

1966

Yorkshire's opening match of 1966, against MCC at Lord's, was played in glorious sunshine. It featured centuries by Geoff Boycott and Ken Taylor as well as a bizarre ending in which Yorkshire left the field thinking they had won, only to be told that it was a draw. There was no time for MCC's last man to come out so the fact that he was unfit to bat was irrelevant.

Geoff was twelfth man, and unusually – for a match in April – it was hot enough for drinks to be called for. Thus it was that Geoff took his first steps onto the field of a first-class match.

> I was doing everything perfectly. It was a hot, hot day, and I got this tray of drinks ready – not a jug but individual glasses all poured out. I had my blazer on, a wet towel over my arm, and I walked through the Long Room, with all the members staring at me. Then I waited near the top of the steps.
>
> At the end of the over I got the signal to come on. The steward opened the gate, and I went down the steps very carefully. But at the bottom there was the smallest of steps, and I didn't realise it was there. So I fell forward and, before I knew it, the glasses had gone flying all over the grass. It was very embarrassing.
>
> "I take it we'll have drinks a bit later then," I heard Fred say.
>
> The next time I came down the steps, a steward carried the tray for me. I just did the towel. My first trip into Lord's was literally a trip.

On they went to Oxford, and Geoff prepared for his Yorkshire debut, only for the early-season sunshine to disappear.

> We just sat in a cold dressing room and watched it rain for three days.

There would be plenty such days in years to come, and he got to know how they all liked to pass the time: Ray Illingworth organising a game of bridge with Tony Nicholson, Phil Sharpe and John Hampshire; Jimmy Binks servicing his car when the rain eased off; Ken Taylor drifting away with his sketch book; and Doug Padgett heading off to the local law courts.

> He took me once or twice. You'd hear two or three cases. Padge would be sitting there, watching the defendant intently, then he'd turn to me: "He's lying through his teeth, this chap."

Around the country, in almost all the other games, there was some play – including at Derby where MCC's newly-formed Throwing Adjudication Committee was filming the action of the fast bowler Harold Rhodes – but at The Parks in Oxford there was nothing at all, not even the announcement of the two teams. Geoff returned to his desk at Wiggins Teape, not a Yorkshire player after all.

Three weeks later he was at Old Trafford, playing the first second-eleven match of the summer. While Lancashire's Jack Bond dominated them with a century, he bowled steadily for 45 overs and took four wickets. Then, against Cumberland at Headingley the next week, he returned impressive match figures of nine wickets for 71 runs.

England had gone down to an innings defeat in the First Test against the West Indies, and at the weekend the selectors announced a major shake-up of the side. The headlines were all about the recall of Tom Graveney, who would be 39 on the first day of the Test, but another less-trumpeted recall – of the 34-year-old off-spinner Ray Illingworth – was of more significance in Yorkshire.

Tuesday 14 June 1966. The county had completed an innings victory at Chesterfield, a win that took them well clear at the top of the championship table, and they announced the team for the game next day at Park Avenue, Bradford against Hampshire. Geoff was at work when he received the telegram from John Nash, the Secretary.

It said simply, REPORT BRADFORD TOMORROW – NASH. Yorkshire never wasted brass.

As far as I was concerned, it was totally unexpected. I had a lot still to learn. I rang Dad to tell him, and I couldn't get him. His pal at work, Wally, said, "He's slipped out, Geoff. He said he'd something to do." Unbeknown to me, he'd found out. He'd taken a half-day's holiday. And he was at home to greet me. We had this arrangement that whoever went to the launderette, the other one did the ironing. But he'd done the laundry, he'd done the ironing. My shirt was immaculate, he'd pressed the trousers of my brown suit. I looked brilliant.

The following day I set off for Park Avenue – The Wembley of the North – and I drove through the gates at about twenty past nine. This was for reporting by 10.30. I parked my car, went up to the dressing room, and I just looked at this empty room. Nothing in it at all.

I went into the corner, out of the way, and got changed. Then I went downstairs. There was still nobody there. And I walked out onto Park Avenue. Ron Healey, the groundsman, was there. "Well done, lad," he said. "I'm ever so pleased for you."

We had a chat. Then one or two of the press came out. There was a guy, Phil Brown, who followed Leeds United everywhere: whatever they did, they were the best side. "Where do you work?" he asked me. "Wiggins Teape." "Oh yes, I know them very well." And he put it in the paper that I worked for a well-known tea firm. That went down exceptionally well with my employers.

Phil Brown reported their conversation: 'The boy tells me he is very keen indeed about county cricket. "I wish I wasn't so excited," he muttered.'

I gradually made my way back to the dressing room. The famous old steps at Park Avenue. You go round the back, in the door, then you go up one to go back one. And when I was no more than four paces from the dressing-room door, it suddenly hit me. You've been picked for Yorkshire. And in that dressing room there would be Brian Close, Fred Trueman, Ken Taylor, Jimmy Binks ... I felt I should have had my autograph book.

I opened the door, and I had my head down. The first thing I heard was this bellow from Fred: "Are them thine?" He was pointing under the masseur's table in the centre of the dressing room to this suit, shirt and tie all rolled up and scattered, and a pair of shoes that were somewhere.

"Yes, they are, Mr Trueman."

He looked at me and he said, "Tha sees that up there, lad ... It's been my peg for the last 15 years and, if tha think I'm changing for thee, tha's another think comin'. You may borrow Raymond's for this match."

I was bricking myself. I went to pick my clothes up, and Sharpy – bless him – said, "I'll give you a hand." I started hanging them up on the peg and, as I turned round, Fred's stood there, and he put his arm round me: "Don't you worry, little sunshine, your Uncle Fred will look after you." And I sat down and cringed.

Then Closey came in. "Morning, lads." He threw a racing paper across the table, flung his kit down, turned round and he looked and saw me. "Ah, so you're with us today."

"Yes, captain."

"Right," he said, "I know you can bat a bit and I know you can bowl a bit, but can you bloody well field?" Those were his words: "Can you bloody well field?"

I said, "I'll do my best."

He said, "You'll do more than that."

I'm absolutely shaking. Big Nick, the big softie, said, "Don't you worry, lad. You're all right with me." The rest came over, and they all made me welcome.

It was a damp day, and that summer some of the matches, like this one, had an experimental rule that restricted the two first innings to 65 overs each. It reduced the role of the spinners on the first day, but Geoff had no thought for that. He was playing for Yorkshire and, full of both pride and nerves, he walked onto the field on that first morning. Fred Trueman took the new ball at the pavilion end, while the bespectacled Roy Marshall took guard.

> I went out – following out, not saying anything. I think I was wearing my Leeds sweater. I'm not sure I'd got my second eleven cap by then. Out I went, and Closey said, "You'd better get off down there." And he sent me down to fine leg at the football stand end in the corner. So I went down there.
>
> Fred bowled, and I remember it as clear as day. Marshall turned the ball off his hips, and it came straight to me. Third or fourth ball. My hands were shaking. I thought, "This is it." So I gave it the long barrier, took the ball cleanly – thank goodness – lined it up and threw it back. Binksy was stood over the wicket, and it landed straight into his gloves. Had his gloves not been there, it would have bounced on the bails. It was pinpoint accuracy. And I thought, "Phew!"
>
> Then I saw Closey coming towards me. When he was about twenty yards away, he said, "Did you enjoy that?"
>
> I said, "I'm doing my best, captain."
>
> "Well, tha best's not good enough. While it were up there, they ran another. Come and meet it, pick it up and throw it in. Just get it there quick. All right?" And off he went.
>
> "Jesus," I thought. I went from shaking to really shaking. Then at the end of the over, when I came in, Binksy was waiting for me. "Did he give you a bit of a doing? … Yes, well, while the ball's coming to you, the batsman is deciding whether to run one or two. Get to it and let it go straightaway. It doesn't matter if it bounces to me or it's slightly wide, I'll get to it. You'll be all right. Gradually it will come. Don't worry about it." That was Binksy.

With drizzle in the air, the players were on and off the field, and the Hampshire batsmen made slow progress. Geoff's day took a turn for the better when he held what *The Times* called 'a fine catch near the ground', providing a welcome wicket for his skipper.

> You wouldn't want to drop it off Closey. You'd be buried in the ground.

He was not offered a bowl, nor was the slow-left-armer Don Wilson, as Hampshire grafted their way to 151 for eight off 65 overs of seam bowling. Geoff's next involvement came on the second morning when, with the scoreboard reading 100 for nine, he went out to bat for the first time for Yorkshire – in gloomy light against Hampshire's quickest bowler.

> This fellow Butch White was charging in, steam coming out of his nostrils. He was hostile and he would let you know what. But, like the majority of cricketers, off the field he'd be a lovely chap. He'd have his pipe, and he'd be a real social animal.

'It was good,' Phil Brown reported, 'to see 19-year-old Cope open his championship account with a nice shot off his legs before White bowled him a rearing brute of a ball at top speed and forced a sharp, low slip catch to end the innings.'

Cope caught Keith bowled White 2

> I think I'd got 0 on all my debuts up till then – for Leeds Schools, Yorkshire Schools, North of England and the Second Eleven – so my two was a success.

On an awkward pitch Hampshire batted a second time, this time with no restriction on the overs, and they set about building a substantial lead. There was a long spell from Don Wilson but, well into the afternoon, though his barber had sent a telegram offering him two free haircuts for each wicket he took, Geoff had still not bowled an over.

> In those days they had a strange system where the Cricket Committee would meet during play and they'd call the captain off. So Closey went off the pitch, and Fred took over – and straightaway he called to me: "Come on, young'un, have a bowl." So I got my first bowl for Yorkshire: five overs, two maidens, nought for nineteen.

The reporter from *The Times* was impressed: 'A tall boy, he makes full use of his height, and looks a good prospect, flighting the ball skilfully.'

> Then Closey came back. "Who put you on?" "The captain." "I'm the captain ... Right, well, tha's had thy bowl, now get back down there." I was sent back down to the boundary, and I never bowled again.

Hampshire had reached 75 for four when heavy rain arrived a few minutes before tea. Soon the pitch was under water, and there was no further play – neither that evening nor the next day. With Ray Illingworth not in the final eleven at the Test, Geoff was not needed for the next match at Headingley.

He negotiated time off work to play three more second-team matches, including one at Workington that was due to start on a Monday morning.

That was a classic. We had to be at Headingley at nine o'clock on Sunday morning, to get on this coach that then went all round Yorkshire picking everybody up. We got to Workington at eight in the evening. Then on the second day the game was all over by 12, and we had to wait till seven for the coach to come back.

He scored a fifty against Durham at Driffield, but he was not called up the next time Ray Illingworth went off to England. There was a championship to be won, and Brian Close preferred to back his experienced players.

At one point, when Ray Illingworth was out injured, Geoff was sent down to Hove to join the team.

I had a letter from the committee that I had to give to Closey before play. He read it and said, "Put that back in your pocket. Tell them you gave it to me at lunchtime. Oh, and you're twelfth man today." I was intrigued by this so I read the letter. It said, 'The committee request you play Geoff Cope in this game to give him experience.'

Closey always referred to 'his' team, and he would support them to the hilt. If somebody was in a bad run, he didn't leave them out for quite a while.

For the final Test, England – 3-0 down in the series – overhauled the side again. This time the selectors turned to Close to captain the team, with Illingworth and Boycott also called up. The Test coincided with two of Yorkshire's last five matches and, with the reigning champions Worcestershire fast closing the gap behind them at the top of the table, they opted to give a first game to Barrie Leadbeater, a 23-year-old batsman with the Bradford club, a second game to Geoff – and to pluck Richard Hutton, whose accountancy training had kept him away all summer, out of club cricket in Surrey.

Their opponents at Scarborough were Glamorgan. Under a dull, cloudy sky, in front of 6,000 spectators, the first day started well enough: Glamorgan all out for 137, Yorkshire 55 for no wicket. Then, in the words of the *Guardian*, 'Batsmen tumbled out, mainly through recklessness and inexperience', and the county ended the day on 110 for nine. Chief destroyer was the evergreen Don Shepherd, whose fifth victim of the evening was Geoff, bowled for nought.

I loved watching Shep. He was superb. He had a bit of a longish run for an off-spinner. His flight and his change of pace was fabulous. And what a super guy! If you picked a side that weren't England cricketers to represent the county game, Shep would be one of the first you would pick. Every day he did his job.

He did me like a cuckoo. It was there to drive, and it wasn't there at all. County cricket was a school, and you didn't have long to learn, not with Yorkshire. You weren't coming into a bottom-of-the-table team. You had all these fine players and a fine history, and the spectators didn't see you as a young lad coming in to do your best. They saw you as a link in the team; you were picked for Yorkshire so you must be able to play. There was no question. You had to perform.

It was a view shared by the *Guardian*'s reporter who noted the performance of the two young bloods in the side: 'The fact that Leadbeater and Cope contributed only one run between them must have set the county selectors wondering what had happened to that old supply of brilliant youngsters waiting to step into the senior side.'

The reporters thought the pitch a good one, yet Glamorgan managed only 91 in their second innings – with Geoff again not bowling – and Yorkshire, needing 105 for victory, were soon in trouble on 28 for three. A recovery followed, led by John Hampshire, but his dismissal – caught at mid-wicket 'off the worst stroke he had made in weeks' – led to a collapse from 83 for four to 99 for eight. Six runs were still needed, with Don Wilson – already dropped at slip – yet to score and Geoff coming out to join him. Number eleven was Tony Nicholson, whose highest score in his last 63 appearances for Yorkshire was 12.

I was in at number ten and Big Nick was sat on the toilet. The wicket fell and somebody said, "You're in." I got up to go with the encouraging words of "I'm in 'ere, and I'm not comin' out. See it through." Oh right! So I made my way out.

Shep was bowling. And Wils greeted me: "I can't understand it. It's as flat as owt, it's doin' nowt, and we're in a mess." Typical Wils.

I said, "I've got a message from Nick."

"I know what his message will be. He won't be in dressing room."

"He's not."

He said, "Just play. Forget everything, forget everybody, just play."

Geoff's scrapbook of cuttings contains several reports telling of the 'cathedral-like silence ... the eerie seaside dusk ... 20 terrifying minutes ... every time a batsman hit it or the ball went harmlessly through to the wicket-keeper a great sigh of relief echoed around the ground.'

Don Wilson, who was batting with strapping around badly bruised ribs, 'got a three off Ossie Wheatley', then Geoff – 'attempting no heroics' – 'snatched a single', then 'a single by Wilson put the scores level.' Finally, 'Wilson drove Shepherd for the winning run', and 'the holiday crowd of 5,000 spilled onto the field ... men and boys jumped up and danced a little dance of happiness.'

I kept my head down as Wils walked me off at the end. "Never a crisis," he said.

The team remained unchanged for the next match at Northampton. On the first day, under Fred Trueman's captaincy Geoff had his first long bowl in county cricket – 26 overs, no wicket for 68 runs – attracting praise from the former England selector Wilf Wooller: 'Cope served up an impressive brand of slow off-spin of good length and line. He looks a good future prospect.'

The next day Brian Close was leading England to an improbable innings victory at the Oval, but Geoff's main memory of the day at Northampton was a chase to the boundary to stop a four.

> I was thinking I was getting there, but there was a slight dip in the ground and the ball just ran away from me at the last minute. The bench was only inches beyond the boundary, and I whacked into it and sent it flying. One of the team came over: "We're not a demolition squad, you know." I got up and, when I looked down, there was blood all over my whites.

On the third day, he found himself in a crazy run chase in which, with Trueman instructing them to keep going, he and Tony Nicholson, the last pair, attempted to score 79 runs in 36 minutes. They had added an extraordinary 45 when Nicholson 'swung once too often and was bowled' – though only three of the 45 had come off 'the sound, straight bat of Cope'.

> Nick was suddenly in a world of his own, thinking he was the finest batsman the world had ever produced and this was his moment to show us. I was just keeping an end up for him.
>
>   If you bowled the ball in the arc of his bat swing, Nick could get runs. But if you bowled it different from that, he was somewhat in disarray.

With Ray Illingworth's return that was it for Geoff in 1966. He had played three times for the summer's champion county, and he had not taken a wicket, not won himself a single free haircut.

> The high point was my one not out at Scarborough – not causing Nick to come out of the loo.

5

Emperor Tojo has been born

1967

Geoff's cricket had moved forward in 1966. Not only had he played five second-team games, as in 1965, he had turned out three times for the first eleven as well as going down with them to Lord's and Oxford and later to Hove. The days away from his desk at Wiggins Teape had mounted up, and the late and unpredictable call-ups, hinging on whether or not Ray Illingworth was in the Test team, were taxing the firm's sympathy.

> My boss was a chap called George Loftus. He played paper-trade golf, but he wasn't that interested in sport. One day after the season I was sat at my desk, and I got the call: "Mr Loftus wants to see you." In those days you put your jacket on, you walked down the corridor, knocked on the door and waited. You stood until he invited you to sit down. He talked, and you said "Thank you, sir" and walked out.
>
> He said, "Look, we've got to have a serious chat. Do you want to work in the paper trade, or do you want to play cricket? If you're going to play cricket, when you leave us in March, you leave us. Nobody will be upset. We'll wish you well." So I was faced with that.

That winter Geoff completed the Advanced Certificate of the National Association of Paper Merchants, gaining a distinction. He was now well versed in the properties of all the different grades of paper and the printing processes, and he had a good career ahead of him, earning good money. So it was not a straightforward decision. At a time when the average weekly wage was over £20, a professional cricketer would struggle if he did not have a proper job in winter – yet, for Geoff, there was only ever going to be one outcome to his deliberation. The dream of cricket had to be pursued.

> You were living on £8 for 20 weeks and £4 for 32 weeks – and match money, out of which you paid your petrol, your evening meals and anything other than your hotel. The first winter I didn't get the £4, and it was hard. It fuelled you with a big ambition.
>
> Dad was very good. He didn't have money, but he looked after me.

The summer of 1967. BBC television broke new ground by transmitting the Wimbledon tennis championship in colour and by co-ordinating the first live international satellite production, linking countries across the globe. Looking to capture the spirit of this new age – heart transplants and supersonic aircraft – the BBC turned to the Beatles to close the show with a new composition.

There's nothing you can do that can't be done.
It's easy. All you need is love.

The 20-year-old Geoff, a full-time professional cricketer, was filled with optimism, but he did not anticipate that it would be easy. He was still learning his craft as a bowler, and he was coming into a Yorkshire side that expected to win the championship again. It helped that Brian Close was England captain for all six Tests and that for the first four Ray Illingworth was with him. As in 1966 that gave Geoff opportunity, and this time he seized it. His scissors were soon busy as the pages of his scrapbook filled up.

His first call-up coincided with the First Test. He was playing in a second-team match at Harrogate that finished on Tuesday evening, after which he had to drive 250 miles down to Bath to join up with a Yorkshire side that had finished their match early at Lord's. With Brian Close away at the Test, Fred Trueman was their captain.

> I got there at half past two in the morning, and Fred was asleep on the settee in the lounge. The night porter said, "Mr Trueman's been waiting up for you. I'm to wake him when you come."
>
> He woke him up. "Where am I? ... Oh, you're here ... It's stupid they didn't let you go earlier." A few expletives as well. "Now you get yourself to bed. You're supposed to be at the ground for ten o'clock. You be there for a quarter to eleven."
>
> The next morning it was "How do you feel? Are you tired?" "I'm OK. I want to play if you want me." "I want you, sunshine." And I played. I thought, "Who else would have waited up?" They're the little things you don't see on the outside.

In three matches in 1966 Geoff had not taken a wicket, and his figures after two second-team matches were two wickets for 159 runs. Yet, after 53 balls at Bath, he had taken two wickets for no runs.

> My first victim was a Virgin – Roy Virgin. He pushed forward a little, and Binksy stumped him. They all knew it was my first one so they came to me and said, "You've broken your duck now so come on."
>
> My second wicket was Bill Alley. When he came in, I looked down with a bit of awe. Fred took Ken Taylor out of the covers and put him behind square on the legside, and I looked at Fred. He said, "What are you looking at?" I said, "Ken's the best cover fielder." "Just believe in me, lad. This fellow will try and sweep you." Sure enough, Bill lapped

me – but he lapped me in front of square, and Ken set off. I reckon at the time he was the best fielder in England. His anticipation was superb, and he ran a considerable way. There was none of this diving; he took the catch running at full tilt by his right ankle, about a foot off the ground. It was a cracking catch. Nobody else in our team would have made it.

Then 'Budgie' Burgess gave me a bit of tap. Fours and sixes. Fred came up to me: "He's frightened of you so he's going to try to slog you out of t'park. But you're better than that. You'll do it. Come on, keep going." I got Budgie finally, caught by Ken Taylor again.

Cope 25 overs, 14 maidens, 57 runs, 3 wickets

'New boy saves champs' pride' read one headline while another report described him as 'bespectacled with a toothy, eager expression ... with a delivery as economical as Illingworth's and an appeal louder than any Yorkshire larynx has produced in the last twenty-odd years.'

Probably just my enthusiasm. I always thought umpires were deaf!

Unfortunately those three wickets were the highlight of the game for Geoff. He took two in the second innings, but – despite opening the batting for his Leeds club – he went in at number ten and was out for a pair of ducks, as Yorkshire went down to an 80-run defeat.

He was joining the fraternity of county cricket, with the match providing the beginnings of a friendship with the great roustabout Bill Alley, 49 years old in *Wisden* though rumoured by many to be even more ancient.

I was walking round Bath on my own one evening, and I came to the big crescent. As I was walking past the hotel in the middle, a window opened and Bill Alley's head came out, shouting, "What are you doing on your own at your age? Come on in here." I went in, and for the next two hours he talked to me. I hardly spoke a word.

The last time I saw him was down at Taunton, not long before he died. He used to hold court in a room above the sports shop, with twenty or thirty people around him. "What do you want?" he said when I came in. "Sit down there. Cross your legs." He sat me in front of him and carried on with all his stories.

"Right," he said eventually. "What do you want?"

"I just want to know how old you are."

"Are you from the tax people?"

"It's down in my book that you were my second victim."

"Yes, well, you would remember that."

"And they brought out a bath chair to take you off."

"Get on with you."

He was such fun to be with.

From Bath the Yorkshire team travelled across the newly opened Severn Bridge to Swansea. Geoff took five wickets in the match, including the vital one of Glamorgan skipper Tony Lewis when it looked possible that the home team might avoid defeat. His bowling earned a tribute from his captain: "This lad will make it all right," Trueman told a pressman. "He's got the right temperament to go with his spinning." For Geoff, though, his freshest memory of the match was the hospitality of their Welsh hosts.

We walked into the dressing room, and on the table were a dozen invitations to go to places. We split up and went to different dos, and Nick, Sharpy and Wils took me off to the Pontardulais Choir. It was absolutely jam-packed. Sharpy was a big man in York Light Opera, and he and Wils started to sing along. "Would you mind," the conductor said. "You'll get your chance later." The choir sang *Delilah* in seven parts. It was fabulous. The warmth of South Wales making you welcome.

Another time we were invited up this valley to a village hall, where the miners were on strike, and it was Richard Hutton, Nick and me. We were met by men in flat caps and waistcoats, with open-necked shirts with a pressed-stud in them. "Good of you to come all this way. Come on in." They were all bustling around us, making us welcome, and then suddenly they said, "We'd like you to start the evening by singing *Ilkley Moor Bah Tat.*"

"I didn't come all this way to make a fool of myself," Richard said.

Of course, Nick set off. He was Frank Sinatra was Nick. His eyes would be shut, and he'd be into a different world. Richard and I made a very poor attempt at supporting him, and the place just erupted. Then they sang all their Welsh songs.

"Oh dear," Richard said, "just think how we performed, and they can sing like this. Oh, Nicholson, what have you done?"

Then we were given a banquet. And the banquet was jam and bread on a plate. They'd stayed out on strike when most of the other mines had gone back, and they had no money at all. Yet they still wanted to share with us what little they had.

I'm not of the political field. Whether they were right or wrong to strike, I don't know. But they invited us. And the warmth of that place is still with me today.

The match at Swansea ended at five o'clock. Then for Geoff it was back to the second eleven, playing 300 miles away next morning at Driffield in the East Riding. Geoff had taken ten first-class wickets in two games and, with that breakthrough behind him, he took ten Durham wickets.

The following week, when Close and Illingworth again headed off for the Test, he played another pair of games. And what games they turned out to be!

In the first, against Northamptonshire at Sheffield, they lost the toss and fielded first, coming off at the end of the morning with Northants on 90 for no wicket. The big-hitting, 18-stone Colin Milburn threatened to take the match away from them.

I came in for lunch, put my blazer on and set off towards the dining room. Fred said, "Oi, where are you going?" I said, "I'm going for lunch." "You're not," he said. "Sit there."

"You're going to bowl this lot out this afternoon."

"But I haven't bowled all morning."

"I'm telling you, you're going to bowl them out this afternoon. Now then, first question. How are you going to bowl at this fella Milburn?"

My first reaction was to think of Mr Smelt. His theory was, "If they miss, you hit." So I said, "Off-and-middle." "No." So I said, "Middle?"

"Come on, think," he said. I thought, "I've never bowled leg-and-middle in my life." I said, "Leg-and-middle?"

"Come on, you're not thinking."

There was silence. I was thinking, "There's steak-and-kidney pie on for lunch. I'm getting nowhere here."

I said, "Fred, can I be honest? ... I don't know."

"There's nowt wrong with what you said if it hadn't have been Milburn. It's a good pitch, and you should be bowling off-and-middle. And we can set a field to that, that's no problem. But this fella Milburn's different. You're going to bowl in at his legs."

I'd never heard this statement "in at his legs". I said, "That means I'm bowling outside leg stump."

"Ah, but he won't get bat round belly to bray thee." Those were his words. "He won't get bat round belly to bray thee." He went on, "Now then, there's only you and me playing this afternoon. Don't look at anybody else. If you've owt to say, say it to me. And if I've got owt to say, I'll say it to you. All you've got to do is bowl. I'll sort the field out. Go on now."

I looked unhappy, and he said, "Trust me, lad, I won't let you down. If you bowl where you were going to bowl, there won't be enough balls here to keep game going till teatime."

After lunch I came on at the pavilion end, and I got away with two maidens. Third ball of the first over Fred said, "Just a minute", and he bellowed at the fielder out at cow-shot corner. "You've moved." He shifted him half a pace. Then the next over: "You've moved back." Then, with his pincer toes, he came up from the football end to greet me. His young protégé. He put an arm round me. "Bowl round the wicket, and I'll just move him a bit further round. Don't you worry." I bowled three or four balls, and I shook my head. I said, "I'm not comfy." He said, "All right, next over, go back over."

I went back over, and I bowled a ball on off-and-middle. It was the first time I'd made a mistake and, because we'd kept him quiet for a while, Milburn went to whack it. And he edged it to Jimmy Binks behind the stumps. And he stood. I thought, "Blimey, even at this level they stand." He walked a couple of paces. Then he stood again, by which time Fred was next to me. And Ollie Milburn said to me, "If you keep listening to that old bugger, you'll get a few more wickets. Well bowled." He knew that I'd not got him out; Fred had.

Milburn caught Binks bowled Cope 61
Doug Padgett slip, Roger Prideaux non-striker, 'Dusty' Rhodes umpire

Fred said, "Come on, there's some more here." And I bowled from lunch to tea. Wils was bowling at the other end, and at one stage I heard Fred in a loud voice – so the batter heard it – say to Wils, "Hey, give him one. I want him back at that end because he can't play Copey." I think it was Brian Crump. "Right, we've got him back," he said to me. "He thought he'd got away from you. You're the one on top." I'd never been in that sort of cauldron before.

Don't get me wrong. It wasn't all smiles. There'd be a few times Fred would come and tell you straight and why. But that game, he just knew everybody inside out. And Binksy kept chipping in with a few comments. "What you saying, Binksy? … Ah, tha's right as usual."

Cope 27 overs, 20 maidens, 15 runs, 3 wickets

Milburn, Steele and Crump were his victims, as well as a moral victory against Mushtaq who was run out for 1: 'The Pakistani became so impatient with being pinned down that he attempted a run that was never there.'

'Stand-in Cope sends Northants reeling,' was one headline. 'He bowled for the whole of the afternoon,' wrote Eric Stanger in the *Yorkshire Post*, 'and his questing length, varied flight and occasional turn was a challenge to the batsmen. No one met him successfully as he nagged away over after over to sap their confidence. It was a most promising performance.'

Boycott, dropped from the England team for slow scoring in the First Test, hit a double century, and Yorkshire won by an innings – with Geoff taking another three wickets, this time for two runs. The victory took them for the first time that summer to first place in the championship table.

Next up was Surrey at Headingley, and again Geoff was among the wickets: three in the first innings; then five in the second when on a damp pitch Surrey struggled in vain to avoid an innings defeat, the final wicket falling only minutes before heavy rain set in.

Those were the days of uncovered pitches. It rained a lot, and the pitch was damp. We got them to follow on, and the openers put on 40-odd. Then it started to dry out and, once we got a wicket, we went right through them. Fred kept changing our ends.

That was the game when Barrie Leadbeater was on as twelfth man, and he caught one in the gully. Micky Stewart, the Surrey captain, walked down the steps in his flip-flops, newspaper under his arm, very, very slowly all the way to the middle and said, "I don't want him fielding there." Turned round and walked back. Leddy had to go out into the deep.

I was bowling a lot with Wils. He was so enthusiastic. He was saying to me, "You and I have got to work together as a partnership. We bowl

Bowling against Surrey at Headingley, 1967
The umpire is Charlie Elliott

for each other. What you do, I get the credit for at the other end. And the other way." I called him Wilfred, after Wilfred Rhodes.

The match was over by mid-afternoon, but not before the arrival of Ray Illingworth, returning from the Lord's Test where he had taken six for 29 in the Indian second innings. He sat and watched as his young substitute took all the local headlines. 'If he shifted uneasily in his seat,' wrote one reporter, 'if he occasionally wore a worried look, there was every justification. For out in the middle his position as Yorkshire's number one off-spinner was being strongly challenged by a 20-year-old unknown.'

Illingworth had played seven times that summer for Yorkshire, Geoff four, and the newspapers were quick to compare their bowling figures:

	Overs	Maidens	Runs	Wickets	Average
Cope	147.3	79	228	24	9.50
Illingworth	210.4	91	355	20	17.75

The headlines in Geoff's scrapbook tell the story the pressmen were creating: 'Colt leads Test ace in Wicket Race' ... 'Young Cope spins a problem for Yorkshire' ... 'It's my turn now, Ray!'

In the *Yorkshire Evening Post* Bill Bowes quoted the words of the great George Hirst: "You can never name a county player of the future. You pick the ones you fancy and hope they'll get over the last little step. It's cappin' how many tummel." Bowes' view of Geoff was that it was 'a great pity he has not had more opportunity. The successful cricketer is seldom the one who has to spend a long time marking time.'

> I was just the youngster looking to learn my trade. Suddenly the press were saying, Yorkshire are going to have to make a big decision soon, but there was never a hint of getting rid of Illy; they were just thinking how were they going to work me into the side.
>
>   I'd had a few games, and I'd appreciated playing in front of bigger crowds, not like the second-team where the crowd was only 50 or 60, maybe 100. It was beginning to gnaw away inside me, "I want to play. I want to be in this atmosphere, at this level."

Yorkshire had a week away from the championship, during which time Leicestershire, captained by the veteran Tony Lock, slipped ahead of them at the top of the table, making the next fixture at Leicester a crucial one. Geoff went down as part of the Yorkshire twelve.

Leicestershire's success was in no small part down to the wickets taken by their two spinners, Lock himself and Jack Birkenshaw, and for this match the pitch, according to the *Guardian*, 'took spin even before an astonishingly large midweek crowd had settled in.' Close, inspecting the surface, left out Tony

Nicholson in favour of Geoff as a third front-line spinner – though, on that first day, when Leicestershire were dismissed for 161, the duo of Illingworth and Wilson was sufficient.

> Illy and Wils bowled them out, and I didn't bowl. It was a result wicket, a big turner, and we had to bat properly to win the match. Padge got some runs. He was as good as I've seen on indifferent wickets. Then the next day Illy batted for hours, and we built up a big lead.

Lock led from the front, having a hand in the first eight wickets – four as bowler, four as fielder – but it was his dismissal of Illingworth, bowled for 60 after four hours of patient graft and when well set, that stays in Geoff's memory.

> Let's just say, it was his quicker ball. Illy had hardly got his bat up when his off-stump went flying back. And at the end of the game, he came into our dressing room with a great grin on his face. Closey was going to be captaining England in the West Indies that winter, and he said, "Good luck, Closey. Give us a shout if you want Sobers throwing out; I'm available." Those were his words: "throwing out". And he was laughing all over his face.

The match was over in two days, Yorkshire winning by an innings. Geoff contributed an unbeaten 0 to a last-wicket partnership of 40 with Don Wilson. Then in the Leicester second innings he took four wickets, playing second fiddle to Illingworth, who finished with match figures of eleven for 79.

> Illy came up to me at one point and he said, "This fella Inman, the left-hander, you'll be all right. Bowl him a couple of off-ers, get him driving into the covers, then give him the arm ball and you'll do him through the gate." So I came up, bowled three that he drove, then the arm ball and he hit me into the middle of Leicester. My head went up, following the ball, with my mouth open and my glasses reflecting in the sun. And when I turned round, there was Sharpy on the floor and Binksy, they had tears coming out of their eyes. Howling. "That's it," Sharpy said. "Emperor Tojo has been born." They said I looked like the old Japanese emperor with my glasses. So I got the nickname Tojo. And that was the making of me in that side. I was accepted.

On Sundays, for variety, they called him the Emperor. It was a nickname that led to a misunderstanding in a hotel in Lakenham, when their Gillette Cup match against Norfolk had to be finished on the Sunday.

> We were packing up to go, and I was coming down the stairs with all my things. Sharpy and Wils were at the bottom, and Wils shouted,

"Emperor, you shouldn't be carrying your bags." I've never seen a reception move so quickly. "Let me take your bags, sir, please."

With six Tests that summer Close, Illingworth and Boycott were regularly missing from the Yorkshire side, providing opportunities not only for Geoff but for other young players – Barrie Leadbeater, Chris Old, Peter Stringer and the slightly older Chris Balderstone – all coming in when Fred Trueman was left in charge.

He won the championship that year by skippering the side as often as Closey – and he did it with some of us kids. I don't think Fred ever got the accolades that he deserved for that.

Fred did his own thing at night. Sometimes you didn't know where he'd gone, and perhaps it was a good thing. But during the day, when he was in charge, he was always around. And he was always with you. He'd talk to you about other youngsters: "Is he worried? Tell him he's all right." And nine times out of ten, if you spoke to him about somebody, he'd say, "Don't worry, I've had a word."

Fred didn't have the physical presence of Closey. He had his broad shoulders and his big beam, but Closey was frightening. If you wanted to have a go at Closey, you always made sure you were between him and the door.

Fred got so much pride out of what he got from his team. That meant an awful lot to him.

Three of Geoff's last four championship matches that summer were ruined by the rain, but the game at Eastbourne gave him a brief glimpse of Fred Trueman as he had been in his pomp.

That was the game when Nick stopped me getting all ten. I bowled Kenny Suttle on the first evening, and the next day the tide was in, the ball swung, and Nick took nine for 62. He bowled superbly.

I got a rollocking from Fred because I'd got a pair of cream flannels that I used to bat in. He said, "Get them off and bin them."

We left them to get 350 on the last day, and we were doing reasonably well till Mike Griffith and Graham Cooper got some runs. It was a flat pitch, and the game was going away from us. I'd been bowling, and Fred said, "Go stand at short leg and go a yard deeper."

Binksy said, "The old boy's going to give it a go." And Fred bowled a very short spell of the quickest I'd ever seen. Binksy went back, and it kept smacking into his gloves. He got Griffith and Cooper out, but he'd given his all, he couldn't bowl at nine, ten and eleven. So he gave the ball back. His spell won the match for us.

Fred Trueman leads out the Yorkshire team

There are times when you need the big players to perform: Illy at Leicester, Fred at Eastbourne. That's how you win championships. And you remember those moments.

Close and Trueman, both born in February 1931, making their debut together in the same match in May 1949, were two of the greatest characters of post-war English cricket. They had their different styles, and the young Geoff could appreciate both of them.

Fred was probably more understanding and was closer to you. Half the time Closey would be saying, "Come on, you should be taking wickets. You're bowling it like a pansy. Bowl it a bit quicker, and don't let them get to you." It wasn't a rollocking, but he'd do it in a more abrasive way. Fred was an arm around you: "Now, sunshine, come on, we've got to …" I responded to that. But don't get me wrong. Closey was the best captain I played under.

The most special moment of Geoff's summer was at the Dean Park ground in Bournemouth, where he met one of cricket's and Yorkshire's all-time greats: the 89-year-old Wilfred Rhodes, now blind and living nearby with his daughter.

He was sat near the boundary edge, and Wils and I went to say hello to him. He was relying on his hearing to picture the play.
"That man's too deep," he said.
"What do you mean?"
"Is he on the boundary edge?" He listened a bit more. "That seems near. Why isn't he half way?"
Wils said, "If he's halfway, the batsman can push it for one or he can hit it over the top for four."
"Well, you're not bowling it at the right pace. *You* dictate how he hits it."
Wils looked at me, as if to say, "I'll have to work that one out."
He carried on, and then he said, "I'm going to ask you a favour. They've asked me down to the local school where my grandchildren are. They've got a new cricket pitch, and they want me to open it tomorrow morning. Will you come down?"
The next morning we walked out together to this artificial pitch, and he said, "I'll bowl the first ball." He touched the stumps, shuffled a bit and said, "Am I about on the batting crease?" He put this newspaper down on a length, went to the other end, took a ball and bowled it. It bounced on the newspaper and went towards the slips.
I looked at Wils and he said to me, "I think it's time we went."

There he was, blind, nearly ninety, his arm low down, and he landed the ball right on the paper.

We said we had to go, and he said, "I'm grateful for you coming. I might get down to the ground later." But he never did.

"Come on, Wilfred," I said to Wils.

To me he was one of the icons of Yorkshire cricket. It was magical just to be near him.

Wils said to me, "We got away with that. And you, you dozy devil. Calling me Wilfred in front of him. If I couldn't have hit the paper, I'd have been a right Wilfred."

Geoff's final game of the season was at Scarborough in a festival match against MCC. On the last day he led Yorkshire to victory with five wickets, once more capturing the headlines: 'Cope turns tide for champions'. In the same editions the newspapers printed the final first-class averages, and in second place in the bowling list, behind Kent's Derek Underwood, was Geoff, his 40 wickets taken at 13.82 runs each. He was still Illingworth's deputy, but what progress he had made in just twelve months!

There was no winter job at Wiggins Teape. Instead, Geoff worked in the office of the Yorkshire County Cricket Club Development Association in the old groundsman's house beside the gate in St Michael's Lane. His task was to keep the ledger for all the ten-shilling cheques that agents sent in for the weekly lottery that they ran. Each afternoon, shortly before the bank's 3.30 closing time, he had to take a bundle of cheques to the National Provincial in central Leeds – where, soon enough, he made a point of standing always in the same queue, to be served by the same cashier, a girl of his own age called June.

> I always seemed to go to the same counter. I don't know why!! And if another queue was shorter, I would say to the person behind me, "Are you in a hurry? You go ahead of me to that one."

Then one day, while June waited for her bus home to Otley, Geoff pulled up in his car. "Do you want a lift?" he asked, as if it was on his way, not on the opposite side of town, and soon enough they were on a first date – at the Cow and Calf, a hotel with a disco, at Ilkley.

The Development Association, which raised more than £8,000 that year for ground improvements, was run on a shoestring, and the following winter there was no vacancy there for Geoff. Instead, Ray Illingworth helped him out by passing over to him some of the shops where he collected annual orders for fireworks and Christmas cards.

> He sent me down to Kent and Sussex. My car went in for service every Saturday. You went to the established accounts, looking for a repeat

order, and that was usually all right. But when you went to the new ones, they'd say, "What are you doing down here?" Raymond, as an England cricketer, might have got away with it.

Of course, he had all the ones round Yorkshire. He sent me round the Bradford ones once. I'd never covered so many shops in a day. "Hello. How is he? Good. Same as last year. Plus this." You were in and out. You went down to the south, though, and you were competing with local suppliers. So that was hard. Illy used to look at my figures, and I still don't know if he took his commission out of them. But it got me by. I was grateful for it at the time.

So is Geoff saying that he lost business because he was a poor substitute for Raymond? He laughs.

Some people thought I was always a poor substitute for Raymond.

6

How long do I wait?

1968

What a time it was for followers of sport in Yorkshire – and especially for those in the city of Leeds. At Wembley, in March 1968, Leeds United – managed by Don Revie – won the Football League Cup, the first trophy in their history, while two months later, on a waterlogged pitch in the same stadium, the Rugby League Challenge Cup was held aloft by Leeds. Both teams went on to win their leagues the following winter – which, with Yorkshire retaining their county title in 1968, allowed the city to lay on a celebratory dinner for its three champion sides. There were speeches aplenty, with Geoff remembering two in particular: those of Brian Sellers, the autocratic Chairman of Cricket at Yorkshire, and Clement Freud, the television chef who had just won a transatlantic race from London's Post Office Tower to New York's Empire State Building.

"Look round this room," Sellers said. "All you people who support all these sports. Do you realise, Leeds United? We've had to wait 85 years for a bloody party till you won a championship."

Then it was Clement Freud's turn. "I know a lot about Yorkshire cricket," he said. "You've won it 31 times. And I know a lot about Leeds United. But my heroes are Leeds Rugby League, because you've won your championship playing two men short."

They were good days; the players all mixed well together. John Atkinson, the winger of Leeds Rugby League, was my best man. Today, if I want to organise a golf day for the Guide Dogs Association, I ring the footballers – Eddie Gray, Pete Lorimer, Norman Hunter – and they say, "Six or eight? Leave it with us, Geoff." And they come back in a few hours and say, "We've got nine. Is that all right?" And they all turn up. And the Leeds Rugby lads, the same. We all get there, and it's just as if it's yesterday.

Norman Hunter was a good cricketer. He played in a game in my benefit year, at Pocklington, and he got 70 or 75. He came in the dressing room, and he said, "I enjoyed that." I said, "Well, go and get yourself some tea." He sat down and, when we went out to field, he came up to me: "I can't move," he said. "My legs are all stiff."

Don Revie always said, "If you want to come and train with us, you're welcome." So I took him up on it; I went down to Fullerton

Park where they trained. He said, "I'll send Les Cocker out to see you on your own first." Les had me running round the pitch numerous times, then he got me doing exercises.

The team came out: "Has he done his stuff, Les?" "Yes, he's done very well. Shall we put him in with our lot for a few minutes?"

"Just a minute," Revie said, and he went off and got a bucket. "I don't give you ten minutes out there," he said. "You're at a different level with your fitness."

"Go and tell Norman that," I said. "He came and played with us."

"He's not a bad cricketer, is he? Is he better than his golf? ... He must be useful."

"He batted and got 75, but he couldn't move afterwards."

It's different aches and pains, you're using different muscles.

Brian Clough once came into our dressing room. He looked at Nick and he said, "If I'd have been in charge of you, I'd have had you shot."

Nick looked an unhealthy specimen, bless him. Beer in one hand, fag in the other, a bit of weight on him. He always had something wrong with him – was always first on the masseur's table, either to have something attended to or to have a sleep. But he had a big, big heart. He ran in and he ran in, and he came back for more and he ran in.

In 1968 the regulars of the Yorkshire first team played 32 three-day matches. In 1969, it went down to 29, but – with the start of the Sunday League – there were also 21 one-day games, a total of 108 days' cricket which, together with the travel between games, were squeezed into a 20-week season. It was a schedule that required a particular kind of fitness.

You reported the first Monday in April, for a pre-season that was up to the last Saturday in April. Fred and Nick would arrive, they'd go out there and bowl for two hours, they'd come in, have a cup of tea and a sandwich, and they'd go out and bowl another hour and a half in the afternoon. They'd bowl themselves fit.

Then some time in the 1970s a new fitness regime started to creep in. We went up to Carnegie and a lecturer there, Dr Jim Golby, who used to play rugby union for Yorkshire, took us for training. He gave us eight individual exercises – press-ups, rope-climbing, step-ups – and we had to do as many as we could in a minute, with a break between each one. Then he said, "Halve the numbers, and that's your circuit." My legs were fairly strong so I could do a lot of step-ups. But not press-ups because my arms were never strong. So for my circuit I'd have to do twenty-four step-ups but only four press-ups.

Tony Nicholson

We ended up running up and down hills, then we did sprints, then this, that and the other. After a fortnight with Jim we were fitter than we'd ever been. Everybody was feeling good.

The next week we went to the gym in the morning, went to the pool to relax, then to the nets in the afternoon. But when we went to the nets the bowlers couldn't bowl. I rang Jim up, and he said, "It's my fault. We should have treated you more individually, strengthened what you needed to strengthen." He was very upset. "You'll be all right," he said. "It won't take long."

I think now they're so much into fitness. They're at such a level, they're like Formula One cars. If they're dead right, they're tremendous. But if they're a fraction out, something goes. I might be wrong, but you get someone who's super-fit and all of a sudden his back's gone, or his hamstring's gone. We used to say Nick was injured every day, but he'd turn up and say, "I'm all right." And he'd go out and bowl 25 overs.

At the end of the day we were fit for purpose.

The cricket of the 2010s is another world from the game that Geoff played in the 1970s, but then the cricket of the 1970s – with its explosion of one-day matches – had moved on a long way from the 1930s. The great Yorkshire batsman of the inter-war years, Herbert Sutcliffe, came into the first-class game in 1919, at the age of 24, and he was still playing in 1939 – still scoring his 1,000 runs every year, usually 2,000, sometimes 3,000. The greatest run-scorer in Yorkshire's long history was a director of Wiggins Teape and, when Geoff went back to the firm in the early 1970s, he had a conversation with him that he has never forgotten.

Herbert used to call in at the office. He worked for the mill sales division that was downstairs; I was upstairs. This particular day I'd gone down to sort something out, and he was there. Immaculate. A real gentleman. "Geoffrey, how are you? Have you time to sit down for just a few minutes?"

"For you, sir, I have."

He'd have a general conversation. "How are you? How's the paper trade?" Then he said, "I admire you at your level now. Do you know, if I played now, it would have taken five years off my career."

"What do you mean by that?"

"The pace it's played at. Bill Bowes used to field at mid-off and, if he couldn't stop it with his foot, then cover had to chase it. Because Bill was there to bowl. The fielders were there to field; he was there to bowl. If I were playing now, I don't think I'd have made the runs I made."

I said, "I think you would."

"That's kind of you, but I'm not sure."

Hutton, Sutcliffe, Bradman, if you brought them in today, they'd still get runs because they were great players. But what is different is the level of fitness, the fielding.

If he thought the cricket of my day would have taken five years off his career, what would he say now with T20?

Perhaps 1968 was the last year of an era. The Sunday League had not started so, apart from one Gillette Cup match which they lost, Yorkshire concentrated exclusively on the three-day game. Yet there was one great change that summer.

Yorkshire's championship title completed a hat-trick of successes, a feat not achieved by any county in almost half a century since, and it was all the more remarkable for coming in a season in which the other counties took advantage of a relaxation of the regulations governing the signing of overseas players. Unswervingly Yorkshire stuck to their Yorkshire-born principle as, match after match, they came up against many of the great names of world cricket: Sobers, Majid, Kanhai, Procter, Asif, Greg Chappell, Barry Richards and more.

Not only this but at Bramall Lane in early July they inflicted an innings defeat on the Australian tourists whose team contained most of the eleven who had gone one-up in the series against England. In controversial circumstances Brian Close had been stripped of the England captaincy at the end of the previous summer, a point not lost on one Sheffield spectator: "Never mind, Lawry," he called out to the Australian captain. "You'll have it easier against Cowdrey and England next week."

What pride Yorkshire folk took in their triumphant cricketers! In the *Sunday Times* Michael Parkinson called for the England selectors to pick the whole Yorkshire eleven, even suggesting the long-gone Johnny Wardle as twelfth man.

The tourist match was a high-point in every county's summer, never more than against the never-say-die Australians, and you had to go back 78 years – and 18 tours – to find the last time a county had beaten the Australians by an innings. 'The crowd cheered the winners in,' John Arlott wrote in the *Guardian*, 'and they drifted out to stare at the pitch before they turned home, smiling and proud, as if they had done it themselves. In a way, simply by being Yorkshiremen, they had.'

Brian Close was out of the team at Sheffield, recovering from a badly twisted knee, and the pride of leading Yorkshire to this historic victory fell to Fred Trueman. Jack Fingleton, the former Australian Test cricketer, was greatly impressed by his field placements, bowling changes and 'rare generalship': 'Here was one,' he wrote, 'who could have led England with distinction.'

Despite such success there were stories starting to appear in the press, rumours circulating that all was not well in the Yorkshire camp. Unlike other counties the players did not have written contracts. They were employed one year at a time on the basis of a verbal agreement and a handshake, and the pay was not generous. There was even a row about this Australian victory, with the committee arguing that the £5 win bonus was just for championship matches. At the heart of every dispute was the Chairman of Cricket Brian Sellers, captain of the great 1930s side, a man with no sympathy for trade-union attitudes or for professional cricketers who did not know their place.

Geoff recalls an occasion when the senior players sent for Sellers to request a bonus in anticipation of another championship title.

Brian Sellers

Sellers would never go near a dressing room unless invited. As he came up the steps, a silence fell across the room. He walked in. There was a big table. He just lent across the table, and he looked around. "Well, the state of what we're in at the moment is not very good. As for thee, Trueman, if tha bowled for county the way tha bowled for England, we'd have had this championship sorted out a long time ago. As for thee, Illingworth, if it looks a flat 'un, tha's always got something wrong with thee. When it's turning, tha's loose and ready. As for thee, Nicholson, I'm amazed tha's awake, tha's so busy going out at night." He continued all round the room.

I was a young twelfth man, and I sat in awe, looking at my heroes being torn apart by this man whom I'd never seen in this light before. It was quite frightening.

"Is there something someone wants to say?"

We all looked to Fred who was our spokesman. Fred was looking at his steel toecap. "Has tha got something to say, Trueman? Let's be having it?" And Fred said, "The captain wants a few words with you."

Closey stood up, and he invented the word 'erm': "Well, erm, Chairman, erm, it's good of you to ... erm ... come and ... Well, erm, the lads have been thinking ... erm ... if we're successful in this game ... erm ... and there's no reason to think we won't be and ... erm ... we know in your era you were a wonderful side and you won seven championships in ten years, well ... erm ... the lads were wondering if there may be some remuneration."

"Remuneration," bellowed Sellers. "You'll get your remuneration on September 24, the day of the sacking meeting. Them that survive, you've done it by the skin of your teeth. Them that goes, well, you've had every opportunity. Now, you lot, listen to me. I'm going over on a boat to France tomorrow, and I want to read in the *Telegraph* that tha's pulled thee socks up, tha's played the cricket that this Yorkshire public demands and that tha's got stuck in."

He went out of the room amidst a stony silence. Six or seven steps. Then he came back and put his head round the door. "And I know what you're all thinking. Bad luck. I can swim."

He went a second time. Then after a while Nick broke the silence. "I take it that's a yes, then." And we all laughed.

Perhaps the most significant of all the disputes that summer involved Ray Illingworth. Now 36 years old and aware of the progress Geoff was making, he sought from Sellers the security of an unprecedented three-year contract, saying that he would leave if he was not offered one. Sellers' gruff response was to tell him to go and to 'take any other bugger with you.' So in the autumn he went, signing as captain for Leicestershire. Fred Trueman, whose powers were waning, retired, as did Ken Taylor. The team that had won seven championships in ten years was starting to break up.

Close had led Yorkshire to four titles in six summers, but he had done this by remaining loyal to a core of twelve men, all of whom had been in the side from his first year at the helm. Together they were growing old, and the youngsters – Geoff, Chris Old, Barrie Leadbeater and others – were playing only occasional games when the first-choice players were missing.

In Geoff's case this was less often than in 1967 because England had no need of Close nor, in the first two Tests, of Illingworth. So, after the euphoria of his success the previous year, he started to wonder what should he do. Should he bide his time or should he go elsewhere, as Barry Wood, now forging a successful career across the Pennines at Old Trafford, had done?

Bob Platt was now the captain of the second eleven. He only bowled a few overs and stood at short leg, but he was very much involved with

Sellers, and he brought in all the discipline of the first team. He made me his senior pro. So he had the first choice of pegs, I had the second, and so on.

We had two games against Cheshire, at Hoylake and at Bridlington. Their captain was Freddie Millett. He'd been captain for years and was on MCC committees. He had an immense knowledge of cricket – and was quite a character; he and Ronnie Burnet swapped wives.

At Hoylake I went out to dinner with him. It was the first time I'd ever spoken to anybody about my thoughts and aspirations. The question was, 'How long do I wait?' As a spinner, I thought I could afford to hold on longer. But one or two counties had made noises; Glamorgan were one. Would I be interested in moving? So I said to Freddie Millett, "What do you advise? What questions should I be asking myself?"

He said, "There's far more to discuss than answering the question as it stands. I suggest that you look at this season. I'll buy you dinner at Bridlington, and I'll be positive in the answer I give you then."

That was in mid-June, at which point Geoff had played only once for the first team – in the pre-season match at Lord's, a rain-ruined affair in which he had not taken a wicket. But, unbeknown to him, that match at Lord's had set in motion a chain of events, the consequences of which only came to his notice a fortnight after the game at Hoylake.

I was at home one morning when the doorbell rang, and there was this fresh-faced reporter standing there. He said he was John Helm from the *Yorkshire Evening Post*. "I wonder if you would speak to me. I understand that you've been reported for throwing."

"I've what?"

I left him on the doorstep and went to ring Yorkshire. The staff there was just Miss Coates and John Nash. "Mr Nash is in a meeting," Miss Coates said. I told her what it was about. "I'm sorry. You know you're not allowed to interrupt ... Oh, all right, if you insist, but be prepared for the consequences."

John Nash picked the phone up. "You know I'm in a meeting." And he went through it all again, how I was not to interrupt. Then Sellers' voice came on. "I'm sorry, lad, we're discussing it at the moment. Don't worry about it. And don't say a word to that man. Tell him to go." His language was a bit stronger than 'tell him to go'.

"I'm sorry," I said to John Helm. "My Chairman is saying I'm not allowed to speak to you."

"I understand, but I am going to have to print something. Please don't take offence with me."

'Spinner Cope is accused of throwing' was the headline. The report went on to say that a decision from MCC was awaited, mixing in rumours that Ray Illingworth was considering a 'very attractive' offer from a Lancashire league club and that Brian Close had been approached by Lancashire.

> It turned out the story was from Ron Yeomans, the Leeds representative on the Yorkshire committee; he worked for the *Yorkshire Post*. He'd gone for a toilet break and made the call. Bill Bowes was their cricket correspondent but he wouldn't do it so John was sent.
>
> Two days later there was a knock on the door, and the same John Helm was there. "What's happened now?" I said.
>
> "I just wonder if I could buy you a cup of tea. I'd like to explain the embarrassment I had at the job I had to do." We spent the best part of two hours together, and he's still my best mate today.

Bill Bowes did reflect on Geoff's problems in his Saturday column, writing that he noticed a change in his action when he watched the pre-season nets at Headingley: 'He was arching his back at the moment of delivery and, although he began the delivery action with left shoulder nicely facing the batsman, he began the swing away far too early. At the moment of release of the ball he was not only "chest on" to the batsman but beginning to get chest on to the cover point fieldsman.'

The letter from MCC stated: 'His basic action shows a slight straightening of the bowling arm immediately before delivery. The committee felt that this fault can be easily corrected.'

Bowes was not convinced that it was any easier to correct a slight straightening than a severe one. But Yorkshire's captain had no such worries.

> I bowled at Closey for half an hour in the nets at Bramall Lane, and he said, "There's nothing wrong with you."

With Illingworth back in the England side, Geoff went down to Cardiff for his first championship game of the summer. He took the field just as Bill Bowes' column appeared in print, the ordeal becoming worse when he discovered that MCC had replaced one of the standing umpires with Syd Buller, a man notorious for his strict interpretation of the throwing law.

> That's when the real pressure was on. I saw him at square leg, then at point, then back at square leg, and I could see him all the time. He wasn't stood as they normally do; he was actually staring at me.

On a damp pitch Geoff was not introduced into the attack till late in the morning, but his impact was immediate, taking seven wickets in 19 overs as Glamorgan crashed from 95 for two to 144 all out. In the second innings he took another five wickets, bowling 34 overs and filling four pages of his scrapbook with cuttings: 'Cope shows the critics' ... 'New-look Cope spins to fame' ... 'Cope storms back' ... 'All clear Cope has Glamorgan reeling'.

> I got severe cramp because it was fairly warm, and I'd not been bowling that amount of overs. But I was happy. I'd performed like that under Buller's gaze. After the game we were crossing the car park, and he said, "As far as I'm concerned, go and enjoy your cricket because I can't see anything wrong." And I walked away with a great smile.

The team were playing at Sheffield the next day.

> Closey said, "Don't stop at Sheffield. Keep going up to Jesmond. You're with the second team. And while you're there, try to improve your fielding a bit."
> I got to Newcastle at two in the morning, We were staying at the hotel opposite the station. There was a blackboard on each floor, and you had to write in whether you wanted tea or coffee and what newspaper – but somebody came in after me and changed it. I got into the room, I looked out the window, the big block of the station in front of me, and I got into bed. Next thing I knew I was getting this wake-up call. I looked at the tray, and I'd got iced orange juice and the Beano. And the clock said six a.m.
> I went back to bed, and I gradually woke up. Twenty to ten. Report at the ground at ten for an eleven o'clock start. I got there at ten past ten, to be taken into the dressing room by Bob Platt and given an almighty bollocking.

Another late night occurred when he received a last-minute summons to go down to Kent:

> Illy had a doubt with his ankle. I got down to Canterbury at three o'clock in the morning, and the guy in the hotel said, "We're full." "But I'm with Yorkshire." "I can't do anything about that." Eventually they found me a room in Herne Bay. I had to go from Canterbury to Herne Bay, come back next morning, then Illy declared himself fit.

Another Test call for Illingworth brought him back into the side against Essex at Westcliff, a call-up that was more expected than that of his fellow colt Barrie Leadbeater, who sat in civvies in the pavilion as Essex's Keith Boyce marked out his run, ready to bowl the first ball at Philip Sharpe. Suddenly the loudspeaker boomed out: "Wait a minute, please." And half an hour later Sharpe was on the M1, driving to the Test at Headingley, and Leadbeater was preparing to face the first ball.

It was a game that got feisty when Geoff came in to bat at number eight and Boyce took to bowling short at him, forcing him to retire hurt.

Boycey hit me all over. On the fingers, on the hand. Fred went in when I came off, and he had words with him. "You wait till you come out to bat," he said. And Boycey's retort to Fred was to tell him, "You used to be quick."

Next day Fred came out with all the sweaters – "Tha sees that, lad, tha gets that for playing for England … this for going on tour … this for playing for Yorkshire. And I won't need many deliveries to sort you out." And he gave him a right working over.

After Fred retired, we'd get the bouncers from other teams. "Has Uncle Fred not come today?" They remembered. But you'd nobody to return it like Fred did.

Geoff played only two more games for the first team that summer: one at Scarborough when for the third and last time in his career he played in a championship match alongside Ray Illingworth; and one at Worcester when Fred was last man out, lbw, to lose by one run. It was the game when the great man took his last ever wicket for the county.

On the first day Fred had opened the bowling and not got a wicket. Then late morning Closey said, "Fred, get yourself loose." Then we got two wickets and Fred never bowled. In the afternoon Fred was out at deep square leg. "Fred, get yourself loose." And we got another two wickets and he never bowled. At the end of the day he'd bowled very little.

The same thing happened in their second innings next day. In the dressing room at the end of the day Fred said, "Have you got a spare sweater, young'un?" "What for?" "Don't worry, have you got a spare sweater?" He walked round, and he got this heap of sweaters in his hands. Closey said, "What's going on, Fred?" He said, "I've just been thinking. I'm going to sleep under the covers tonight so, when new ball's due in morning, you don't miss me." The whole dressing room collapsed.

For Geoff those sessions at close of play were a vital part of his education.

For half an hour at the end of each day there'd be a drink in the dressing room, and you could raise any cricket point you wanted. Then somebody would say, "It's nearly seven, lads." And that was the end of the cricket conversation.

You'd go out into the club bar, and there were always members. It would be half past nine, ten o'clock, before you left. If you walked in with five for 30, they'd say, "Well bowled, lad." And next day, if it was nought for 60, it would be "Well, you never could bowl."

You'd mix with the other team: "Have you come across so-and-so? ... We bowled off stump against him." That's how you learned. It went all the way round the circuit. It was a wonderful era.

Between the game at Scarborough, when he bowled alongside Ray Illingworth, and the game at Worcester, he played the return match against Cheshire at Bridlington, looking forward to his evening meal with Freddie Millett. He was top of Yorkshire's championship averages, but he had hardly played. He needed to have that conversation.

The Bridlington club was where Geoff had spent several happy weeks in his school holidays, staying with Jim Wood, the local headmaster, and his family. He followed Geoff's career closely, and he was there for Yorkshire's second-eleven game. It was he who broke the all-important news to Geoff.

Just before tea I was out in the middle, batting against Freddie Millett, and Jim walked out at the end of an over. He said, "Geoff, Illy's going."
I had no idea. "He wants a contract, and they won't give him one."
Freddie said, "I presume that means I won't have to pay for dinner."

Illy was going. For Geoff, that changed everything.

7

You're one of us now

1969-1970

An era had come to an end. No one knew it at the start of 1969, but Yorkshire's dominance of the county championship was over. Since 1900 they had won the title 26 times in 59 summers, including seven of the last ten, but they would not win it again in the 20th century. Overseas stars strengthened all their opponents, two per side through much of the 1970s – and, in the case of some counties, taking advantage of the small print in the regulations, as many as three or four. Warwickshire won the title in 1972 with four West Indian Test cricketers in their eleven, Leicestershire in 1975 without a single county-born player in their first-choice side. Yet, all the while, Yorkshire stuck proudly to their Yorkshire-born policy.

The loss of Ray Illingworth, Fred Trueman and Ken Taylor at the end of 1968 took crucial experience away from the team, and the departure of Jimmy Binks the next year left Brian Close without any of the senior lieutenants on whom he had depended during his years as captain.

> You'd run through trenches for Closey, and he'd run through them for you. But I do think he'd lost his rudder with the lads who'd gone. They weren't just people in the dressing room who'd got experience and knowledge. They were friends. When he looked round the dressing room, there wasn't a lot left of what he had, and I think that as much as anything drove Closey down. I'm not sure who he knew to turn to, to talk to. He respected Fred, Illy and Binksy, and I don't know if he had the same respect for those who were left.

Close went at the end of 1970, Doug Padgett in 1971, Don Wilson played little after 1972. It was a time of great upheaval.

> Eight or ten years is a long time to be one set of players. Then they all go, and suddenly you're looking around and you're thinking, "I'm nearly a senior player." Chris Old, myself, Leddy, we were nowhere near senior players. But we had the responsibility.

The summer of 1969, Geoff's first as a regular in the side, did not go well. Yorkshire won only three championship matches all summer, slumping to an unprecedented thirteenth place in the table, while Geoff took just 43 wickets in 23 matches, only three more more than he had taken in fewer than half the matches two years earlier. The team were beset by injuries, not least to Close himself, and it did not help that, within weeks of starting out as captain of Leicestershire, Ray Illingworth was appointed captain of England and summoned to his side not only Geoff Boycott but also Phil Sharpe and John Hampshire.

It was the first summer of the 40-over Sunday League, in which Geoff played only once, and Yorkshire's mediocre results in that were not helped by Close's refusal to take the competition seriously.

> What was it he said? "You throw down some sawdust, put on red noses and top hats, and you've got the John Player League." I was twelfth man for one of the first games, against Glamorgan at Neath. "This will never last," he said. He didn't have the enthusiasm for it that he had for the three-day cricket. There were some games he didn't play. He'd say, "I'll have a rest today."

By contrast, across the Pennines, Jack Bond's Lancashire – galvanised by their overseas stars Clive Lloyd and Farokh Engineer – were drawing great crowds as they carried off the trophy in each of its first two years. They clinched the title in the second year in a Roses match at Old Trafford in front of 33,000 spectators, a game in which Geoff did appear.

> The gates were closed hours before the start. A jostling, noisy crowd. There were so many on the grass that, when I walked out to bat, I had to fight my way through them all. I think I entered the field a good thirty yards to the right of the gate. It was very different from anything I'd ever played in before.

The one silver lining in Yorkshire's dismal summer of 1969 came at Lord's on the first Saturday in September, when they beat Derbyshire to win the 60-over Gillette Cup. Geoff was in the squad but did not play.

> Closey came in the dressing room. "I've lost the toss, but we're batting – but that's only to keep the game going till tea. This lot are frightened to death of us." It was all Closey's psychology: "Who are we playing? Just go out and win it." When Closey was like that, it rubbed off on everybody around him.

On the Wednesday at Hove John Snow had fractured a bone in Geoff Boycott's hand, putting him out of the final, and on the Friday his opening partner Barrie Leadbeater, taking a spectacular catch, had chipped a bone in his left hand, an injury only discovered shortly before the start of play at Lord's. They strapped it up, and he went out to hit a gritty 76 runs that won him the Man of the Match award.

It was his breakthrough innings and, with the 20-year-old fast bowler Chris Old topping the championship averages, it was no surprise when the following week at Scarborough the two of them were presented formally with their county caps. But, alas, there was no such promotion for Geoff.

I confess I went round the back of the pavilion and had a bit of a cry.

"I hope one day you'll bring home a Yorkshire cap for your dad," had been his mother's last words, and still he had not done it – though once, in a never-forgotten moment, he had worn one.

> We were playing at Bradford, and I came in at lunchtime. There was nobody in our dressing room. I went through the toilets and the shower areas, and there was nobody in their dressing room either. So I locked their door, and I came back and I locked our door. Then I took a cap, a Yorkshire cap, off the peg, and I put it on in front of the mirror. I said to myself, "I want one of these."
>
> I took it off quickly, put it back and unlocked the doors, and I still feel guilty to this day that I did that. It was a cardinal sin. I had no right to wear that cap. It was everything that every Yorkie dreams about, and I'd broken the dream by doing that.

September 1969. While Geoffrey Boycott nursed his injury in the Lord's pavilion – "All I need now to round off a perfect season is to fall down a big hole," he said sorrowfully to Michael Parkinson – Yorkshire were winning their eighth out of county cricket's 18 trophies of the 1960s. Were they really about to go 13 years, and 50 competitions, without further success?

The summer of 1970 began badly for Yorkshire. Their defence of the Gillette Cup ended before April was out, in a match at Harrogate so cold that at one point snow stopped play. Their Sunday League venture started with four defeats, in the second of which Brian Close damaged his shoulder, an injury that kept him out for a month and handicapped him for the rest of the summer. Things were no better in the championship, with three heavy defeats putting them back where they had ended the previous year – in 13th place in the table. The *Guardian*'s Eric Todd called the third of these defeats, against Gloucestershire at Bradford, 'the most depressing experience ... but the way things are going, there are plenty more on the horizon.'

Jimmy Binks had gone, and Yorkshire had started the season with Neil Smith behind the stumps. He was 21 years old, and he had been playing in the second team, often with Geoff, since he was 17.

> He was the true Yorkshireman, from Ossett. He spoke like a Yorkshireman, he acted like a Yorkshireman. A great team man, with a wonderful sense of humour. He was a biggish lad. He could stand up

Yorkshire 1970
standing (from left): GA Cope, G Boycott, N Smith, CM Old, RA Hutton, JH Hampshire,
B Leadbeater, JD Woodford; sitting: D Wilson, PJ Sharpe, DB Close, DEV Padgett, AG Nicholson

to the wicket to anybody. I can't recall him missing anything. He was immaculate. Really he was the rightful number two to Binksy.

But for the Gloucestershire match the county called up the 18-year-old David Bairstow, a sturdily-built redhead who was playing at Undercliffe in the Bradford League. He was in the middle of 'A' level exams at Hanson Grammar School and, on the second morning, he sat an English paper from 7 to 10 a.m., was driven by his headmaster to the ground and not left unaccompanied till all the other candidates around the country had sat down to the paper. Off the day's second ball he caught the former England opener Geoff Pullar and made such a good impression that Neil Smith hardly played for the county again.

David came in with all this fanfare – did his exams early morning. He was the life and soul of the dressing room, he won everybody's hearts with his personality, and that counted for a lot.

Stood back, he was a good keeper. He threw himself about and came up with some nuggets. Some of the older ones thought, 'Binksy would have taken that without diving.' But he was entertaining, he was a bundle of energy, and he was a much better bat than Neil.

I felt for Neil. He'd not done anything wrong. Whenever he could, he would go up to the stumps. I remember with Nick once, he came up. "What are you doing that for?" Nick said. "Well, it's only a slow pitch." Next thing he'd stumped somebody. "How embarrassing," Nick said.

I think I would have got more wickets if I'd had Neil. There were a few "Sorry"s with David when he missed stumpings off me. When you'd been brought up with Neil in the second team and you were used to them being taken, it made a lot of difference to you, especially in first-team county cricket. You'd create a chance, then you had to start all over again.

If you could have mixed the two together, you'd have had a world-class keeper. All in all, I think Yorkshire made the right decision.

Bairstow was still keeping wicket for Yorkshire twenty years later, but he never experienced the joy of winning the championship – unlike Smith, who moved down to the little-fancied Essex.

Neil became a bit more vocal at Essex, but you had to when you were playing with Easty and Fletch and Lever. The Essex lads were delighted with him. He stood up to Pont and to JK, and he retained his Yorkshire humour.

Gradually, through the summer, Yorkshire rediscovered their winning ways. At one point, with matches in hand, they were favourites to win the title once more, but their challenge faded in late August. In the thick of their improvement was Geoff, never more so than against Essex at Colchester's Garrison Ground in late July.

They won the toss on Saturday morning and opted to bat, watching as Essex's veteran captain-keeper 'Tonker' Taylor, cricket's ultimate sergeant-major, gathered together his young side.

"Boys, boys, I want you in 'ere now," he said. They went in the dressing room, and we could hear him speaking to them. "This fella Boycott can't 'ook. So, Boycey, third ball you bounce him. Lever, fine leg, you catch 'im. Right?" "Right."

Boycey ran in third ball, Boycs went for the hook, gloved it, and Tonker dropped it. Eight players fell on the floor laughing. Typical Essex. One G. Boycott then went to 260 not out. On the Sunday he got 98. Then he fielded Monday and Tuesday, and in all that time there were only two overs in the four days when he wasn't on the pitch.

We bowled Essex out in the first innings. I got three for 44. Then in the second innings, the third morning, the clouds were gathering, and I was innocuous for six overs. Suddenly Closey came up, and for once it was different. He put an arm round me. "Now then," he said. "Every pitch you play on is a different surface. You're bowling as if you're bowling on a good wicket. Your line's good, your length's good, but you need to bowl it a bit quicker. I've been watching you. I could have got to every delivery you pitched. If you bowl it that little bit quicker, I wouldn't be able to."

The score was 49 for no wicket, with Brian Ward and nightwatchman Ray East at the crease.

East went on the back foot to try and hit me. And it turned and got a top edge and went to backward point where Richard Hutton took the catch. The next ball Edmeades played bat-pad, Closey dived forward, rolled over and said, "That's better" and threw the ball at me.

That was the end of the over, and off the first ball of my next over Saville tried to play the ball with the spin and was caught round the corner by John Hampshire. He took it slightly behind him. A fabulous catch. And that was a hat-trick.

Fletch blocked the next three balls. Then Closey caught him, diving to his left. A bat-pad that went forward, landing on the fringes of the wicket. Gordon Barker came in. First ball he tried to sweep me, and it went off the bat, round the corner at pace and Hamps took another fabulous catch. I'd taken five in eight deliveries. The next ball I bowled I was on a hat-trick again, but Boycey blocked it.

Cope 18.1 overs, 8 maidens, 36 runs, 7 wickets

The match was over shortly before lunch and, according to JM Kilburn in the *Yorkshire Post*, 'the players had scarcely left the field before heavy rain began to fall.'

'Cope's hat-trick gives Yorkshire title chance' was the *Telegraph* headline, 'Yorkshire's bid for title set up by Cope' that of *The Times*.

Despite the triumph, Geoff had another challenge awaiting him that day – chauffeuring his captain into London for the game next day at Lord's. That summer Ford Motor Company had donated a fleet of 21 of their new Capris to the Test and County Cricket Board, with each county taking one away. Most counties, like Yorkshire, gave their one to the captain – though, in the case of Brian Close, Ford were soon having to send out a replacement.

Brian Close, always a risk-taker

There's a junction at Norman Cross on the A1 near Peterborough, where you go out at one o'clock. Well, Closey went straight on, and he wedged this Capri into a tree. He got out, and he flagged a couple of lads down. I don't know how many of those Fords he went through.

There was another time, we had a do at Fulford. "I'll pick you up," he said. He had this mat with rubber pimples on it on top of the dashboard. He was driving along, and he got a flask out, opened it up and got out a tea bag. We were racing up the A64, and he was mashing tea. "We're all right," he'd say. "Stop worrying."

The day I got the hat-trick at Essex, he said, "You can drive." So I was driving his Capri while he was reading the racing paper. "Where are we? … Get a move on. … Oh for God's sake, stop this car and get out." It was frightening. "Do you realise this car's never been above 45 mile an hour all the way here?" He got in the car, and he went with handbrake turns and everything through London, by which stage I'd lost quite a bit of weight.

For Geoff there was not just a match to play at Lord's. His bowling action had been questioned for a second time, film had been taken of him at Leicester, and now he had to attend a meeting. Brian Sellers and Ticker Mitchell, Chairman of Cricket and Head Coach, were coming down from Leeds to join him,

Covering Geoff's triumph at Colchester for the *Daily Telegraph* was EW Swanton, and he stated his opinion with his usual air of authority: 'Cope's arm looks straight enough to me – and, incidentally, it is at maximum height, almost brushing the right ear. He makes free play with the wrist, as all good bowlers should.' John Woodcock in *The Times* used almost the same words: 'The offending arm looked straight enough to me.'

"How long are we likely to be here, boss?" Ticker said when he got to the ground. Sellers said, "Not long, I hope." "Right. Is there a pub with Tetley's round here?"

We walked in this room, and Sellers used several expletives about "this young man's career". He suggested I was being tracked, followed, done and dusted, and nobody had any concrete evidence. He really let off. Donald Carr was there to show us the film, there was no committee. All Donald would say was, "The committee feel that …" "Who's on this committee?" "I'm not able to divulge that." "Well, if I send these two out, will you?" "No, that's not fair, Brian." "Well, tell me next time there's a meeting, and I'll come down. If I believed the lad threw it, he wouldn't be playing for Yorkshire. I'm here because I don't believe he does – and, unless we can argue with somebody, this is ridiculous. This is a young man with a professional career, and all we're doing is making it hard for him." He walked out, and I was taken with him.

Donald Carr came to me afterwards. He said, "I really feel for you. I'm talking to you as a friend, not as TCCB secretary. If there is anything I can do to help. It's a horrible business, but unfortunately those are the rules." I liked Donald.

As in 1968, Geoff was allowed to continue bowling, with Yorkshire asked to make a minor correction to his action. The crisis was over for now.

The match at Lord's had a further significance for Geoff. His father had taken Thursday and Friday off work and had driven down to London. For the first time in his life, having turned down the possibility of joining the Arsenal, he was in the capital.

We were about three-quarters of an hour into the day, out fielding, and this head appeared around the sight screen: the deputy organist at the chapel where they'd hardly ever had an organist for 47 years, and he shouted across at me, "The car's in the middle of that grass back there, and it's not moving unless you move it."

At the end of the day I said, "We'll have a look round London." He said, "Well, you're driving." I started driving, and the first thing he did was to pick the newspaper up and put it in front of his face.

Through Sharpy and Wils we were very friendly with the Black and White Minstrels. So we went to the pub by the stage door of the Victoria Palace, and one of the dancers whom we knew, Mary, came out in a crocheted dress that didn't leave a lot to the imagination. It was just too much for my dad.

We went into the theatre, we were plonked in the star seats at the front and, if he got one mention, he got four. His little face lit up. He loved his music. We met them all afterwards, and he was just in seventh heaven. That was his highlight. He'd been to a show in London. Then he put his newspaper up, and I drove back to the hotel.

He watched the game on the Thursday and Friday, and he came up to see us at Northampton on Saturday. Enid, who was the daughter of Dad's cousin Ivy, came with her husband John to the game. Then Dad went home, to get back to work for Monday.

Saturday was a good day for Geoff. He finished with 52 not out, his second fifty of the summer. Then on Monday, when he was out finally for 66, things got even better.

At lunchtime Closey threw a cap across the dressing room. "Here, lad, catch that. They've given you it." And that was it. None of the ceremonies that you see at Scarborough. Just "here, catch that."

I sat and looked at it, thinking what Mum had said the day she died. I went through my pockets, found all the coins I could and went out to the phone. "It's Geoff, is my dad there?" … "What's the matter? Why are you ringing me now?" "They've given me my cap." And there was nothing down the phone. The coins went in, and there was just silence. He couldn't speak.

I went back into the dressing room, and I was ready to go back out. I was wearing my second-team sweater, and Hamps said, "Hey, you're not going out like that. You're one of us now." And he gave me his sweater. So I went out with Hamps's sweater which was, shall I say, a size bigger than I should have had – but it didn't matter. I'd got it.

Closey turned to me. "Now you're capped, you're expected to do it." The apprenticeship was over.

8

This one's going steadily downstream

1971

As a captain Brian Close was always at his best when attacking, when making things happen. You did not win the championship by avoiding defeat, you won it with adventurous play, taking risks. By instinct he was a gambler, and that instinct was not confined to the field of play.

> He always did the gee-gees. He knew so many people in racing. In 1969 when we won the Gillette, we went from Lord's to Middleham to play against some jockeys on the Sunday. We took the cup round the ground. Then after the game we went back to a trainer's house for a superb spread.
>
> If you were twelfth man Closey would have you ringing numbers, with coded messages being given down the phone. "This one's going steadily downstream ... Clodderhops is working hard to get upstream." You never got a conversation, just "Tell him so-and-so" and that was the end of the message. It put me right off betting. If you said some horse was upstream, he'd get the paper out and start marking it. He got Mike Bore going with it: "Have you been to the bookies? Well, now's your chance. Get your money on this one." Always the *Sporting Pink* under his arm.
>
> Some of his ashes were scattered outside the bookies at Guiseley because that's where he lived at the end. He'd be there in winter in a light-medium sweater, stood outside with no coat on, with a plastic cup of coffee. His hand would be shaking, his cigarette would be shaking. "Brian, why don't you go inside?" "You young 'uns, you don't know what it's like. You're brought up soft." He'd always give me that line.

On a damp day in mid-September 1970, at the Circle ground in Hull, Brian Close led the Yorkshire team from the field. He had scored a good 68 in an innings victory over Somerset that lifted the county to fourth place in the final table, and all that remained was to say the end-of-season farewells. The summer was over, and they made their way to their various winter jobs – Geoff Boycott, John Hampshire and Don Wilson to the MCC tour of Australia, Brian Close to a company manufacturing automatic machines and Geoff – after three winters away – back at Wiggins Teape.

> The assistant manager, Colin Stanley, rang me one day: "You're going to get a call from Mr Loftus." They'd replaced some experienced

salesmen with youngsters, for their enthusiasm on the phones. But within three or six months the youngsters would say, "When do I go on the road? When do I get my Ford Anglia?" That was the in-car for reps in those days. They started to leave when they realised they had to learn the trade and, if they went to sell sweets, they could get a car straightaway. So the office was having to have a rethink.

"He'll ask you if you want to come back. If he offers you a job for this winter, say 'Why can't it be for every winter?'"

"He'll probably bite my head off."

"Well, he might not. You don't know, but he got a ticking-off from head office for letting you go. It was all about you being an expense on his books at Leeds, and head office would have taken that on."

Len Hutton had worked for Wiggins. Herbert Sutcliffe had worked for Wiggins. They were very much a sports-oriented head office.

I got the call from Mr Loftus, and I went up to see him. He knew that I had had two winters of hardship. Was it worth it for the game of cricket? I said, "Yes." I held my tongue, not wanting to say he didn't know what he was talking about.

"Perhaps this winter I'll be able to help you." He told me the offer, that I'd be back on sales. "Is that all right?"

I said, "Well, can I put something to you? The time I was here, I enjoyed it. I liked the people, I enjoyed the industry. Would it be feasible to come back each winter?"

"Oh, oh, dearie me," he said. Anyway he sent me out: "Go and talk with your friends. I'll ring head office."

I went straight to the telephonist. "Is Lofty making a call?" She looked at the board. "No," she said. Then suddenly the phone went. "Is Geoff about? Send him back in."

"I've spoken to head office," he said. "What's been agreed is that they will take on your costs. I have first choice of you but, if there's a bit of a crisis elsewhere, say Manchester or Newcastle, we'll send you there – but for no more than a month at a time and no further south than Birmingham. If you do that, you'll be getting good experience."

That was the deal. And I went straight back to thinking of Mum: "If you've got something to fall back on." That's when it really hit me that her words were the best advice I could have been given. Yet she died with me being a little bitter towards her. I was young, I didn't understand properly, and I just wanted to play cricket. Now her words all fitted into the jigsaw, and she was so, so right.

"See you in April," the Yorkshire players will have said when they parted in September 1970. Yet there was one man who did not come back: Brian Close. In late November, in a move that sent shock waves through cricket, the committee decided to dispense with his services both as captain and as player. One reason only was given in their public statement – 'his often-stated dislike of one-day cricket, a form of the game which becomes increasingly important as the years go by' – but in the background there were other factors. He had stayed too loyal to his established players at the expense of bringing through promising youngsters, there had been an incident during the full-house Sunday League match at Old Trafford when he had been rude to the Lancashire President Lionel Lister, and – perhaps most tellingly – he would turn 40 in February, he had struggled with a shoulder injury all summer, and a consultant's report offered the opinion that he would be fit to play only one more season.

> Closey had taken a lot on his own without talking about it to people. He was never one to sit in the dressing room, moping about what had happened in the committee room.
>
> I think it was right probably for him to go at that time. You believe a consultant. I can see the reasons.
>
> It's never easy when you get rid of somebody. He'd had the utmost pressure for a long time – 22 years at the highest level, all the time in a cauldron of expectancy, with highs and lows – and all of a sudden this rug had been taken out from under him. It hurt him a lot, and he took that hurt to the grave with him.

With hindsight it has come to look a terrible decision. Close went down to Somerset where he played for another seven years, even earning a recall to the England team at the age of 45. He brought through a group of highly talented youngsters, including Viv Richards and Ian Botham, and, but for an agonisingly close run out on the last ball of the season, he would have led them to the John Player League title, the county's first ever trophy, in 1976.

> His wife Viv was a Devon girl, the county weren't doing an awful lot and he was able to clear his head – in an environment that was very friendly. They were delighted to have got him.
>
> He just wanted to play, but you can't not ask him to captain the side when he had the ability that he had. The time he had there was long enough for Closey not to get over Yorkshire because he never did – but to accept what had happened. Then I think it hit him: this is an environment in which I can enjoy myself, I can relax. The committee are offering me drinks instead of giving me bollockings. At the end of the day his eyes were opened.

When you saw Closey down at Somerset the chuckle was back, the laughter was back. There were things you saw that were typical Yorkshire that they didn't know how to handle, but they saw they had a leader, somebody who was going to take them on the right road. You saw a difference in the team you played against from what you played pre-Closey. And they became a better and better side.

That extended Closey's career by several years.

There was no question now of Yorkshire beating Somerset by an innings, as they had at Hull at the end of 1970. In their first encounter of 1971, at Taunton, the West Countrymen won by ten wickets with Close hitting a near-faultless century.

He just played the V. You could see his eyes: "I'm going to show them." He got himself in. And when he was in that mood, when his mind was set, he was a fine player.

I was batting, and Closey was fielding in so close I had to walk away from my stance. "Closey, if you bend down, I can't actually get in position." He said, "You just get on with your batting."

Kerry O'Keeffe was bowling, the Australian legger. He bowled it fairly quick. Closey was giving him all these expletives. "Come on, if you can't bowl this fella out, how are you going to get wickets?" I played the ball down, and he caught it with his hand on my right boot. I'm not kidding. Then he threw the ball at O'Keeffe and said, "See." And O'Keeffe broke down in tears. He couldn't handle Closey at all.

I walked away and I thought, "Nobody else in the world would have caught that." Somerset people suddenly knew what it was all about. They got the biggest awakening of all time.

On the day of Close's Yorkshire sacking, John Arlott wrote of him that he was 'the most successful, passionately involved, tactically astute, intuitive, determined, personally brave, hasty and stubborn of modern cricket captains.' Of his appointed successor, Geoffrey Boycott, he wrote that he 'has not Close's drive nor flair, but he will make fewer mistakes and probably fewer enemies.'

Out in Australia Boycott celebrated his promotion with a glass of champagne. "It is the greatest thing that ever happened to me," he said.

I thought initially it would be Padge, Wils or Sharpy, one of the senior players. Sharpy had the background to be captain, but he was one of the lads and he was quiet. When he was on the committee he got splinters on his backside because he sat on the fence so much. Wils would have given it a bounce, it was always a laugh with him, but he was more of a playboy. So it was down to Padge. And Padge was the little man in the corner who went out for a pint at night. One to one, he had a lot of knowledge and he was happy to chat. But he wasn't Closey.

Nobody stood out. So they gave it to Boycs.

'It will be interesting to see how the side plays for him as captain,' John Woodcock wrote in *The Times*, 'and whether he can overcome a natural introspection.'

Alas, any hopes that a fresh captain would bring a change of fortune for Yorkshire were soon dashed. They were knocked out of the Gillette Cup straightaway, they finished two points off the bottom of the Sunday League, and in the first-class fixtures they set a new county record by going 17 matches without a victory. Only a win in the last championship fixture lifted them from second-from-bottom to 13th place. In the blunt words of Bill Bowes in *Wisden*, 'Yorkshire had the worst season in their history.'

They began the summer at Bradford with a match against the champions Kent, which could hardly have gone worse. Boycott, who had returned from Australia with a broken arm, surprised everybody by announcing that he had not sufficiently recovered to play, and he was joined on the sidelines by Barrie Leadbeater, who had broken a bone in his hand during a practice match, and Tony Nicholson, who had strained a leg tendon. During the match, which they lost by an innings, Phil Sharpe reactivated an old shoulder injury, Chris Old twisted a knee and Geoff, trying to sweep a ball from Derek Underwood, retired hurt with a double fracture of the nose.

Geoff Cope nursing his broken nose at Bradford yesterday.

It was a rain-affected pitch. Andrew Dalton played. He charged Underwood and was stumped by about six yards. He came in and said, "I shouldn't be expected to play on wickets like that."

Of all stupid things I attempted to lap Underwood and got a face-full. I think I'm the only person that Derek has actually maimed.

I went to Bradford Royal but, by the time I got there, I was so swollen they couldn't do anything. Then, when I went back, they broke the nose again to reset it. I came out with plaster of Paris across my nose and on my forehead. I looked a right beauty with my glasses stuck on the end of this plaster of Paris.

Colin Cowdrey wrote me a lovely letter. Typical Cowdrey.

In the Sunday League match that took place between the first and second days, Yorkshire brought in the young opening batsman Richard Lumb but, before he had scored his first run, he fell and fractured his wrist. And, on top of all this, Don Wilson, standing in as captain, had his own problems.

Wils went to Australia and, when he came back, he couldn't pitch the ball. Some would go right over the top; some would double bounce. He'd bowled that much in the nets, he couldn't bowl. He'd lost all co-ordination. He was worried stiff.

It was not the start Geoff Boycott had dreamed of when he had drunk champagne in Australia, and the strain took its toll. In late May, on the last day of the Roses match at Old Trafford, he left the field early and did not bat. Run out in a mix-up in the first innings and having got himself embroiled in an argument about Lancashire's bowling tactics, he was diagnosed with 'nervous exhaustion' and missed the following match.

You just felt it wasn't going right for him, and he took himself out of the firing line.

Such was Boycott's single-mindedness of character that he came back to score a big hundred in an innings victory over Nottinghamshire, and he ended the season with 2,503 runs at an average of 100.12, the first English batsman to average 100 in a summer. Yet even this remarkable achievement was not entirely appreciated by his team.

His final innings of the summer, the one that took his average into three figures, came at Harrogate against Northamptonshire. Ted Lester, the Yorkshire batsman of the 1940s and '50s, was the scorer, and Boycott liked to pick his brain whenever possible.

Northants had been bowled out for 61 on a pitch that traditionally took turn later in the match, and on the second morning, with the weather set fair, Yorkshire were building a healthy lead: 266 for two, with the bowlers expecting to have a lazy afternoon.

> Nick as usual was on the toilet. I was by the window in flip-flops and shorts. Some lads had their heads down, laying down. And suddenly they were walking off. We said, "Hang on, is it lunch already? What's going on?"
>
> Boycott walked in, and he said, "I've declared." "You what?" Nick came out of the toilet, blazing. "What do you mean, you've declared? You know what Harrogate's like on the last day?" And he said, "I've spoken with Ted and, when I reached 121, I was averaging 100 for the season."
>
> Nick said, "Just listen to this." And he walked out the back, threw something down the toilet, pulled the flush and said, "I've just washed you down there. You big shit." He was livid. The whole dressing room was livid and mystified.

Boycott's declaration worked out fine. They completed an innings victory before the day was out and thus brought to an end their 17-match winless sequence. But the accumulated failures of the summer had taken their toll, and Geoff – who was far from the least sympathetic to Boycott – found himself having one blazing row with his captain.

The episode began on the final day of the Roses match at Sheffield, with the team due to travel south – to Canterbury, then to Swansea. Play was abandoned at lunchtime, before the Cricket Committee had met to select the side for the next games.

> Boycott instructed so many people to come prepared for the away trip. The dressing room was full not just with the side but with lots of second-team players. There were bags all over the place. The Cricket Committee were meeting, and we sat there for over an hour, waiting to know who'd been picked. It went on and on. Finally Boycs came in and, as he passed me, he said, "And you can go home."
>
> I said, "Hang on, what's going on?"
>
> "Do you want to see the Chairman?"
>
> "No, I'm asking you. What's …"
>
> "Do you want to see the Chairman? No? Well, just go home then."
>
> Others were sent home in a similar manner, often those who weren't playing in the game but had been told to come, expecting to be picked.
>
> At that stage of the season none of the bowlers had really performed. But nobody had gone for a lot of runs. We'd all got similar wickets. So why me? He wasn't prepared to tell me.

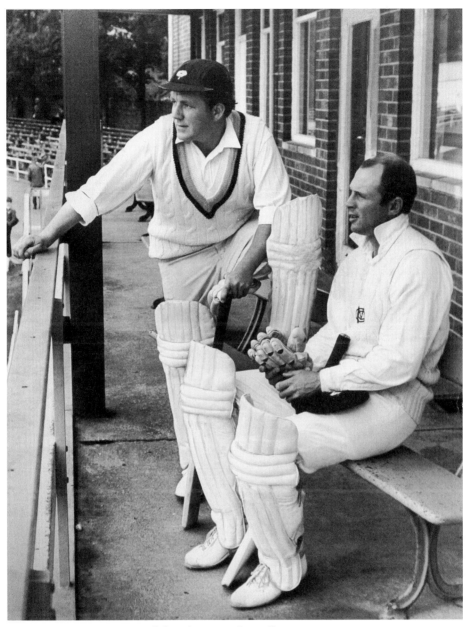

Philip Sharpe and Geoffrey Boycott

I went to the next second-team game. In those days, the committee arrived five minutes after you'd started, went for lunch ten minutes before you did, so you never had a chance to speak to anybody. I played in the league on Saturdays, but the matches went by and I'd still heard nothing. So I rang Sellers at his printing place, and this typical voice came down the phone: "What's up with you?"

I said, "I wondered if I could see you."

"You can see me any time ... I'm coming to Castleford, I'll see you there."

He came to Castleford on the first day. Sellers and Ticker were walking round. Ticker went to the gate, and Sellers came round to me. "Right," he said. "He's going to the pub opposite. He's ordering two pints of ale and, if there's no top on it when I get there, you're in bother. So what's up?"

I said my piece, what Boycs had said, and Sellers started: "He never spoke to you? He didn't explain why? ... Right, I'm going to the pub. You bowl this lot out, and don't you worry. The reason is, you're the youngest and you're learning your trade still. Even though you've got a cap, you're learning your trade. Nicholson and Wilson are old enough, they've got enough experience to sort themselves out here. None of you are bowling as well as you could, but I don't want you to lose your confidence. And that's all it's about. Confidence. Get a few more wickets, and you'll be back in. Now get on with it." And off he went.

It hurts, you don't want to be dropped, but the way Sellers put it, it was understandable.

Three and a half weeks had passed since Geoff had been sent away so abruptly from Sheffield, but his return on the final Saturday of August showed the county's communications in no better a light.

The classic of all classics. I was planning to play for Leeds, and in the morning I got a phone call. "Geoffrey, it's John Nash here. ... You should be at the Oval, and I forgot to tell you. What's the situation?"

I said, "Well, it's fairly grim. I did my washing last night, and I'm doing my ironing this morning for what I need this afternoon. And finishing the rest off later."

"Well, how long will it take you? Can you get down for lunch?"

"I'll do my best."

I put the phone down, got back to the ironing, and the phone went again: "Where the effing are you?" It was Boycs. And he went on:

"You can't rely on anybody." Gave me some grief. "Get here when you can." And put the phone down.

I finished the ironing, threw everything in the bag, filled up with petrol and drove all the way to London without a stop. I got to the gates at twenty to two and tried to explain that I was playing. "No, it doesn't work, lad, that one." "But I am, I am." Luckily Kenny Barrington was walking round the back and saw me.

I got parked, got up to the room. "Right," Boycs said. "Get changed, get out there and practise."

"What about lunch?"

"You're not having any lunch. Get out there and practise."

So I went out to practise, and one of the umpires came down: "Geoff, you're not allowed to practise on the field during the match." So I went back up to the dressing room, and Boycs did his nut.

Then, as we came down the steps, just getting onto the field, he turned to me and he said, "Nobody talks behind my back. Pick what end you want and set your own field." And he walked away. I bowled 29 overs on the trot, and he never spoke to me.

Afterwards I took him in the junior pros' room, got him out on the balcony, and for the first time I really went for him. I was livid.

"What are you saying about me talking behind your back?"

"Well, you've been to see the Chairman."

"If you recall, I asked you why I'd been left out, and you sent me home. You said nothing."

"Well, I'd that much to deal with. How could I?"

"That's not the point. You let me down badly."

I told him what Sellers had said.

"Well, that's sensible, isn't it?"

I said, "It would have been far more sensible if you'd told me. You caused me all this turmoil. And now, with this cock-up, I've driven all down here, and you treat me like that."

It's the angriest I've ever been in my life. It really upset me. All I wanted him to say was, "I'm sorry. I should have told you." But he wanted to argue the point and to accuse me of doing wrong.

He said, "And what else is there?"

I said, "Are you going to take me for dinner tonight?"

"You've blazed off like this, and you're saying, 'Am I taking you for dinner?'"

"Well, you've got your captain's expenses, and you haven't spent them."

"All right," he said, and he took me for dinner. We sat and talked about what had happened in the games I'd missed.

The team had changed since Geoff had first played in 1966, for all sorts of reasons, and the change was not helping his development as a bowler.

Those first years I came into a side that was on top of the world, with expertise in all areas. I was allowed to attack and try to take wickets, with a cauldron all round the stumps – Sharpe, Binks, Hampshire, Trueman, Close – that was not bettered anywhere else.

Then people started to disappear, and suddenly the side was not the same. The word 'attack' disappeared. I was in the side as the stock bowler, bowling a lot of overs for not many runs. It took away a lot of aggression. Johnny Wardle used to say, "Never be afraid to give a batter ten or twelve runs if you know you're going to do him." It got to the point where I thought, "I daren't give that twelve away because, if I don't get the wicket, I've got to pull it back."

You were always that bit more defensive. And with the overseas players coming into all the other sides, if there was a Test match on, you weren't playing an average side as you used to do, you were playing an average side with a star player in it – or two or three. And because we'd stayed as we were, the game became far more difficult. You can't replace experience, that's for certain.

Close, Trueman, Illy, Binks, Ken Taylor, you've got more than 2,000 appearances there. And you're replacing them with the likes of Barrie Leadbeater, Chris Old, me, and we've got fifty games between us at this stage.

Away from the cricket field, there was some good news for Geoff that summer. On 5 June, on what would have been his mother's 58th birthday, he became engaged to June Burnett, who by now was the manager's assistant at the bank.

9

It was like going to MI5

1972-1973

Yorkshire's fixture list for 1972 had a strangely late start, with no game – first-class or one-day – till Sunday 7 May when they were to entertain the touring Australians in a three-day match at Park Avenue, Bradford. It left Geoff free on the Saturday to play for Otley, the club for whom he tried to fit in a game or two each year. It was the day of the Cup Final at Wembley, with Leeds United playing Arsenal.

I'd left a message with Jack Harker, the Chairman, to tell him I was available, and I rang him on Saturday morning. "Where are we today, Jack?" And there was a silence down the phone. I said, "Jack, you've forgotten I'm available, haven't you?" "Yes, but don't worry. I'll sort it out." "No way do you tell anybody they can't play. I'll watch the Cup Final." "You know what it's like. All sorts happen. I know what a game of cricket means to you. I'm sure I'll come back to you."

Three-quarters of an hour later, the phone went. "All right, lad. It's sorted. Half past one. Red Lion, Otley. They'll be waiting for you." I drove down to the Red Lion, and by this stage it was raining quite hard. I looked around, and there were three elderly statesmen of the committee and a schoolboy side waiting to go and play their game. I stood there for a bit, then I went across to the committeemen. "Jack told me half past one. There's nobody here." "We're here, Geoff. It's the third team. We're playing at Weston. This is the team."

Weston is the back road to Ilkley. At the corner you do a right turn, and you go through a farmyard. And beyond the farmyard is this cricket ground, with an electric wire fence around the square and a 'pavilion' which is canvassing around an oak tree. We got out of the cars and into the canvassing, and it was fairly wet under foot. One of the young lads said, "Excuse me, Mister Cope, do you think we'll get back in time for the Cup Final?", obviously thinking the game was going to be abandoned.

A voice from the other side of the canvas said, "Tha's not laiking with county, tha'll be on in half an hour." We looked through the so-called plastic window in the canvas, and there were these two characters in wellies with forks, climbing over the electric wire fence and putting a few fork marks in. There were cows in the outfield, and they moved them into another field.

As one of the senior players I got one of the nails in the tree so I hung my kit up on this. We batted first, and I was allowed to go in at number five. I was in with a youngster who batted a bit like Boycs and ran like him, too. He'd hit the ball and, if he could get to the other end, he'd shout "Run". At about five to four, we were only about 82 for three, and everybody was walking off.

"What's going on?"

I made my way back to the pavilion, and I saw them putting the wire fence back up. Then the cows were brought back through the field to be milked and, after they'd gone through, they took the fence away, and we commenced play again.

We played through rain, but we kept going and, afterwards, I went back to the local hostelry. Then on the way home I called on June at her mother's house in Otley. "Where have you been?" she said.

John Helm had started a cricket round-up programme on Radio Leeds, every week from six to nine, giving out all the local scores, and he'd said that there had been no cricket played within a 30-mile radius of Leeds. I undid my bag and tipped out the whites – and it wasn't just grass stains, it was brown patches. "Well, we played," I said. And we sat there and howled with laughter.

The following day we played the Australians. I can't really explain it, but I think you know which game I enjoyed more.

The match against the Australians was, in fact, washed out on the first day and, with the ground not fit for a proper contest and a large crowd present, the teams opted to spend Monday and Tuesday playing two 50-over games. Geoff appeared only in the first one, bowling four overs before the rain returned. The Australian captain Ian Chappell was at the wicket for some of this time and, if Geoff's suspicions are correct, it might have been better for him if the rain had arrived half an hour earlier and he had not bowled to Chappell.

Four weeks later, while Geoff was playing at Lord's, his bowling was filmed once more, and within days Yorkshire had received a letter from the TCCB. Two captains and two umpires had questioned the legitimacy of his action, and the Adjudication Sub-Committee would meet to discuss the matter on 29 June.

In the meantime Geoff continued to play. Yorkshire had made a much better start to the season: in contention near the top of both the championship and the Sunday League tables and, by the time of the Adjudication meeting, through to the final of the new Benson & Hedges Cup. The first-class averages told a happier tale than in 1971, with four Yorkshiremen among the top ten bowlers: Richard Hutton, Tony Nicholson, Chris Old and Geoff. Alas, for Geoff, that was where it stopped. This time, unlike in 1968 and 1970, there was no talk of a minor fault; the film was studied, and he was suspended with immediate effect from bowling in first-class cricket.

I got a phone call from Joe Lister, the new Yorkshire Secretary – you're suspended from now. You don't know who's reported you. Nobody says a word. You see the camera arrive. Half the time they'd no idea and would set up right in front of the sight screen.

The press were on my back. Jim Laker and Fred Titmus were telling people that they'd help me. I don't think I'd ever talked to Tittlemouse. Jim I did know. He used to do the Sunday League. He'd walk round with a cigarette, and he'd talk about Saltaire and Shipley where he'd played. But I don't think he was doing any coaching. He was just doing TV work.

Then I got this call from Fred Trueman: "Now then, sunshine, what's all this bloody nonsense? ... Right, get yourself in your car and come up here. Nobody will get you up here. You need to settle down, gather your thoughts, see what you're going to do. Your Uncle Fred will look after you." He lived in Flasby, near Gargrave. I didn't think twice about going.

He sat me down with a coffee; his big dog was around. "Come on, come and bowl a couple of deliveries on the front lawn." So I bowled. "I don't know what they're on about. Have they given you any clue?" "No." "Listen, I know the man. I don't think you should be going all the way down to Titmus or Laker. There's only one fella to put you right. Wardle." That was the first time Johnny was mentioned. "He knows more about the game than anybody I've known."

Fred rang him. It was clear that they didn't speak on a regular basis. "I'll help him," Johnny said, "but it needs Yorkshire's blessing. I'll do it as an individual with pleasure, but I don't want to get into bother with them suddenly finding he's down here."

I went home to find a message to ring Joe Lister immediately. "Why have you gone to Trueman? He's only doing it so he can get an exclusive for *The People*." I said, "Fred doesn't work like that." "I'm telling you." "I'll ring him back." "No, the damage is done."

I rang Fred back: "Jumped up second-team cricketer, what's he think he's doing? This is your life at stake." Fred rang Joe, and Joe rang me back. "It's in order for you to see Fred." "What about Johnny Wardle?" "I'll leave that to the committee." He rang back later and said, if that was my choice, I could go. So I arranged to see Johnny.

Time has passed, and little film of Geoff's bowling survives. There was clearly something amiss in his action, but was it bad enough for him to be forced out of the game? Opinions differ on that. Pat Pocock, the Surrey and England off-spinner who had played with him in that schoolboy game at Hastings in 1962, wrote in his autobiography that he thought even then that Geoff was a 'thrower', a conviction that 'grew firmer with the passing years'. Geoff's Yorkshire team-mate John Hampshire, later a respected international umpire, took a more balanced view: 'In total honesty I have to say that most of us in the side thought there was something slightly imperfect about his action, yet at the same time I don't think one could genuinely say that he chucked it. It was very much a borderline thing.' Under the modern system, where a straightening of up to 15 degrees is allowed, it is almost certain that he would be free to bowl.

John Arlott, always sympathetic to the professional cricketer, reflected thoughtfully on Geoff's ban: 'Few bowlers have ever deliberately or even consciously employed an illegal action. It is possible to bowl faster by "jerking" than by orthodox means; but it is doubtful if more than two bowlers of modern times have consciously done so. ... Some cynics have said that all finger-spinners who turn the ball appreciably throw to some degree; and there is a germ of truth in that.'

> Every off-spinner straightens a bit. If we get really technical, I'd say to you that, on a turning wicket, Illy threw it. But if you think I was a Muralitharan, gee whiz no; I'd have shot myself by now. I never knocked stumps out of the ground.

Johnny Wardle, a slow-left-armer who could bowl both finger and wrist spin, was a legendary figure, one of only seven men to have taken 1500 wickets for Yorkshire. But in 1958, still in his prime, he had lost patience with the inexperience of the amateur captain Ronnie Burnet and was sacked by the county. In the 14 years since then, he had continued to play cricket with outstanding success – for Cambridgeshire and in the Lancashire League – but the rift with Yorkshire had not healed. He did not come to matches, and Geoff's only contact with him had been when he had joined the team for an end-of-season tour of Bermuda. Don Wilson had a coaching appointment in South Africa and, in his place, once more the Yorkshire slow-left-armer, was Wardle.

> He came out to Bermuda with Edna, his wife. He was quite rotund, and he was pulling on his Capstan cigarettes. One game we were playing in a quarry, and there was this Bermudan who had taken a fancy to me and to Johnny. He slogged fifty in no time, in 20-odd balls. Johnny was out at deep midwicket for my bowling, and there

was a big heave by this fellow. Johnny set off, his little legs pumping away, he was in his late forties at this stage, and he threw himself forward, rolled over and up he came. A brilliant catch!

The chap went off, and the new batter came in and took guard. I was waiting to bowl, and Johnny said, "Just a minute, umpire, do you mind if I leave the field?" "Have you been caught short?" "No, I'm off down the road to get the ball back." There was not one person in the ground who didn't think he'd caught it. The batsman came back in, laughing. He was so confused, he got out two balls later.

Another time the batsman hit the ball down the pitch. Fred was at mid-on, and Johnny shouted at him, "Get on after it." Fred went running off, and after a bit Fred shouted, "Where's the f...ing ball?" The batsmen were going up and down, and Wardle turned to them, "Have you two had enough?" He'd caught the ball and put it in his pocket.

Johnny Wardle and Fred Trueman in Bermuda

I said to Fred, "This fella is amazing." He said, "Don't you try and emulate him. To do that, you've got to be a genius. And you've got to be at the top of your game."

He had a fabulous action. He looked over his right shoulder and, when he'd finished bowling, he was right round. He bowled one ball that went right through Binksy for four byes. "When tha were a young'un," he said, "tha couldn't read me, and tha still can't. When my hankie's out, it's chinaman. When I scratch back of head, it's top one." No wonder they were talking about this fellow being a hard nut, but now he was saying it with a grin.

He lived in Thorne, north-east of Doncaster, on a triangular strip of land he and Edna had bought with his benefit money. At first they had sold snacks and fishing bait for the anglers using the fishponds, but in time he had converted the site into a country club, the Ponderosa, with a dance floor and a restaurant, and alongside it he built a wooden cricket shed where he coached. They lived there with their sons, John and Gerald.

It was a super spot, and he built it up, really made it hum. They had a band, and in the evening Johnny would be in his black tie, peeling spuds in the kitchen, then coming out to talk to people.

I went down there on the first day, and we had a good chat. On the second day he arranged for the press to come. He got them all lined up near this shed on the lawn near the gate, and he said, "Right, you can ask what you want to ask." Then, as it was drying up, he said, "Have you finished?" "Can we come back?" "No. There's the gate. It's shutting. And if any of you come back, I'll shoot you. The lad's got a lot of work to do, and he doesn't want bothering. It's a serious situation, the lad's career is at stake, and I ask you to respect it. And don't forget ... you'll get shot." And off they went.

"Come on," he said to me. "We'll go and have a bacon sandwich."

I started going on a daily basis. He told me what he was hoping to do, and he took film with his cine camera. He said, "If you fail, *we've* failed. If you succeed, *you've* done it." In other words, you take all the glory, I'll take the flak. He was brilliant. "Don't be down," he said. "You'll get through this. And when I finish with you, you'll play for England." There I was, looking into a deep hole in the ground, wondering if I had any future in the game, and he was saying, "You'll play for England."

At Yorkshire Padge had taken over from 'Ticker'. What did Padge know about bowling? Not a lot. And there was Mike Fearnley. He was a schoolteacher, fully qualified, lovely man, second-team sweater on, and he was trying to help. But Johnny knew so much. He started talking about cricket, and I just sat there. And memorised. I'd never heard the knowledge that was coming out – from anybody previously.

I was looking for this fellow who was supposed to have been a destructive element in the Yorkshire side, and I couldn't find him. This guy was warm, he was caring, he was helpful, he was everything I wanted. Some people react to hard words; some people react to a kind word and an arm around. And he knew how to deal with me.

Wardle's finest hour had been in South Africa in 1956/57, though it still frustrated him that in the crucial Test at Durban his captain, Peter May, had not pressed for victory on the last day, instructing the left-armer not to bowl out of the back of his hand. Unbeknown to May, but all too apparent to the keeper Godfrey Evans, he did still slip in the occasional chinaman.

Peter May said to Johnny, "We'll only survive if you bowl it tight." So he bowled a lot of overs for not many runs. Then a wicket fell, and Roy McLean came in. Johnny bowled him three of the orthodox, then a wrong'un, and it went through the gate and bowled him. Peter May came up to him and said, "There you are. If you keep it tight, you'll get your reward." Johnny said, "You go back there and don't interfere. Ask Godfrey later what I bowled."

"Never be afraid to give away a few runs," he used to say. And also: "It's up to the bowler to educate his team-mates into his way of thinking."

They got into a daily routine.

Get there for nine, bacon butty was on; half past nine you went in the shed; half past twelve or one o'clock, he'd send me home. Then some days he'd say, "We're going to have a walk" and we'd just walk around. And we'd do two to five. There was even a time when I had three sessions in one day. It was a round trip of 100 miles, but I didn't care. I just wanted to be there with him.

His lad John mainly, Gerald sometimes, they held a bat. They didn't need pads on. It was embarrassing. You were walking up to bowl, or you stood there, and you hit the net above, you hit the side net, it was dreadful. The green mat in the middle might as well have not been there.

It was like riding a bike. When you first learn, you keep falling off. Then when you do it, it's easy. After a while things started to become better. "That's it," he said. "You've hit it three times now. Now I want six times. Come on." He put a paper down. You hit the paper, then he halved the paper.

It wasn't just Johnny. It was Edna. It was John. It was Gerald. They gave up so much time. John was a teacher and a good cricketer. He bowled left-arm spin, but he had a short arm. Gerald ran the Ponderosa with Johnny; he'd go to bed at two or three in the morning, and often he'd not get up till eleven or twelve. You were part of the family. And Edna was lovely: "Ee, I'm glad you've come. He hasn't given me a bollocking since you've been coming."

Before the summer was out, Geoff played three times for the second eleven, trying to bowl in the new style that Johnny Wardle was developing, trying to be less chest-on at the point of delivery. But the feedback to the Adjudication Committee was not sufficiently positive for the ban to be lifted.

Chris Clifford, a schoolteacher who played for the Scarborough club, took his place in the Yorkshire team, as Geoff pursued the lonely road to rehabilitation – through the rest of that summer, through the winter months when he was back at Wiggins Teape, then into the next summer.

I was on my own. I didn't see anybody. Just Johnny. He was an oasis in a very large, open desert. If I went out, people would say, "Hello, there, Chucker, how are you?" They'd think it was funny, and it wasn't. It hurt.

At the back of my mind, always there was this feeling, "I might never play for Yorkshire again." And, when I was working with Johnny, struggling, I'd think, "How do I do this and still bowl at Garry Sobers?"

It's times like that when you find your friends, and John Helm was one. He was always there for me. And Yorkshire were supportive. They put a lot of trust in Johnny and kept in touch with him.

I got games all over the place – for the Yorkshire Gentlemen, the Wharfedale Ramblers. I played at Otley but only as a batter. For a time I felt the whole world was completely agin me.

It was a painful time, and Geoff's memories of it are a jumble. At one point he was invited down to Lord's for a meeting with Gubby Allen, the still-powerful MCC treasurer who lived in a house adjoining the ground.

I just wanted somebody to put his arm round me and say, "Geoff, this is what we think is the problem." But the Adjudication Committee never told me what I was doing wrong. Johnny was more infuriated than I was. All the time he was putting right what he thought they were thinking, but he could have been putting right the wrong thing.

I went down to Lord's, and it was like going to MI5. I went to see Donald Carr, and Gubby was in with Donald.

Cope tries Wardle way

GEOFF COPE, the Yorkshire off-spin bowler in search of an action free from suspicions of throwing, tried a new method during the Colts' Roses match at Harrogate yesterday. In these Yorkshire Post pictures (top left) Cope adopts the style used by his mentor, Johnny Wardle, by bringing his bowling arm from behind his back at the start of his delivery action. Top right: Cope shows a straight right arm at the moment of releasing the ball. Above: Cope talks with Wardle after bowling three overs for two runs.

Donald's secretary said, "Quick, Geoff, quick, through here. You mustn't be seen with Mr Allen." And Gubby disappeared.

Donald said, "Just have a coffee with me, and we'll go and see Gubby in a minute." Then, when we went out, I was hiding behind walls, making sure there was nobody there.

When we got to the house, the door opened, and a voice came: "Quick, quick." We went in, and he said, "It's your leg, you know. It's so high. That's your problem. Thank you for coming."

That was the closest I got to anybody telling me what was wrong. Nothing in writing at all.

Under the system in place since 1966 it was not necessary for umpires to no-ball a bowler, only to send in a report – which two of them had done, though Geoff was never told who they were.

> You have suspicions, but you don't know. You meet an umpire, and you always say, "Good morning, how are you?" They smile and chat to you. And two of them have reported you. They're probably thinking, "He doesn't know I've reported him." That side of it's not good.
>
> Equally, if you did know, you'd think, "I'll bowl with him at my end." And you wouldn't respect the guy in the right way. So I can see the point of keeping the umpires quiet.
>
> What I've never been able to accept is that a committee can turn up at a meeting, look at a film and they are not there to say what you're doing wrong. At what point is the arm straightening? Show me. You've got to be able to talk to somebody. All I got was the statement.

One person did later admit to having been on the committee: Peter Parfitt, the Middlesex batsman. He told Geoff how he had told them that he could not see how, with his longish hair, Geoff could bring the ear out from behind his hair if he was bending his arm. Parfitt bowled occasional off-breaks himself, and his action was hardly out of the MCC coaching manual.

> "Parf on the Adjudication Committee?" Richard Hutton said. "That's the equivalent of Rommel being the Lord Chief Justice at the Nuremberg Trial."

It was the worst of times. Geoff had married June in September, and he spent much of his spare time during the winter driving back and forth to the Ponderosa Club. Yet it finally proved worthwhile, and he was the better for it, not least for all the expertise and inspiration he had received from Wardle.

A happy day amidst his troubles, 16 September 1972

I was playing in a league game at Abbeydale, and he was walking round with his camera and tripod. His hands were waving, doing all sorts, and the umpire said, "There's a gentleman over there. I think he's trying to attract your attention."

He said, "Aren't you thinking about this game? Can't you see he can't play to the on-side? Get a man in there and there, and bowl it this line." Three overs later the batsman hit it straight at them: "I told you, but you need to work it out yourself." He saw so much that was different.

In May Geoff was filmed bowling for the second eleven at Chester. Then at four o'clock on the afternoon of Monday 4 June, more than eleven months after his ban, he received the phone call that told him he had the all-clear from Lord's.

'When I heard it was OK,' he told one newspaper, 'I simply felt, well, a bit exhausted. All the pressure of these last months suddenly being lifted was hard to believe, hard to realise. I just feel a bit empty – delighted, of course, but a bit unreal somehow. After the worrying time I've been through, I don't think any batsman will really worry me again.'

In another interview he paid tribute to his mentor: 'Johnny has been like a father to me. He has cut special wickets in his garden, bowled with me, spent hours talking and watching and coaching. He's talked about aspects of cricket I did not know existed. Now I have to find out if I can put it all into practice.'

Yorkshire waited till the end of July before reintroducing him into the first team – in a game at Bramall Lane against Derbyshire. He bowled just two overs in the first innings but, in the second, Phil Sharpe the stand-in captain gave him 31 overs and he took one wicket for 83 runs.

> I came on to bowl at the bottom end and, when I looked across at the old stand, I could just see this one face, Wardle, looking intently at me. Every so often he'd be making hand gestures or he'd put his thumb up. I bowled a lot of overs in that innings, and I was tired. But by the end he looked as if he'd bowled twice as many as me.

It was another bad year for Yorkshire: down to 14th in the championship table and, in the Gillette Cup, suffering the humiliation of losing to Durham, the first time in the competition's history that a major county had been beaten by a minor one. Geoff's return was welcome, but his four matches produced only seven wickets for 338 runs and, in *Wisden*, Bill Bowes was not impressed: 'Cope, when finally satisfied that his bowling action would not be censured, failed to show any of his old ability to spin the ball viciously.'

Geoff was starting all over again, and he had a long way to go if he was to live up to Johnny Wardle's prediction: "You'll get through this. And when I finish with you, you'll play for England."

10

I'm enjoying it again

1974-1976

The summers from 1974 to 1976 were the best of Geoff's career. He missed only one first-class game for Yorkshire, and his total of 239 wickets was just five fewer than Eddie Hemmings, the leading English wicket-taker across those three seasons. In the long hot summer of 1976, when the pitches grew dry and dusty, Geoff took 93 wickets, more than any other bowler, and thus joined *Wisden*'s list of 'Leading Bowlers in an English Season', nestled among such greats of the game as Bishen Bedi, Andy Roberts, Mike Procter and Derek Underwood.

> 1974, '75, '76. I've come out of the wilderness. My confidence is up, I'm getting wickets, and I'm starting to get recognition. I always played the game to enjoy it and in those summers, after all the problems I had, I'm enjoying it again.

In his darkest days in Johnny Wardle's shed he had wondered how he would cope if he ever again had to bowl at Garry Sobers, yet at Worksop in July 1974 he was doing so once more – though not for long.

> We got a wicket, Sobers came in and Boycs came up to me: "Come on, this is your moment. You're the only one who can get this fella out. Concentrate. Your ability, my brain." He always used to say that. And I bowled Sobers first ball.
>
> A few years later Garry came to a dinner, and he'd been talking for ten minutes when he saw me: "What are you doing here?" "I came to hear you talk." And he said, "The last time I saw this man, I came in to bat at Worksop. I took guard. And he opened me up like a tin can. I was looking to play him through mid-wicket, it pitched about leg-and-middle and took the off bail. How do you play those first ball? It was a magnificent delivery."
>
> "I love your version," I said, "but I seem to remember that it was a half-volley that you brayed onto your boot and that rolled back onto the stumps."
>
> *Sobers bowled Cope 0*

He never mentioned the 1,000 runs he'd taken off me previously. He hit me for five fours in an over once at Headingley. Like going round the clock, anti-clockwise. He hit me straight, he hit me between cover and mid-off, he hit me through extra cover, he hit me square, and I thought, "Where do you bowl at this fella?"

Then there was Colin Cowdrey at Dartford the next May.

Colin would come in, take his guard, have a look round the field, and he'd play the V. You'd think, "I'm bowling well here." Then you'd look up at the board, and he'd be 40 not out, and you haven't realised because he's not taken you apart. He's just worked you.

It was like a game of chess. You'd have four men in the covers and bowl it a bit wide, with a straightish mid-wicket and a straight mid-off. But he'd still get it through and work it round.

First ball at Dartford he clipped me off his toes. Leddy caught him at square leg and apologised. "Sorry, Colin, I love watching you bat."

Cowdrey caught Leadbeater bowled Cope 0

Sobers and Cowdrey, two great batsmen. Both of them retired soon after. They'd got to the level of me getting them out.

A very different style of batsman was Clive Lloyd.

You bowled the best ball of the day at Big Hubert, and he'd go down on one knee and whack you for six. You'd think, "Gee, that's a big hit." Then there'd be a swish and a miss. A big shout for l-b. Another big hit. And you'd think, "Jeez, how many's he got?" You'd look at the board, and he'd only have 25. Yet you felt as though he'd taken you apart.

He made you concentrate in a different way from bowling at Cowdrey. You'd think: "Where's he going to hit me? If I bowl wide, he's going to hit me across there or he'll go for the launch. You've got to bowl it straight." Off-and-middle, not even middle. You'd really got to concentrate. One six at Old Trafford. Against the turn, down on his left knee, he hit me over cow-shot corner, and it went an awful long way.

But I did him once in my 'leg trap'. Chris Old caught him at deep square leg, eighty yards away. 'Chilly' was the tallest player on the field, and he jumped up a foot and caught it. It was just flat, still on its way up. Tremendous power.

Lloyd caught Old bowled Cope 20

A similar challenge was posed by Viv Richards.

With Viv, if you had four men in the covers and bowled it a foot wide of off-stump, he'd whip you through mid-wicket. You'd take a man out of covers, put him on the leg side, and he'd hit you through the covers. And you'd think, "Where are we going with this one?"

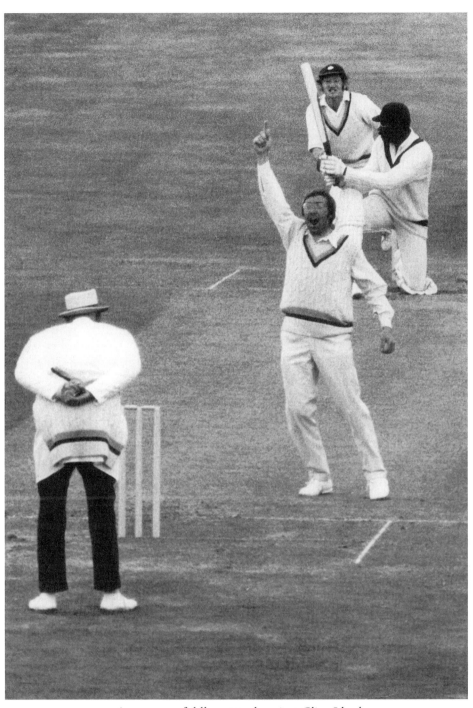

An unsuccessful lbw appeal against Clive Lloyd
David Bairstow is the keeper, George Pope the umpire

You'd be on your mettle all the time. You'd be running up, but you'd be staring at him, because you were waiting for a movement, to give you that split second: "He's coming for me. Push it down a bit, or bowl it a bit wider." You'd only the slightest split second to make that decision. And if he did you, you'd think, "What was wrong with that delivery?" – and the answer would be "Not a lot."

He got a double hundred against us at Harrogate. Then in the second innings he was run out. I was next to Dickie Bird at square leg. Viv ran ten yards past the wicket, stopped, looked at Dickie, and Dickie nodded. And Viv set off. That's all. He did nothing worse than stop and look at Dickie. And, when he got near the pavilion, there was this voice that was uncouth, rude and awful. It was Graham Stevenson's uncle, shouting, "Get off, you cheating ..." It ended up with 'Both' and Brian Rose jumping over the wooden rail, to escort Viv off.

I was on a hat-trick to win the match, with one ball left. Five for 25 in 23 overs. AA Jones was the last man; he was six-foot-odd. I'd been bowling at a little fellow, and I bowled far too full at Jonesy. It was a complete waste of time.

The next time we played Somerset at Harrogate, Viv got 90-odd in the first innings, a lot of them off Graham Stevenson. He played this one shot off Stevo. He just clipped it, called "Come one" and the ball sailed over the pavilion. Then in the second innings I was bowling when he came in. He charged me, and he smacked the ball straight up in the air. Stevo was underneath it, he had boils on his face, and he went from red to green to blue to purple to white. Then he caught the ball, and his colour came back. "I'm ever so glad I caught that," he said. "We all are." "Aye, but not for you. It means I don't have to bowl at him."

Richards caught Stevenson bowled Cope 0

Don Wilson played his last games in 1974, a shadow of the bowler he had been in the glory years of the 1960s, and his place as Geoff's spin partner was taken by the slow-left-armer Phil 'Fergie' Carrick. In the summers of 1975 and 1976 the two of them took almost half of all Yorkshire's wickets.

We got on very well. I respected him as a cricketer and as a bowler.

The umpire took him off at Bradford once because he was running on the pitch. "What do I do?" he said. I said, "Go and see Wardle." "I don't know him." So I rang Johnny up. "I know why you're ringing me," he said. "Go and get a saucer." He got me to roll the saucer. "That's how Carrick bowls." We straightened him up and off he went.

In 1975 Carrick took 79 wickets, ten more than Geoff; only Bishen Bedi among spinners took more. Yet late the following summer, when he had passed the 50-mark again, the county had still not awarded him a cap. It was playing on his mind, coming to a head in the penultimate match of the summer at Old Trafford.

> One end was turning, the other was fairly flat, and Boycs was keen to have the left-armer bowling into the turning end. Fergie bowled for an hour and a half, possibly more, and, whilst he was beating the bat, he wasn't getting the wickets. I was bowling at the other end, tight, not giving anything away. I was frustrated so I called Boycs over. "You've got to switch us round." "But he's beating the bat." "He hasn't got a wicket yet, Boycs. If we try it for a bit and it doesn't work, we can switch it back. We've got to keep the pressure on." So we swapped ends. I got David Lloyd caught behind, coming down the track. It turned quite a bit, and I finished up taking the last six wickets.

> Cope   18.2 overs, 10 maidens, 37 runs, 6 wickets
> Carrick   27 overs, 13 maidens, 50 runs, 0 wickets

For a few weeks Phil had been mumbling about a cap. "Don't you think I've done enough for a cap?" I came off, and he was sat down, dejected. I sat beside him. I talked to him about partnerships in the same way Wils had talked to me. When we played Kent that summer, Mike Denness had said in the *Yorkshire Post* that we were the best pair of spinners in the country. I was buoyed by that because we were a pair.

I said to Phil, "Just be glad you're not a capped player." "What do you mean?" "If you'd been a capped player, they'd have said you should have bowled them out." "I did my best." I was very hard on him, and I'm not used to that sort of speech with anybody. And I left him for a bit.

We went to Scarborough, and I got hold of him the night before the game. "What did I say? Did that hurt?" "It brought it home." "Well, now I'll apologise. There was no intention of hurting you. It's part of your learning. I think you're the best spinner we've got, and I think you'll have a long career. But it's times like that when you have to say: 'We bowled them out.'" "Well, you got six, I didn't get one." "Listen to me. *We bowled them out.* That's what you've got to think about."

In the match Carrick took seven wickets and was finally awarded his county cap, along with the left-arm fast-medium bowler 'Rocker' Robinson. Up to that point in the summer, with Chris Old out with a bad knee, Geoff had been the only capped bowler in the line-up.

*Phil Carrick and Geoff leave the field
after bowling out Nottinghamshire at Park Avenue, Bradford, 1976*

For Geoff it meant a lot of bowling – more than 1,000 overs in the 20-week season – and he felt the strain during the great heatwave of August.

> "What's up with you?" Johnny Wardle said to me. I said I was feeling a bit tired, mid-late August, and he said, "What are you on about? I bowled 1,000 overs in eight weeks once."

The batting was also short of experience, with both Boycott and Hampshire sustaining injuries that summer, and on several occasions the county turned to Geoff, the former opening batsman at Leeds, to go in at the top of the order. He had done it in Boycott's absence the year before at Hove, when John Hampshire had been standing in as captain.

> We played the previous game at Harrogate against Derrick Robins' XI. A lad called Andrew Townsley played. He'd got runs for the second team, he'd got runs for Castleford, he was a very good league cricketer.

Barry Stead and Clive Rice were bowling – 'Steady' off ten paces, Clive Rice off eight, half pace – and Andrew bricked it. "Jeez, aren't they quick?" he said. I said, "How are you going to go on at Hove if Snow decides he wants to bowl?" "They shouldn't expect me to open, should they?"

I talked with Hamps, and he said, "You can go in first with Lumby." I said, "Thanks very much." We fielded first and batted for the last hour. Snow bowled three deliveries at me, and he stood. He said, "Is somebody taking the Michael?" His face was straight. I never answered. He went back and said, "Round the wicket, please." And he steamed in.

I saw him off, and I got out to Greigy with five minutes to go. I came back in the dressing room, and I just sat there for a few minutes. Then the lads came down from the watching area, and they said, "Well done." I said to Hamps, "Were that quick, or were that quick?" He sat beside me, and he said, "Just tell me. Did you answer him when he spoke to you?" I said, "No, I didn't say a word." "Well," he said, "the answer is, that were quick. I thought you'd said something and wound him up."

Cope lbw Greig 17

It was a different story in the second innings when Geoff again opened, this time with the team chasing 195 for victory.

It was a rain-affected pitch, and Snowy bowled off four paces. Greigy said, "What are you doing?"

"If you want off spin, you bowl." That was typical Snowy. "If I bowl on here, I'll kill somebody." And he didn't want to know.

We then got Greigy trooping in, bowling these great loopy things. They were flying all over the place. They'd beat the bat and the keeper. There were 28 byes. He should have bowled us out. It was a spiteful pitch. I got hit everywhere. Hamps came in: "We're all right, pal." He was the only one that made it look as though you could play on it.

I batted two hours for 39 – nudges, grafts, anything I could get. It was certainly a knock that stays in the memory.

But my innings at Chesterfield was my pièce de resistance. It started on the Saturday night when I came in as nightwatchman. We finished the night on 33 for three. Very shortly on the Monday we were 46 for five.

We were on, off, on, off all day. Arthur Jepson, the umpire, was calling me Herbert. "'Erbert, come on." They had Ward, Hendrick,

117

Barlow. Every time they came off, they put their feet up, then started again. 'Bluey' Bairstow got 44, then Stevo came in. It wasn't a green, green wicket, but because of the dampness and the cloud it greened over just enough and it was fizzing through.

"We'll play for five," I said. "That's one hit," he replied, but for once he kept his head down. The stand developed, so we started playing for ten, and he reached a most unlikely fifty. Then there was a bowling change, they brought Keith Stevenson into the attack, and Graham said, "He's got to go." I said, "You're playing so well. Every run here is worth two." But Stevo couldn't resist. He smashed him for 28 or 29 in two overs. Then he smacked one up in the air and was caught.

He walked all round the square-leg umpire to avoid meeting me at the bowler's end, with his head down. But, in the context of the game, it was a super knock.

Stevenson caught Swarbrook bowled Ward 83

I kept going, and finally at twenty to six I was lbw to Miller. Arthur Jepson looked at me, and he said, "Herbert, I've had enough. You've had enough." I came out to field, and I was aching in every place possible.

Cope lbw Miller 61

'Cope's innings,' wrote Terry Brindle in the *Yorkshire Post*, 'developed, matured and became a grandfather knock, a bewhiskered antique of an innings which salvaged Yorkshire's pride minute by defiant minute ... If it was Cope's greatest innings, it must also have been his dullest to watch.'

Cope to rescue

Tail-ender holds out to save Yorkshire

By PETER JOHNSON

NIGHTWATCHMAN Geoff Cope put in a day's overtime guarding a 19-year-old Yorkshire record yesterday.

Cope, a tail-ender with an opener's patience and aspirations, had been asked to face three critical overs against Derbyshire at Chesterfield on Saturday night.

Instead, he stayed for 72 overs, making 61—just five short of the highest score of a career that began ten years ago.

It was not the biggest and far from the most exhilarating contribution to Yorkshire's 251. Both those distinctions went to young Graham Stevenson's career-best 83. But it was Cope's sheer cussedness that dragged Yorkshire clear of the follow on.

GEOFF COPE . . . saved follow-on

In the winter I had to speak at Wombwell. When it got to question and answer, this fellow stood up. "Now then, tha's talked about characters, tha's talked about entertainment. I were at Chesterfield the day you got 61 in four-and-a-half hours. I've never been so bored in my life. I took a day's holiday, and tha played like that. All I ask is, if you're gonna to do it again, will you tell me, and I won't book any holiday."

I'd given blood, sweat and tears.

Geoff's walk to the wicket was not one that emptied the bars as, say, Graham Stevenson did, but there were occasional moments when he hit out. He reckons he hit nine sixes in his career, the best of them on a damp evening in early May at Bradford Park Avenue – in a Benson and Hedges match against Surrey.

Robin Jackman was bowling at the football end. He came steaming in, and somehow I managed to hit the ball straight back at him. It was still rising when it hit the sight screen behind him. He ducked as it flew past him, and he finished up on his backside on the ground. He lay there for a while, and someone – Geoff Howarth, I think – said, "What are you doing, Jackers?"

"I've just been contemplating," he said. "If it's come down to Tojo hitting me for six, maybe it's time for me to retire."

At Scarborough, against Kent in 1974, Geoff was at the non-striker's end with one ball of their allotted 100 overs left and his partner, Barrie Leadbeater, on 98 not out. Eight years on from his debut, Leadbeater was playing his 180th first-class innings, and he had still not scored a century. He glanced the ball down to fine leg, and Geoff set off like a hare.

I was more than halfway down the pitch for the second, and Leddy sent me back. I said to him, "Why did you do that?" He said, "Well, 99 not out is better than 99 run out." I'd run nearly three.

Another innings that Geoff recalls, albeit a brief one, was at Sheffield's Abbeydale Park against the West Indians in 1976. The pitch, according to *Wisden*, had 'pace and uneven bounce', and on the first day Chris Old took seven wickets as the tourists managed a meagre total of 103. Late on the second day Yorkshire were on the verge of a famous victory, needing only 110 to win.

The West Indians had turned up at the beginning of the match and just gone through the motions. Now suddenly they realised they could lose to a county, and all they did was to up the standard to Test cricket. They did nothing that was nasty. They did nothing that was out of the ordinary. They just played at Test match level.

We had about an hour's batting on the Thursday night. We finished at 10 for one, and extras were about eight. Leddy had one not out. On the way home he crashed his car and couldn't come back on the Friday. We sent him a telegram: "We thought there were other ways of avoiding the bouncers."

I was in at number ten. I had a good net in the morning, and I went out with the score on 75 with an ashen-faced Phil Carrick at the other end. As I walked past him, his lips were moving, but there was nothing coming out. I said, "Are you trying to say something?" He said, "They're trying today."

I took my guard. Michael Holding, 'Whispering Death', was way up the hill, with seven in the arc in the slip cordon and a short leg so close he was in danger of being trampled on. Michael set off, and from the side his action was perfect. His head was still, his arms rotated slowly, his thighs went the same way, and gradually his pace built up. All the time he was running in, he was showing you that red piece of leather. I was convinced that I'd picked my bat up, when there was a thump on my hip. The ball went down to fine leg, and Phil Carrick shouted, "Run." I got to the other end. Michael was in the middle of the pitch, and he looked at me and smiled. He said, "Umpire, did Geoff play a shot?" There was a moment of hesitation, then the umpire, Eddie Phillipson, said, "Michael, he was thinking about it."

I played a few, then suddenly this one went past fairly sharp. And I looked at Michael. He said, "Always in your half, pal. I understand."

From that day at Abbeydale, Michael and I have always got on. I was in South Africa last year, walking down the street with a few others, and there was a tap on my shoulder. "Always in your half, pal, always in your half."

Yorkshire all out 90 (Cope not out 2)

At that stage we had one or two lads who were beginning to think they could play this game. And whatever you say, the word 'experience' is probably the most important word of all. That half an hour on the Friday morning was a far better experience than any net session you could wish to have. They saw the level. Hang on, they were thinking, I'm striving to play county cricket. If I want to play Test cricket, I've got to go up four more notches. It was the biggest education of the lot – and a fabulous game of cricket.

There were plenty of good games in those years, with the ones against Mike Brearley's Middlesex regularly producing grandstand finishes. Geoff missed the tied match at Bradford in 1973, but he was in the thick of it two years later at Lord's.

> There was torrential rain on the Thursday night. The water level was from the edge of the square. As we looked out from the boxes at the top of the Tavern area, the people were walking to cars with their trousers rolled up.

It was 2.30 on Friday afternoon before play resumed. With the spinners Titmus and Emburey running amok on the drying pitch, Yorkshire lost their last eight wickets within the hour, leaving Middlesex to score 158 in two hours. In the 40 minutes to tea the openers raced to 63 for no wicket.

> Wiggins Teape were part-sponsors of the game, and one of their directors, a fellow called Hetherington, an MCC member, was there. When we were bowled out, he was standing at the gate, one foot on the grass, one on the step, having drunk quite a lot of wine, mockingly saying: "If you get yourselves out of this, there's a case of champagne."
>
> We went out to bowl. Cooper and Sidebottom two overs each, then I was on, with Phil Carrick at the other end. Brearley and Mike Smith plundered the sweep or slog, and runs were scored, not in a legitimate manner: off the gloves over gully's head, off the back of the bat, top edges that stopped two yards in front of a fielder. It was like a Wednesday night slog. They were trying not to let me settle, and they got away with everything. But the runs kept going on, and we hadn't a lot to play with.
>
> I came off at tea, and this idiot was waiting at the gate. "Ah-ha, you're not going to get your crate, are you?" I said to Boycs in the dressing room, "Go away. Go away. Leave me alone." I realised I was supposed to win this match, and I'd got to work it out.
>
> First ball after tea I bowled Brearley, and we were back to playing proper cricket. But the game kept edging away from us. It was frustrating. We'd beat the bat, they'd nick the ball, but the wickets didn't come.

With three overs remaining, and Graham Barlow and the Trinidadian Larry Gomes scampering quick singles, Middlesex were 148 for five, just ten runs from victory. Then Geoff struck twice in two balls, bowling Gomes and Tim Lamb; Barlow got into a muddle with Fred Titmus and was run out; Titmus himself was lbw, and, off the fourth ball of the penultimate over, with six runs still needed, Mike Selvey was run out by a direct hit by Peter 'Squidgy' Squires, the England rugby wing.

Squidgy never quite made it as a batsman, but as a fielder you'd put him in the top ten, maybe the top five, in the country. To me he was a mini-Ken Taylor. Very much down at ground level but light on his feet.

In ten balls five wickets had fallen for four runs and, according to Brian Chapman in the *Guardian*, 'Yorkshire ran off amidst a positive orgy of back-slapping and hand-shaking.'

I came off for the champagne, and he was nowhere to be seen! I got a call back at work some weeks later: "We understand Mr Hetherington owes you a crate of champagne. Is this right?" "Well, yes, by the time it's taken him, it should be two." And sure enough, he paid up.

It was a cracking game, the sort you played from time to time on rain-affected wickets. You see these flat pitches now, and you think what the rain-affected ones brought you. A lot of very interesting cricket. Batters had to be good players to play on those pitches. And there was something in it for the bowler.

Phil Carrick matured because he had to bowl in these tight games. It was part of the learning pattern. You felt this tension all the time when you were on the field, but you learned how to live with it.

The next meeting of Middlesex and Yorkshire, the following July, provided a finish even more dramatic than the one at Lord's – and this time it had the added tension of being played out in front of a partisan and highly critical Bradford crowd.

They shouted some rubbish at you. It was regular and it was often. A chap gave me almighty abuse between lunch and tea in one particular game. "Tha never could bowl, Cope ... Get yourself sorted out." After tea we bowled the opposition out, Fergie and I. And as we came off, this chap's stood up and he's saying, "Well bowled, you two." There was a little man sat next to him all the day, and he just nudged this chap: "That's my lad." My dad.

In those days the players knew the members. You'd go for a drink in the bar afterwards. The bars would be humming. Nowadays the bar's shut, and everybody's gone home in five minutes. They were never backward in telling you how poor you were. Then the following night you'd be their best mate because you were a star.

Middlesex needed five to win when the last man stepped out – and the last man that Tuesday evening was their opening batsman Clive Radley. He had broken a finger in the field on Saturday and gone home, only to be summoned back on Monday night 'in case of emergency'. His left arm in a black sling, he took guard as a left-hander to face the medium-pacer Mike Bore. Then, after surviving an appeal for a catch by keeper Bairstow, he discarded his sling, turned himself back into a right-hander and chopped a ball down to third man for three runs. Now it was one for the tie, two to win, and he was on strike against Geoff. But, in the words of Brian Chapman, 'There was no fairytale finish. Radley was drawn forward by the fifth ball of the over and was stumped gleefully and noisily by Bairstow.' Yorkshire had beaten Middlesex, that summer's champions, by one run.

> Bradford was a good cricket wicket. Always the spinner came into it in the second innings; nine times out of ten you got a result. If you batted well, you got runs. If you bowled well, you got wickets. We had so many good games there.

Runs, wickets, thrilling finishes. Through these three summers Geoff was ever in the thick of Yorkshire cricket. He had been banned in mid-1972, when only 25 years old and still a learner in the Yorkshire eleven, but by 1975, with so many of the senior players gone – Don Wilson, Richard Hutton, Tony Nicholson and Philip Sharpe – he had become a senior player.

That summer of 1975 Yorkshire played their best championship cricket for some years, finishing second to Ray Illingworth's Leicestershire in the final table. It was the summer of cricket's first World Cup, and it was not without significance that Yorkshire's biggest three victories came in the month of June when the overseas stars around the counties were playing in the Cup. With the South Africans Richards and Procter also out of action, injured, they came up against a Gloucestershire eleven without Procter, Zaheer and Sadiq, Warwickshire without Kanhai, Kallicharran and Murray, and Hampshire without Richards, Greenidge and Roberts, comprehensively triumphing over the three all-English teams: once by an innings, twice by nine wickets.

> They were three of the biggest employers of overseas players, and we beat them all easily. We got more pride out of that than anything.

11

You're going to be in charge of the Bovril

1976-1977

The first indication that Geoff was under consideration by the England selectors came when he received a telephone call from Ken Barrington in November 1975. Would he be free to join Derrick Robins' team for a five-week tour of South Africa, starting in January?

> The agreement I had with work was: "If England came for me, they'd do all they could – but if Swanton came for a gin-and-tonic tour, they'd hope I'd say no." So, when Kenny rang me about Derrick Robins, he said, "Let me explain. Because it's South Africa we can't go as an England side. Derrick very kindly lets us use his name. We invite four or five players from other countries to make it a bit of a global, but the England selectors have a big say in who goes."

Barrington spoke to Colin Stanley, Geoff's boss, and the deal was done. The Gleneagles Agreement, banning sporting contact with apartheid South Africa, was still to come, and these private tours were cricket's way of maintaining contact – with matches against non-white and mixed teams built into the schedule. Geoff, with no interest in politics, was going to play cricket, but he soon realised that you could not escape the unpleasantness of the country.

They started with a one-day match on matting against a 'South African African XI' in the township of Soweto, where Geoff took eight wickets.

> We smashed 200 and plenty and bowled them out for 120. It was men against boys, but afterwards we were given a civic reception – a plate with jam and bread on and a chipped cup, no saucers. They gave you everything they'd got.
>
> One lad got a fifty, and he played very well. I offered him a beer. "No, master. No, master. Can't." Then their President shook my hand, and he said, "This is what this is all about." The black hand and the white hand together. And he said to this lad, "Please, have a drink with your new-found friend." The whole day was a wonderful experience.
>
> The following day we played at the Johannesburg Wanderers Country Club against the Staggerers, where it was 100 guineas membership with 100 guineas per sport. It reeked of money. All these whites. And this lad who'd got fifty was serving. I called him over, and I said, "You played against me yesterday." "Yes, master. Yes, master." And this guy

came up and said, "Get back to work." He had a cane in his hand. "Just a minute," I said. "This lad played against us at ..." "I don't care what he's done."

Phil Carrick was out there coaching, and he joined us. He frightened me to death. The first meal we had was a lunch. We were having steaks after soup, and somebody had got a steak that was a bit burnt. "Ey, you, give that steak to the dogs. Get it changed." "Who are you talking to?" "That's how you talk to them here, Geoff. Otherwise they'll try it on with you." I said, "I can't live with that."

I did things on that trip that maybe you shouldn't do. The grounds at that time were nine-tenths for the whites. The railing was only a foot high, and this black lad walked onto the pitch from his sector. He was swaying so I went over to him, put my arm round him and started walking back. I stepped over this white railing and put him down, and he just fell asleep. When I turned back, there were about twenty police with these four-foot bamboo canes. "Don't do that anymore. Just leave them to us." It was awful. It opened my eyes tremendously.

Geoff's tour began well. Against Natal he took wickets, including the crucial one of Barry Richards. Then against Western Province at Cape Town, in tandem with Phil Carrick, he bowled long spells in both innings, dismissing the young Allan Lamb.

At Soweto it was warm, but at Cape Town it was warmer. There was a fabulous breeze coming straight down the pitch, and I bowled into it for most of the day. It was the best part of 110, but because of the breeze you just thought it was a nice English summer's day. Some of the non-players decided to sit out, but they ended up being badly burned.

The next morning I didn't feel so good. At the ground Ali Bacher came in, put his hand on my stomach. Pop! "You've got a double hernia, possibly more." The next thing I knew, Kenny was saying, "You're going home."

Geoff arrived home on a Saturday at the end of January, arranging to go into hospital on Monday. But on Sunday, while he and June were having lunch with their friends Colin and Julia Graves, he felt much worse – and he was rushed into hospital with acute appendicitis. The hernia operation came later, and the talk was that he would miss the first month of the cricket season. In fact, despite being unable to run at the start of pre-season training, he missed only the first game.

The West Indians were the summer's visitors, with the England captain Tony Greig telling the television cameras that he intended to make them 'grovel'. In preparation for the series the England selectors picked two sides for a Test Trial at Bristol in late May.

In the 1960s England had been spoilt for choice when it came to off-spinners, with Ray Illingworth, Fred Titmus, David Allen and John Mortimore, so much so that Glamorgan's Don Shepherd took over 2,000 wickets and was never called up. But, ten years on, there was a gap. The ageing Illingworth, as captain, had kept the role till 1973, thwarting the development of Surrey's Pat Pocock. Greig had proved a surprisingly effective part-time fill-in in the Caribbean. Then the selectors – with few options – had turned back to the 42-year-old Fred Titmus for the 1974/5 tour of Australia.

There were plenty of slow left-arm bowlers – Derek Underwood, Norman Gifford, the young Phil Edmonds – but in the first-class averages for 1975 English off-spinners were thin on the ground. Geoff, with 69 wickets at an average of 21.86, stood out, so it was not a total surprise when he was selected for the Test Trial – and not just for the trial but for the first-choice England eleven, bowling in tandem with Derek Underwood. They were playing against the Rest, whose spin was in the hands of Edmonds and the young Derbyshire all-rounder Geoff Miller.

> We were at Barnsley for a one-day game, and somebody said, "You're in the England team to play against the Rest." I went down to Bristol, and I bowled reasonably in the first innings. Bristol was a bit like Harrogate: a good pitch for the first innings for both sides, then it began to turn a bit. I got 20-odd with the bat. We declared, leaving them not a lot to win, and we bowled them out for 48. Derek took four for 10, and I took five for 27.
>
> On the Thursday night, after play had finished, Greigy was in the dressing room. I used St Peter's equipment; they were at Horbury, near Wakefield, a lovely family firm. They made the pads and gloves for Gray Nicholls and Slazengers; then they started to make bats, and they signed Greigy. He said, "I'm going to do a promotion for SP. Do you want to come with me?" We got in his Jaguar, and we drove to this promotion. And in the car park, as we were leaving, he said, "I'm going to tell you something now. You can't discuss it with your wife, you can't tell anybody. You'll be in the First Test against the West Indies. Well done. Promise you won't say a word?" "Promise."
>
> How do you deal with news like that? You're up there in Cloud Twelve, and you can't say a word to anyone.
>
> Friday, I bowled. Saturday passed. On Sunday I sat in the car on my own. They announced the England team. I was sat in the car,

having been told I was going to play for England, and I wasn't picked. Nobody called me, nobody said a word.

The team contained only one front-line slow bowler, Derek Underwood, and, when the England selectors did call up an off-spinner for the Second Test, it was not Geoff but Pat Pocock. At the same time news filtered out that cameras had been in action filming him at the Oval. "That's a complete surprise to me," he told the *Yorkshire Post*. "I don't know anything about it."

Pocock remained in the squad for the Third Test, with *The Times* reporting a rumour that Greig, who had successfully pushed for the recall of Brian Close, was now pressing for the return of the 44-year-old Ray Illingworth. Geoff, it seemed, was off the radar, and nobody had explained to him what was going on, least of all the England captain who was playing a county match at Headingley when the squad for the Third Test was announced.

> I did Greigy in both innings, and he never spoke to me other than in a group. This went on, nobody said a word. In the end I rang John Smith, a hotelier I knew. He knew the umpire Charlie Elliott well, and Charlie was a selector. "Will you ring Charlie and tell him I desperately need to speak to him?" Within half an hour Charlie rang back. I said, "I've got worries, but I don't want to talk over the phone." He said, "I'm coming to Chesterfield."
>
> At Chesterfield I told him, and he went ballistic. Then he said, "I'll be honest with you. Greigy was right. You were in the twelve and were probably going to play. But at the last minute we decided to send the cameras and get you filmed, to get ourselves sorted out for good. We sent them out, and there's absolutely nothing wrong. You're fine. But you don't want to be involved at the Oval and finish up playing one Test. You're best off out of it. I'll tell you now, I promise you, you're going to India."

But would he be selected this time? Geoff could not be certain.

> The side was to be announced at 11. I was at home creosoting a fence, something just to take my mind off things. The phone rang, and it was John Callaghan from the *Yorkshire Evening Post*. He told me I'd been selected.
>
> You freeze on the spot, thinking "Where am I going? How have I got here?" June had been brilliant. She'd helped me through the troublesome times, and Dad was always there for me. Then I rang Johnny Wardle up. By this time cars were driving up; the press were arriving. Johnny said, "Just go and enjoy yourself. Then ring me up when you've got a bit of time, and I'll tell you how to bowl out there."

The first call I got was from Derek Underwood. Derek and I had always been mates, and I kept ringing him: "What do I need?" He said, "Listen, you're going to be in charge of the Bovril. You need two big jars." I thought, "Is this a wind-up for the junior player? How do I play this?" Every time I rang him, he would say, "Don't forget the Bovril."

Inoculations. Medicals. Down to London and back several times. We met up at Lord's, got the rest of our kit. Off to the hotel. Met the press lads. Meal at the Clarendon. Peter May spoke. "It's not just about the game. Remember you're representing your country." I thought, "Aren't we going out there to win?"

Among those boarding the coach from Lord's to the airport, mingling among the players, was the journalist Frank Keating. Geoff sat and told him how grateful he was to Johnny Wardle, repeating his mentor's words of guidance: "When things get on top of me out there, as they are bound to for a spinner, it will be Johnny's parting advice that I will think on: 'Patience and straightness, patience and straightness.'"

Packing for India

Chris Old and Geoff wear their brand new MCC touring blazers

We arrived at Bombay airport at about 4.30 in the morning. There must have been 10,000 people there. We got in this coach after we'd done the press and the photographs. We were driving to the hotel, and there were folk standing on the back of scooters, banging on the windows, just to wave to us. It was the biggest culture shock I'd ever had. Everybody had told me that we'd see a difference, there'd be rich and poor.

We got to the hotel, and we went to kip. Got up for a late lunch and had a run round the garden. The Taj Mahal Hotel, like a letter E facing the Bay of Bombay. Bernard Thomas took us round for 'light exercise'.

I thought, "If this is light, I don't know how I'm going to go on." Then food. Then someone said, "Shall we have a walk round the block?" Five or six of us went, and immediately it was "Rupee, master, rupee." At Calcutta you saw children with their arms bent the wrong way round and their legs taken off, all to make them professional beggars.

But I enjoyed every part of India.

The first few games they swapped you around for room-mates. I had Dennis Amiss – 'Sacker' – at one point. Poor old Dennis, he'd go to bed early. He'd lay in bed and he'd say, "No, no, you come in when you want." I'd tiptoe in, I'd creep about, and Sacker'd be in bed sleeping. Then boom! He'd sit bolt upright and start saying things. Then he went back to sleep. I thought, "What have I got here?" He said, "I'm sorry, I tend to do that. I just hear something, but I don't wake up."

Then there was Derek Randall. Three o'clock in the morning I woke up, and he was in front of the mirror, with his pads on and his bat.

Bernard Thomas used to organise the rooms, and he did it well. You never shared with your own county. Then after a fortnight, three weeks, you stayed with somebody longer. Derek Underwood was my first long one – 'Deadly'. "You've got the Bovril, haven't you?" I said yes. "Good. We don't need it yet. You keep it."

There were four warm-up matches before the First Test. The first at Poona saw all the party's three off-spinners – Geoff, Geoff Miller and Tony Greig – in action on a flat pitch, and the *Guardian*'s Henry Blofeld was clear which of them had been the most impressive: 'Cope bowled well, keeping to a tidy length and line. Miller did not and was probably guilty of trying too hard. Greig's off-spinners were not tight enough either.' The next game at Jaipur brought further praise from Blofeld, this time in the *Sunday Express*: 'I believe Cope will become an important member of this side. He has superb control and should take plenty of Test wickets.'

But little in Geoff's life has remained straightforward for long, and the team had barely landed in Ahmedabad for their third match than his happy start to the tour was shattered.

It was two in the morning. I was rooming with Derek Underwood, and Greigy, Bernard Thomas and Kenny came in. They woke me up and, when I saw them, they didn't speak. I just looked at Kenny, and I said, "It's my Dad, isn't it? He's died." And Kenny said, "Yes, he has. I'm sorry." Ironically Derek had shared with Pat Pocock when Pat's dad died.

130

One newspaper reported Geoff as saying, "Now he'll never know if I play for England or not." His father was only 65, not long retired, and he had that autumn moved into a cottage in Crossgates.

> Just before I went away, he started to complain of headaches. Every time it was in the morning that he wasn't so good, and he got better in the day. We went to the GP and to the opticians, and everything was all right. So I said, "Cheerio, Dad, I'm off."
>
> June had said to him during the week, "Are you coming over for your lunch on Sunday?" "Aye, lass, but if there's any snow, I'm staying at home." He didn't like driving in the snow.
>
> There was nothing more than a sprinkling of snow. "Do you mind if I don't come?" She put the phone down and heard no more.
>
> Then in the evening there was no organist at the chapel, and somebody went round to the cottage. There was this red glow in the room, and Dad was on the settee asleep in front of the fire. They had to knock the door down. He'd died in front of the fire. Some months before Dad had bought the cottage, a new gas fire had been fitted, and the man had bricked up the flue. So he died of carbon monoxide poisoning; that was the reason for the headaches. He'd had his lunch, and his ironing board was up, but he hadn't finished the ironing.

When he arrived back in England, Geoff was surprised to be met by John Arlott.

> John had adopted me that summer at Portsmouth, during the game when Leddy got his only hundred for Yorkshire. I'd walked into the press box, looking for Terry Lofthouse of the *Evening Post*, and there was only John there. "He's just gone to the shops," he said. And, as I turned to go, he said, "I don't think we've met." And he sat me down. "Tell me about you, Geoffrey. I love being in the company of cricketers." We started talking. He'd got that black tie on, and he told me about losing his wife, losing his son.
>
> The next time I saw him was at Heathrow. He made sure I was all right for the train to Leeds.

Geoff's father was his last close blood relation, and he stayed in Yorkshire for eight days, organising the funeral. Then he caught the train down to London where he was met by Donald Carr and, once more, John Arlott.

> And John's last words to me were, "Geoff, you've been through great difficulty. But you're going back. And, as you call him, 'the little man' will not be prouder if you play for England. Because if you do, he'll

know. He'll want you to do that. We want you to do that. We're all with you." I'll never forget that.

Geoff flew through the night to India, arriving in New Delhi at seven in the morning. The First Test was due to start the following day.

I was having some breakfast in the hotel, and the lads started wandering down. Bernard Thomas said, "Are you going to bed?" "No," I said. "I'm going to the nets. What time are they?" "Ten o'clock." "Well, I'm going." "Are you sure? … Well, I'll go and find your kit."

I went to the nets, and I just bowled everybody out. And when I came in, Kenny said, "Are you all right? Do you feel all right?" "I feel well." "Good. Did you have a net while you were home?" "No. Should I have done?" "I'm amazed at you. You've come back, you've dropped it on a sixpence, and you've caused trouble to everybody."

"He bowled marvellously," Tony Greig told the *Daily Mail*'s Alex Bannister. "It was unbelievable." At 12.30, at a team meeting, his name was read out in the twelve for the next day.

Kenny said, "We're delighted. You've come back, you've made a lot of people sit up, you've been a true Yorkshireman and you've shown us what grit you've got."

A fuller tribute was paid next morning by Terry Brindle in his 'Man Friday' column in the *Yorkshire Post*. Reflecting on the difficulties Geoff had overcome in reaching this point in his career, he wrote: 'Cope's trials – and they have been almost literally that – may have toughened him and threatened to defeat him, but I doubt they have embittered him. He has a zest for people and a concern for others which demands your attention because you know you have his. Beneath an outer skin of deceptive vulnerability, he has a core of exceptional self-belief and determination.'

But, alas, the fairy tale of his return to India stopped at this point.

Next morning I woke up, and I felt good. I could see a lot of discussion going on. They looked at the pitch. They looked at the Indian squad with Bedi, Chandrasekhar, Venkat and Prasanna so it wasn't going to be a seamer's wicket. Greigy made the decision in the end not to play me. He was frightened that jet lag would set in. That's all he said. "I'm not happy that we're going into a Test match for five days and you might suddenly be not right. It's a big gamble." So I didn't play.

Kenny spent a lot of time with me. He said, "This is what it's all about. You've put the pressure on the others. Keep going. I know you're keen to play, but not everybody can."

England, with an attack of three seamers plus Underwood and Greig, won by an innings, and, despite Geoff taking seven wickets in the match that followed, they stuck with the same line-up for the Second Test at Calcutta, where they won by ten wickets. Forty years on, among Geoff's most prized possessions, is a beautifully carved table made especially for him during the match.

> There's heavy carving around the ball in the middle, and the glass is perfectly square. It was made by a little man with a sackcloth round his bottom. "The glass will be square, master." Every day we came back from the Test, this little guy was sat on the pavement chipping away: "I finish, master, I finish." The fourth day: "What colour you require?" He wanted a fiver, and I gave him ten pounds. And he thought I'd given him the world.
>
> My doctor in Otley took it back for me. I'd never have gone in a shop in England and bought that. They did everything with their hands. Bombay Railway Station, all built by hand. Wonderful architecture.

Geoff also acquired two pairs of shoes.

> Bernard Thomas had been a few times before. He said, "Do you want some shoes?" At the end of one day, this Chinaman in the main street drew round our feet and, when I opened the door at quarter to eight next morning, "I bring you two pairs of leather shoes, sir." They lasted longer than any pair of shoes I've bought in England. I took them for soling and heeling, and the man said, "£17.50." I said, "Hang on, they only cost me £3.50." I had them for years.

From Calcutta they travelled up to Nagpur to play a Combined Universities and Under-22 XI, captained by a young Dilip Vengsarkar.

> On the bus Underwood said, "Today is the day for the Bovril. You've got it, haven't you?" "I've got it." And I'm still thinking, "I'm being set up here." We ended up in the army barracks where we had a board for a bed, one sheet, a pillow and a mosquito net – and the choice of six curries. So we got the Bovril out and had Bovril drinks.

After Nagpur came the Third Test at Madras, a ground where the pitch had a reputation for taking more turn than any other, and the newspapermen were full of speculation that another spinner would be brought into the team. But would it be Geoff or the young Geoff Miller?

> That was a pressure moment. They put Mills and I together for that university match, and the build-up was "Madras is the big turner." I was desperate to play. For once I started believing the press. Everybody

The Calcutta Test

who'd been before – Alex Bannister, John Woodcock, Pat Gibson – they were all saying, "You'll be all right, Copey. Madras will turn square."

At Nagpur Geoff took six first-innings wickets while Geoff Miller, at the other end, took only two, and the press were certain what it meant: 'Cope's 6-41 points way to Test place' ... 'Indians just can't Cope' ... 'Cope stakes Test claim' ... 'Watch Geoff Cope – He'll make it hot in Madras.'

But when we got to Madras, we got this uneven concrete strip, and we'd won the first two Tests with seamers so we kept an unchanged side and hammered them. That was a disappointment.

But I had to go back upcountry and keep performing. That was tough at times. Charades came in about 4.30, that was our entertainment, and the food upcountry was very poor. They had outside caterers, and you didn't know what you trusted. You were desperate to go back to the main centres.

Kenny Barrington was fabulous as manager. I came back, saying, "He must be the most southern Yorkshireman we've got." (a) You

134

were able to talk to him, and (b) he'd played at the highest level, he knew the game.

We played one or two games between each Test, and naturally the lads who weren't in the Test team were giving it their all. I remember one game when I'd been bowling quite well and was on top. This lad was batting; 'Sacker' at mid-wicket gave it a lazy lunge and missed it, and the lad got away from me. I gave Sacker the stare, but nothing was said.

Tea was about a quarter of an hour later and, as I sat down, Kenny came and sat next to me: "Here's a cup of tea, lad, get this down. I know," he said, and he tapped my thigh. "I know. We'll have dinner tonight, you and me. I saw, he should have fielded it. But it's hard sometimes when you've played in a Test match, you're probably not concentrating one hundred per cent. I was watching. I know what you've gone through. Don't worry." You've got to play the game to watch and realise, and he was watching the game.

In the nets he put money on his stumps. "Right, there's rupees on my stumps. You'll never get me out." I said, "I bet we do." It was fascinating to watch him because he'd not had a bat in his hand for a long time. He had this net, and he just hit mid-on and mid-off. That's all he did. Boom, boom, boom, boom. It was getting boring. Then finally he came down and missed, and I said, "That's it. Stumped. Pay up." "No, no, no, stumpings don't count," he said. We had a laugh about it.

With victories in the first three Tests, it was – and remains – the most successful tour of India ever by an England team, and, to add to the joy, the team were popular wherever they went, nobody more than their charismatic captain Tony Greig and their 'Clown Prince', Derek Randall – or 'Rags' as they called him.

He came on the tour to South Africa the previous winter. We had a trip to a game reserve 40 or 50 miles outside Cape Town: Andrew Kennedy, Rags and myself. First thing we did, we went through a no-entry door and we saw the little lion cubs of two or three days old. Then they arranged a cheetah feed for us. And right at the end they said, "Would you like a bit of fun? Do you want to go and play with the chimps?" The chimps tried to stop us going through, bur Rags started swinging from tree to tree. The only thing I'd ask is, 'Did the real Derek Randall come out of that chimp's cage?'

There were so many people at the games in India; it was like a religion. In one of the early non-Test matches, there were 55,000 in the ground. The batsman top-edged the ball down to deep square leg, and Rags turned round and took the catch behind his back. He was there with this grin, and bananas and all sorts came onto the field. Of course he started eating one, pretended to be sick, and they ended up carting him off. Then, when he got near the pavilion, he jumped off this so-called stretcher, knocked off the umpire's cap, did three cartwheels and went back to fielding.

After that, we were playing at home. What with Greigy as the white god and Rags doing what he did, you'd be having five hundred outside your hotel all the time.

In Calcutta we went to the market, five of us including Randall. "Please you sit down ... please you have a drink" so you have a Coke. The goods were brought out, and the bartering started. Then they all started following us. Rags said, "Right, this is it. When I stop, we all stop." Stalls, the lot went flying. He caused absolute mayhem.

All they wanted was a photograph with him. There wasn't the slightest murmur of "You've knocked my stall down."

He just went round the whole of India as the Pied Piper.

Crowds outside the Grand Hotel, Calcutta, waiting for the England team to board their bus

For the Fourth Test at Bangalore England stuck to their three seamers – Bob Willis, Chris Old and John Lever – but, on a pitch that took substantial turn, Greig was an inadequate foil for Underwood, and the match was lost. So, when Chris Old withdrew on the morning of the final Test at Bombay, Geoff's moment seemed finally to have come. Away from the Tests he had taken more wickets than anybody.

> Everybody said, "Get yourself geared up, Geoff, it'll be you." Then Derek came in and put his arm round me: "I'm sorry, you should have played, but they're playing Mike Selvey." He was a good mate, Derek. When he sees me now he says, "Hello, Roomy."
>
> I said to Kenny, "I feel I've done all I could do." He said, "You've done all and more besides. They just fancied an extra seamer because we've beaten them with seamers."
>
> I went into a quiet corner, had a reflection and thought, probably that was it. I had that feeling, "Perhaps I'm never going to play." I was very low.

Geoff Miller was the only other one who had not played in the Tests, and he at least had won a cap back in England during the summer.

The Test was drawn, and Geoff had the consolation of playing in the unofficial Test in Sri Lanka. There followed a magical fortnight in Australia – with a match against Western Australia in Perth, followed by the Centenary Test at Melbourne, though Geoff played in neither, the dark shadow of his questioned bowling action appearing in view once more.

> When I got to Aussie, Greigy called me into his room and said, "I'm sorry, but you won't play either of these games." I said, "Well, I wasn't expecting to play." He said, "Yes, but it's not quite that. Gubby Allen's here, and he says he has an agreement with Australia that anybody who has a doubtful action will not be selected."

Geoff's mind went back to the day at Bradford when he suspected that Ian Chappell, the former Australian captain, had reported him. After all that had happened, he could have been forgiven if he had given way to bitterness. But he did not.

> The whole two weeks were the best of my cricketing life. We finished in Sri Lanka, they were very kind to us, the people were as warm as you could wish them to be. Then we went to Perth, where I made my friendship with one D Lillee. Then we went to Melbourne. Functions morning, afternoon and night but only one formal dinner, where the speaker was Sir Donald Bradman and there were 200-odd Test

cricketers. There were only two people who didn't qualify to be there: one was the President of MCC, and the other was me.

You looked round the room at all these Test cricketers. Johnny Wardle was there, and he said, "Give us your menu." He took my menu, with several pages inside, and he got it signed by everybody: Bradman, Hassett, Miller, Lindwall.

Bradman spoke. "I look across to my right, and there's Jim Laker with his 19 wickets at Old Trafford." And there was a ripple. "There's Fred Trueman, with his 307 wickets." Another ripple. "Len Hutton, with his 364." He went through ten or twelve people. Then he said, "And there's my old friend over there, Bill O'Reilly." And the room just stood up. It erupted. Leonard Hutton was on my table. He leant across, put his hand on my arm and said, "He could bowl." That's all he said.

In the great match itself Geoff was privileged to witness one of cricket's greatest innings, a breathtaking knock of 174 by Derek Randall.

When we got rolled over in the first innings, Rags came in, and he sat on his coffin. He tipped his cap back. Kenny was around: "What's the matter?" "I've worked him out. That fellow Lillee. He does you because he's short. It's all to do with bounce. He bounces it from a different level."

In the second innings he took guard and he started playing. And the balls he left were unbelievable. They were going over the top by barely an inch. He played him on bounce. Then he started getting his runs.

Lillee hit him on the head, and he went down like a sack of potatoes. Bernard wanted him to come off. "No, no, I've got to see it through," he said. Next ball Lillee came in and, about five yards from delivery, Rags stopped him: "Dennis, Dennis, just a minute." Lillee glided through: "Is there a problem, Derek?" And Derek said to him, "I'd just like to tell you, that last one were a bit quick."

When he got out, there were two aisles and he came through the wrong gate, went past the Queen and all the royalty and bowed. He came into the dressing room: "Hey, she looks a grand lass." He was barking mad.

I liked the guy as a bloke, but he was very much as I think I am myself. He won a few games for us at six. Then they asked him to bat three: "I'll do it." They had nobody to open: "I'll give it a go." There were other players of the same ilk who would say, "I'll bat three or three." But all Rags wanted to do was to play for England, to put those lions on.

There had been eleven Tests since Tony Greig had told Geoff in Bristol that he was going to be in the team, and for one reason and another he had played none of them. Yet his spirit in adversity had been noted.

There was a pre-season lunch back at Headingley with a speech by the President, Sir Kenneth Parkinson. "Never have I been prouder of a Yorkshire player," he said, and he played the tape of an interview I'd done with Christopher Martin-Jenkins. CMJ asked me, "How do you feel, Geoff? You've been to India and Australia, all this way, and you haven't played a Test match." "Quite easy," I said. "Just think of the people who are at home, in bed or just getting up. How many of them would like to be in my position today? It's disappointing. You have moments when you think you might play. But at the end of the day it's an experience anybody in their right mind would swap you for. I'm just honoured that I'm here." And Sir Kenneth said, "That was a Yorkshireman speaking."

Now, after months of travel, he was back home, and there was time to reflect on the loss of his father.

I thought I'd got over Dad. But I hadn't. I haven't got over it today. When I got back to Yorkshire – and by Yorkshire I mean the county, not the club – suddenly I had everybody talking to me about my dad. "Sorry, Geoff, about what happened. Are you all right now?" It was always there that summer. I used to love it when he came to watch me, and he wasn't there any more.

It was the first time that I realised I was an only one. I'd got June as my only family but we had no children. We'd waited a while, and nothing had happened.

There was a sadness in his soul, but there was also a hope, stemming from something June had said to him after his father's funeral.

When I went back to India, she said, "When you come home, we'll have a child. He's taken one to give one." I've never, ever forgotten those words.

12

Me, captain the side?

1977

On the day that Geoff was named in the tour party for India, he spoke to the press. 'My selection,' he said, 'is the fulfilment of a dream and an honour, which I feel I would never have attained but for so many people at different parts of my career.' He went on to pay especial tribute to two men: his mentor Johnny Wardle 'for his invaluable advice in sorting out my action' and his county captain Geoff Boycott 'who in spite of having problems of his own has given me tremendous encouragement and guidance. Without him I would never have been given this chance.'

That summer of 1976 was Boycott's sixth as captain of Yorkshire – and, though injuries, not least to Boycott himself, prevented them from mounting a challenge for the championship as they had done the previous year, there was still a sense among the county's supporters that the team was moving forward. They had lost several experienced players – Phil Sharpe, Don Wilson, Tony Nicholson and Richard Hutton – but there were high hopes for their young replacements: Bill Athey, Jim Love, Phil Carrick, Graham Stevenson and Arnie Sidebottom.

The old guard who had left, men who had come through under Brian Close, had found it hard to adapt to Boycott's new order. Tony Nicholson disliked the way 'he talked to grown men as if they were kids' and 'was only concerned with his own performance.' Richard Hutton recognised 'his tactical awareness' but thought 'he was lacking in an equally important part of captaincy – the ability to get the most out of his people.' Yet the newcomers, who knew nothing of Close, came without preconception, and there were signs by 1976 that the team played better when Boycott was there than when he was out injured. His stand-in, John Hampshire, 'was by no means a failure,' John Callaghan wrote in *Wisden*, 'but leadership is a matter of practice and confidence as well as knowledge and experience, so it was not surprising that he lacked Boycott's touch.'

It helped Boycott's captaincy that, through 1975 and 1976, for a mix of reasons that have never been fully understood, he had withdrawn himself from Test cricket and was giving his full attention to Yorkshire. They were two of the driest, hottest summers of modern times, and Geoff prospered – with pitches that suited him and a captain who had an understanding of spin bowling, a captain who approached the game with relentless professionalism.

One thing that Boycott wanted to understand better was the playing surface, how you could read its likely behaviour before the toss on the first morning. It was an aspect of the game of extra importance for Yorkshire whose ten home championship matches were spread around six grounds.

Ray Illingworth, now down at Leicester, was the grandmaster of this.

> Illy used to say, "It will turn at twenty past three tomorrow." And he'd start loosening up about ten past.

But for others there was a frustrating unpredictability.

> It's like Len Hutton is supposed to have said at Brisbane. "Looking at wickets is like looking at a woman. Until you've wed her, you don't know the true facts."

It fascinated Geoff, who was keen to learn as much as he could.

> I started going out to look at the pitch every day. I'd look at it and try to assess what I thought it would do. And I would talk to the groundsmen.

Soon enough Boycott decided to make use of Geoff's interest, summoning him on an evening at Lord's when Geoff had other plans.

> I was going for a meal with a dozen supporters. It was an annual thing. At the meal they drew straws, and the lad who got the short straw would arrange the following year's venue and bring a guest. But until you went in the Tavern that evening you never knew where it was. And you didn't know who was going.
> "I want to see you in my hotel room," Boycs said.
> I said, "I'm going out. I've got this meal."
> "This is more important, the cricket. Cancel it."
> So I went to the Tavern: "Boycs wants to see me. I'm sorry."
> They all went off, and I went back to the Westmorland. Knocked on Boycs's door. He was sat there with his little book, writing up – he was very professional with his notes. Mushtaq – who bowls well against him? And he'd worked out I'd done him six times. "What do you do?" "I just bowl as tightly as I can." He'd write it all up. Things like "Gatting tried to bowl an out-swinger." He's writing these notes up, and I'm stood there.
> I said, "You wanted to see me?"
> "Oh yes. Why do you go and see these pitches?" And he's still writing.
> "I just want to see if I'm right in my thinking. I can perhaps get to know the game a bit better."

"Right. Well, in future don't let anybody see, but go out and do the pitch. Come and tell me what you think. And I'll put you right."

That's Geoffrey, that's how he spoke. I'm stood there, and he's writing up. He said, "Yes?"

I said, "Well, you wanted to see me."

"That's what I wanted to see you about."

"But I was going out for dinner."

"Well, you're far better going to find a restaurant on your own, analyse how you bowled today."

This difference between Boycott, the single-minded professional, and the more gregarious members of the Yorkshire team led to a bizarre passage of play at Oxford in an early-season match against the university in 1974.

> We had a few Yorkies watching us, including some students. We arranged to go for a drink with them at the end of the second day, then to go back to their digs for some food and a bit of a party.

All was going to plan when, with the clock ticking towards the close, the University reached 45 for one in their second innings. Then there was a flurry of wickets.

> They were five down, and we were all walking off when Boycs said, "Hold on a minute. I'm claiming the extra half hour. We can bowl this lot out." I think he was the only one who didn't know the party was on.
>
> Oxford let us down badly. They lost four more wickets. That left the Right Honourable Tim Lamb to come in and save the day. As he passed me, I said, "For goodness sake, laddy, don't get out." "Why's that?" I told him: "And you can come with us as well."
>
> At the other end 'Bluey' behind the stumps was saying to him, "Don't let it past the bat. I'll tell you if it's an offie or an arm ball. Just stick your pad out. Nobody will appeal."
>
> Boycs was at mid-wicket: "Come on, you can get this chap out."
>
> I said, "I'm doing my best."
>
> Finally Lamby survived, and we got to stay in Oxford overnight. To get one wicket. We had a good time.
>
> Next morning it was: "Who's capable of bowling straight?" And Lamby was in no better shape. It was all over in two minutes.

A close examination of Boycott's first-class record reveals that he played five or more innings against 32 opponents – including the other 16 counties, the six Test match countries and the Rest of the World – and the only one of the 32 against whom he failed to score a century was Oxford University. In the

1974 match he was bowled for 89 by Imran Khan, but four years later, when he next played the fixture, the students' attack was a good deal more ordinary. Conscious of the gap in his record, he approached the match with purpose.

Alas, it did not work out for him. In the first over of the game he was caught and bowled for nought by a theology student Stephen Wookey, only to spend most of the day watching the next two batsmen, Love and Lumb, hit hundreds. Then, on the second evening, when – despite a lead of 343 – he opted to bat again, he was caught for three off a young Australian called Gregory Marie.

> Instead of declaring, he made us bowl at him in the nets all the next morning. It was embarrassing. We finished up with a horrendous lead. And he said to us, "Right, now you bowlers have got a bit of pressure. It's up to you to win the game" – which we didn't.

At all times Boycott was determined to be his own man, even to the point of not making it easy for the county's officers to contact him when he was at home.

> At that stage I was probably the only person with his telephone number. The Chairman or the President or the Secretary, if they wanted Geoffrey, they had to ring me at home and give me a brief outline of what they wanted to be discussed. Then I had to ring Geoffrey after a quarter past nine and he'd say, "Right, I'll ring him" or "I won't bother with that." So I'd ring them back and say, "I don't think it's favourable from what I've heard," and they would get very frustrated.
>
> There was one day when it was serious. I had both the Chairman and the Secretary. It was ten to nine, and Joe Lister was insistent. "I'm not supposed to ..." "Geoffrey, it's very important." So I rang, and Mrs Jane Boycott – the world record-holder for most runs scored for Yorkshire and all with a stick of rhubarb, the eighth wonder of the world – she answered the phone. "Quarter past nine," she said and put the phone down. At quarter past Geoffrey answered: "You know you're not supposed to ring." "Well, I'm told it's very important. They want you desperately." "Well, what about?" "They just need you desperately." Mumble, mumble. And off he went and rang them.

In each of the first seven years of his captaincy, from 1971 to 1977, Boycott was the leading English batsman in the first-class averages. Always there was a suspicion that, as captain, he played too much for his average, but there were moments when the team stirred him beyond his natural caution. One such came at Middlesbrough towards the end of the long hot summer of 1976.

> Glamorgan got 300-plus. We got 300-plus, and they left us 300-plus. Boycs came in and said, "Who wants some practice?" "What are you

on about?" "Well, it's a stupid declaration." "What do you mean, we can win this." "How long have you played this game?"

It was a flat pitch at the end of August. The groundsman was Keith Boyce, and he did such an excellent job there that he took over at Headingley when George Cawthray retired. And in February and March that year his daughter Ann had gone round and round the outfield on the roller in her duffel coat when she was studying for her exams. All her hard work created the flattest outfield we'd had there.

Hamps said to Boycs, "I'll go in with you" and slogged 30-odd in no time. Then Jim Love. We said, if Boycs gets to 70 by teatime and we leave ourselves 140 in 25 minutes and 20 overs, we'll win it. We ended up talking to him. "Look, Boycs, you're a world-class player, you're the only one who can go out there and do it."

He felt embarrassed, but he went out. They had this chap Gregory Armstrong, and we slipped it to him that Boycs couldn't hook. Boycs got 156, and we won with an over to spare. It was the day when you saw what he was capable of. He played fabulous.

'It seemed an impossible task,' *Wisden* reported, 'but Boycott, whose last 99 runs came from only 81 balls, timed his effort to perfection, the winning runs coming with ten balls to spare.'

Days like that, with the sun beating down, kept Yorkshire folk happy, but the summer that followed in 1977 was a damp, cold one, and by August the county captaincy had become a matter of public debate with the stirrings of a discontent that would ravage the club for years.

Quite unknown to Geoff during his winter tour of India and Australia, several of the England team, including the captain Tony Greig, were signing up for a rebel World Series Cricket, to be staged by the Australian television mogul Kerry Packer. At one point, till he realised that it would cut across his commitment to Yorkshire, Boycott was set to join them.

It was a time of division and confusion in English cricket. Brearley took over as England captain from Greig, and the selectors finally persuaded Boycott to return to the fold. Against an Australian side also in the turmoil of Packer, he made his comeback at Trent Bridge, running out the local hero Derek Randall before scoring a match-turning century. It was his 98th first-class hundred, and at Edgbaston, in his only match for Yorkshire before the next Test, he added a 99th, sending others out to bat ahead of him in the second innings. Was that coincidence, or was he already lining himself up to hit his 100th hundred in front of his own people at Headingley?

In many ways it was the best of Boycott. He had all the pressure of public expectation, the first man ever to hit a 100th hundred in a Test match, the crowd on the first day filling the ground long before the start, and with unswerving determination he reached the landmark shortly before six o'clock. In that moment, for those who knew their statistics, he joined the pantheon of the all-time greats.

As he drove the four through mid-on that brought him his hundred, his Yorkshire team-mates were in the field at Hove.

> We all jumped for joy, and the supporters thought, "What a great spirit this is." But we were cheering because Arnie Sidebottom had bet that he'd get three hundreds in three knocks to get his 100th hundred at Headingley. He won a lot of money.

The county had started well in the championship, top of the table late in June, but Boycott's revived interest in Test cricket came at the same time as a dip in their results. For his vice-captain John Hampshire, it was not a coincidence. 'When he came back from Trent Bridge,' Hampshire wrote six years later, 'the conversation was now all about Test cricket, money, records and the England captaincy. The more pressing matters at hand seemed to have no real place in his thoughts.'

Boycott's departure to Trent Bridge left Hampshire in charge of the team for Yorkshire's match against Middlesex at Abbeydale Park, Sheffield, and what a disaster it was! On a pitch of dangerously uneven bounce and with the West Indian fast bowler Wayne Daniel roaring in, five of the team were out of action by the middle of the second day, including skipper Hampshire with his arm in a sling from a heavily bruised elbow. Geoff was now left to take charge, for his first taste of the Yorkshire captaincy.

> It was a bad pitch. Arnie Sidebottom broke an arm, and Hamps did his elbow. We took the field with five subs. Chris Old had turned up for treatment on his injured shoulder and ended up fielding for four hours. Graham Stevenson, Mike Bore, Arthur Robinson were the bowling attack. I'd lost the rest. I bowled 40 overs.
>
> And we played in the darkest light. You couldn't see anything in the field. I got swept to backward square leg and Colin Johnson was out there, a fine fielder. He was running towards mid-wicket like mad, and the ball was going the other way.
>
> Bill Alley was umpiring. I said to him, "Are we allowed to appeal against the light?" And Bill said, "Never mind you appealing, Geoff. I want to appeal." He went off to ring Lord's, and he came back, saying, "It's up to the batsmen." We were in a complete circus.

With John Hampshire out of action, Geoff was left in charge for the next match – at home to Hampshire at Headingley. His first task was to meet two of the Cricket Committee – the chairman John Temple and the former England wicket-keeper Don Brennan – to assemble a side. Immediately there was an argument about Barrie Leadbeater, who had been playing much of the summer in the second team.

> I said, "The first person I want is Leddy." And John Temple picked out a sheet of paper and said, "He's averaging so-and-so. His last four knocks were … I don't think so." And Brennan said, "Look, John, if he wants him, we must give him our support."
>
> That was Temple. He was Chairman of York Cricket Club; he worked at Ogdens, the excavation people at Otley. He was Chairman of Cricket, Chairman of the Club, and he never missed a gin and tonic in his life. It wasn't good.

The team had only four capped players – Barrie Leadbeater, David Bairstow, 'Rocker' Robinson and Geoff – and they were up against a Hampshire side that contained two of the finest players in the world, the West Indians Gordon Greenidge and Andy Roberts.

> I spoke to the lads on the Saturday morning, and Brennan was in the room. He asked if he could come in. I said to them, "We wouldn't choose to be in this situation, but for those of you who are playing it's an opportunity. You've got to relax, you've got to play your own game and play as you want to play." I told Leddy the day before in a phone call, "Look, you're back. You're going in first, and you play as you can play." There was no "do this, do that".
>
> Boycs didn't say too much before matches, but I felt with younger lads coming in and people who were coming in from the outside, the thing to say was: "Just look round this room. This is Yorkshire. You know who you're representing. Get your chests out. Be proud. And go for it." I remember that fairly vividly.
>
> Brennan turned round to me and he said, "Good luck" and he walked out. I think he was coming with a view to saying something, but he never did because of what I'd said.

In the event they were outplayed. Roberts took four wickets in each innings, Greenidge hit a double century, and they lost by eight wickets. But Barrie Leadbeater hit a good 63 on the first day, Geoff hit a cheerful 44, and the young bowlers stuck well to the task.

> In the last half hour of the first day Greenidge came in. "Come on, Stevo," I said to Graham Stevenson. "Let it rip." And Greenidge just went down on one knee and swept him flat for six; it never went

that much above the ground. In those days we had those little white railings beyond the boundary rope, and it cracked into one of those. He got 200 the next day. But we bowled well because we bowled them out for 300-and-a-few. We brought in Steve Silvester, and he bowled well; that was a big plus.

Even in the moment of defeat he struck a positive note when he spoke to the *Yorkshire Post*: 'It has been a great consolation to me to see how everybody tried. Even when Gordon Greenidge was going mad yesterday afternoon, everyone wanted to bowl. It would have been so easy to drop our heads but no-one did. They gave me everything I could expect.'

A week later, with John Hampshire still recovering, he was back in charge at Hove, and once more events beyond his control made life difficult.

We played at Warwickshire before, and Chris Old had gone off injured. Boycs said to me, "You're going to captain the side at Hove." And Chris was a bit miffed because he thought he should have done.

I said, "I'm only taking Chilly with me if he's a hundred per cent fit, and I want him to tell you that he's fit. I don't want any comeback."

Boycs said to Chris, "What's your state of fitness?" He said, "I'm fine, I'm fine. I need to be there, anyway, to help Geoff sort things."

At Hove Chilly bowled five overs, then went off the field. Came back on with his plimsolls on. "What are you doing?" "I can't bowl anymore." I said, "I could at this stage say 'Go home'." "Well, you need me to help you."

We had lunch, and Callaghan the Prime Minister came. We players had steak-and-kidney pie; he had steak. And not long afterwards a lot of our team started leaving the field. They were running on and off. It was mayhem. Chilly didn't bowl. We were in total disarray.

Of the two umpires Ron Aspinall survived fairly well, but the one who kept going off was Jack Crapp!

With John Hampshire joining them for the next game at Worcester, that was the end of Geoff's spell as captain: most of the disastrous match at Sheffield, followed by the two further defeats at Headingley and Hove. Yet his few days at the helm set in motion events that were still reverberating ten years later. His first inkling of the trouble came three weeks after the end of the season – and it came from the man who had sat in on his team talk at Headingley, Don Brennan.

I got a phone call at quarter past or half past seven in the morning; I was still in bed. Joe Lister: "Have you listened to Radio Leeds?"

"I haven't even got up, Joe."

"Well, I suggest you turn it on now. I'll ring you straight back."
There were some classics with Joe.

I listened, and it was Brennan going on about Boycott. "I've seen Geoff Cope and the way he comes over. He's got the feeling for the county. Boycott's only got the feeling for himself. I trust Geoff Cope to get everybody playing, the way we expect everybody to play for Yorkshire."

I just thought, "What's going on?"

I rang Joe back. "What have you got to say?"

"Well, it's the first time I've heard it. I don't know anything about it."

"You've not been seeing him? You've not been ... ?"

I said, "Joe, you see him. You go for a gin-and-tonic with him most nights."

"We're not being flippant."

"I'm not being flippant. I do not see the guy, other than when he turns up at cricket. Certainly I know nothing about this. Me, captain the side? I've got enough on at the moment."

The story was all over the local papers, with quotations from Brennan's interview: 'Geoff Boycott is a great player, but to my way of thinking he is not a leader ... What I have seen of Geoff Cope gives me the opinion he is the type of player who would put everything before his own personal achievements.'

'SACK BOYCOTT'
Selector Brennan wants Cope as skipper

The sadness for Geoff is that Brennan's interview soured the working relationship, such as it was, that Geoff had established with his captain.

We were Yorkshire cricketers, and we had a job to do. I had to give what help I could. I wouldn't say I was a hundred per cent with everything he did. But I didn't go around shouting about it. Playing in a team, I've always felt that you should give your all to that team.

149

There was difficulty between senior players, I know, but I was trying desperately to be in both camps, to be a team-mate to everyone.

I did what I could to help Boycs. The Brennan thing threw that part-relationship backwards.

Brennan's hamfisted intervention sparked the formation of a protest group which got up a petition calling for a special general meeting and a vote of no confidence in Brennan. But, this time round, matters did not need to go further. Don Brennan resigned from the committee, who duly reappointed Boycott as captain for 1978.

While Geoff had had no part in the call to remove his captain, he did take part in talks about the restructuring of the team's management.

There was a meeting in the Grand Hotel in Scarborough. Boycs, Hamps and myself, and there may have been others there. We'd got fed up with John Temple and the Cricket Committee not being there on a regular basis. John Temple was renowned for walking around in his blazer, with the averages in his inside pocket. Last four knocks, that sort of thing. He was a long way adrift as far as a lot of us were concerned.

We thought the team needed a manager – or a senior person who travelled with us. Ted Lester was possibly in Boycs' thinking at this stage. Whether he could carry on scoring, would be something to be decided. Ray Illingworth's name also came up. We were saying, "No, there's nobody that we want as an individual. But the likes of Ted Lester, who's there every day. Or somebody like Illy."

We talked to Michael Crawford, the Chairman, and Joe Lister, and they agreed to consider it. Michael was a gentleman, you could talk to him. He listened and thought there was a lot of sense to it.

The committee appointed Illingworth to the new post of cricket manager, giving him a three-year contract. Ironically it was the very thing Brian Sellers had refused him when he left for Leicestershire. He could not start for twelve months, however, so for the summer of 1978 they would carry on as before.

13

I'm not sure that I caught it

1977/78

The summer of 1977 had been a disappointment – for the weather, for Yorkshire and even, to an extent, for Geoff. The leading wicket-taker in England in 1976, he was barely in the top thirty in 1977, his 56 wickets a long way short of the 87 and 81 taken by fellow off-spinners Geoff Miller and John Emburey, both of whom were five years younger than him.

It did not help that his spin partner Phil Carrick had a dismal summer, losing his place in the Yorkshire team. As a result, with no slow-left-armer at the other end, Geoff was often deployed as a stock bowler, keeping the runs down. His economy rate was better than those of Miller and Emburey, but his strike rate was worse. Though Greig and Underwood had signed up for Packer's World Series Cricket, it was not obvious that the England selectors would need him in Pakistan and New Zealand.

> The tour was a thought at the back of my mind, but it was never at the forefront. I arranged to work that winter.

Geoff also had a first child to look forward to, as June was now pregnant. "He's taken one to give one," she had said after his father's death, and she was due to give birth in February.

The England selectors had the toughest of tasks. Of the sixteen who went to India the previous year, Packer had recruited Greig, Underwood, Amiss, Knott and, just two days before the selectors met, Woolmer. There was even a rumour that Bob Willis was going to sign.

It was a time of turmoil. There were proposals to ban all Packer players from first-class cricket, with unpleasant divisions opening up in the dressing rooms of some counties. Geoff was among the majority of county cricketers in disliking what Packer was doing, though some years later, through his friendship with Derek Underwood, he came to see both sides of the argument.

> I started to work with Hovat, a subsidiary of Wiggins Teape, in 1981. Their base was in Sevenoaks so I rang Deadly: "Come and stay with us," he said. When I got to his house, there was this amazing note on the door: "Dear Geoff, We won't be long. We're just going for our hour's dancing lesson." All I saw was Deadly, with his ten-to-twos, doing the quickstep.

When he came back, I said to him, "So this is Packerville, is it?" And he said, "I thought you'd have something to say." He said, "Can I talk to you about it?" I said, "Course you can. You're a pal."

"Do you know," he said, "by signing up for three years my daughters and my family are secure, and that's the only reason I did it." That took a lot of the bitterness away from me. Here was Deadly, saying he did it for the family; it was a pay deal that wouldn't come along again. That gave me a different edge to it.

I still think the way it was done was wrong. It was said that it would secure the future of all cricketers in England, but it didn't. It secured the top 15 or 20. I used to say, "What about Rocker Robinson?" Big Arthur was a pal of mine, the type of person you wanted in your side. He turned up every day, his talent wasn't world class or Test class, he was a good solid professional, as honest as the day comes. "What's going to happen to Arthur?" "He'll be far better off because of Packer," they said. And I kept looking for that. When is he going to be far better off? The top few creamed off the money while everybody else stayed where they were.

The upheaval led to a new-look England squad for the winter's tour. Mike Brearley was now the captain, and the chosen party included two from his Middlesex side: Phil Edmonds, taking over the slow-left-armer's role vacated by Derek Underwood, and the 20-year-old Mike Gatting, who was yet to score a first-class century. It was a time to rebuild, to look to the future, and there were first tours for Ian Botham and, to everybody's surprise, the wicket-keeper Paul Downton, whose first-class career to date consisted of seven matches standing in for Alan Knott at Kent.

Yet, for John Woodcock in *The Times*, the emphasis on the future did not go far enough. Instead of the Somerset left-hander Brian Rose, he would have chosen the young David Gower, of whom his county captain Ray Illingworth had said that, in his 25 years in the game, he had never seen a better timer of a ball. The *Times* correspondent called this 'a remarkable commendation. I shall be surprised if Rose goes on to make quite as much of a mark as Gower.' He would also have chosen three young spinners – Edmonds, Miller and Emburey – and not, as the selectors decided after a lengthy debate, left out Emburey in favour of the 30-year-old Geoff. 'What swung it in Cope's favour,' he ventured, 'was his accuracy, there being an idea that this could compensate for Underwood's absence.'

Steve Whiting in the *Sun* put it more bluntly: 'The truth is that Cope gets the trip because, now that Underwood has gone, the selectors were frightened to depend on anybody else.' Whiting went on to quote Alec Bedser, the Chairman of Selectors: "We had to have somebody to take over from Underwood, somebody who could bowl straight and on the spot."

John Arlott in the *Guardian* was altogether more enthusiastic about Geoff's selection: 'He was a reliable member of the side that toured India last winter. He bowls a length and a well-regulated line; he spins the ball and has artful variety of flight; there is no more consistently effective off-spinner in the English game. He can also catch well and, at need, bat above his station.'

This last point had been emphasised only a week earlier at Middlesbrough when Geoff, going in as nightwatchman, had hit a career-best 78 against Essex.

> I batted with Lumby; we got runs in the morning session. Then Hamps sent a message out, "Get on with it", and I got out trying to slog Easty.

'Cope had a century there for the taking,' Mike Stevenson wrote in the *Daily Telegraph*, 'but he holed out at deep mid-off to East's flighted one.'

With June six months pregnant, Geoff left in late November. For the first time they were touring not as MCC but as England, though they were still dressed in the George and Dragon blazers, not the Crown and Three Lions.

Ken Barrington, on his 47th birthday, is presented with a cake by Pakistan Airways, with Ian Botham looking on. Heathrow, 24 November 1977.

My England blazer, cap and tie arrived in the post some time after I got back to Yorkshire.

Once more Kenny Barrington was the tour manager and, when Geoff was selected for only one of the three warm-up games, Barrington took the trouble to explain the thinking.

> He said, "Geoff, you're only playing one because we know what you can do. And we can rely on you."

To Phil Edmonds, who with Geoff Miller was picked for two of the games, it looked as if they were the first-choice spinners. Perhaps they were in some minds. But on the flattest of pitches at Faisalabad Edmonds bowled in tandem with Geoff and, while Geoff's 22 eight-ball overs brought him two wickets for 53 runs, Edmonds' 11 overs conceded 56 runs without a wicket. The consequence of this disparity was not lost on Edmonds, as became clear to Geoff soon afterwards.

> Where we were billeted there were nine of us in the room, which included Edmonds. I had the strangest conversation with him one day. It was mid-afternoon, he came in and kicked the newspaper, and he laid on his bed. Things appeared not to be right.
>
> I looked across and I said, "Are you all right? Is everything all right?"
> "No, it's not."
> "Well, what's wrong? Can I help?"
> "Help?" he said. "You've taken my place." Ooops!
> "Hang on," I said. "We're here as a unit. The team hasn't been picked."
> "Well, it's fairly obvious you're going to play and I'm not."
> So I said, "Well, don't blame me for that." He went off, and I thought, "I'm not sure about this." So I spoke quietly to Kenny. And Kenny said, "Leave it with me. Don't you worry about anything."
> That was a being-on-tour situation. He was thinking: 'Underwood's gone, I'm going to play.'

Edmonds was right. When the team was chosen for the First Test at Lahore, he was not playing. The spinners were Miller and Cope.

> My life changed. You play your cricket. Two days before the Test you go for a net, do a bit of fielding. Then the next morning, the day before the match, you have nets in the morning and you go back and have a team meeting and dinner together. And the team is announced. But, of course, being Pakistan, the first thing that's said: "All 16 are selected. Because anything can happen overnight. You've all got to be prepared."

The team was read out in the order. And it got to Cope. And I thought, "Yes. Yes." Then it's congratulations to those playing for the first time. No presentation of caps, there's nothing to give in that way.

I rang June. She was obviously chuffed as houses. We talked about Dad, what he wanted. June was the only one I'd got.

Then I rang Wardle, and the words were "Dad, I've done it, thanks to you." "Right," he said. "Let's get started. When you get on to bowl, make sure that field's in the right place. Have you worked out who your good fielders are, who's got a left arm, who you're going to put at mid-wicket?" He knew. He'd bowled every ball I'd bowled so far on the trip.

We had this wonderful conversation. "Good luck, lad, you'll be all right." I said, "Johnny, when I came to your place, you said, 'By the time I've finished with you, you'll play for England, and you'll have done well. And if we've failed, we've failed.' And Johnny, we've succeeded." He said, "No, you've succeeded. You've done it."

'A blank cheque from Kerry Packer himself could not have bought the contentment that filled room 423 of the Intercontinental Hotel here last night,' wrote Pat Gibson in the *Daily Express*. 'Room-mates Brian Rose and Geoff Cope were sharing the satisfaction of becoming the first new England caps of the post-Packer era.'

It was a magic time. You just wanted to be in your room, on your own, reflecting. Mentally settling yourself down for what was to come. We were playing eight-ball overs, which I'd never played before. You tried to get the first one or two in right. If you got clipped for four first ball, then you bowled a bad one and they got another four, suddenly you'd gone for eight, and you'd another six to bowl. It needs a lot of concentration to bowl eight-ball overs. Johnny gave me advice: "Bowl a ball at a time," he said.

I'd never seen wickets like it before. They were just rolled mud. They watered the outfield, what you could describe as an outfield – very, very bare. They put water on it so the mud would stick together. It was tacky mud initially when you went out. Then it gradually dried, and by the end of the day it was dust. You couldn't bowl in studs. The ground wouldn't give so you ended up bowling in rubbers.

There wasn't a lot of pace. They prepared these pitches that were the most boring things you could wish to play on. If you put men round the bat, they'd hit you over the top. If you put men out, they just blocked you.

England lost the toss and were sent into the field.

> Bob Willis bowled the first over. He got so wound up, 'in the zone', he gave it everything. Fourth ball. I was at mid-off, looking up, and I was thinking about my dad. "Dad, whatever happens, they can't take it away. I'm on the field for England." And boomp! Someone threw the ball at me, it hit me on the chest and fell to the ground. "Look after that new ball," Bob shouted. "It's not going to last long."

The crowd – 3,000 at the start, swelling to 20,000 after lunch – saw 63 eight-ball overs bowled during the 5½ hours of the first day, at the end of which Pakistan had crawled to 164 for two, with their opener Mudassar Nazar on 52 not out. Geoff had bowled 12 overs for 23 runs.

Haroon Rashid batted with greater enterprise, completing his hundred next morning, but Mudassar continued at the same pace, his eventual century – in 9 hours 17 minutes – the slowest in the history of first-class cricket. To make matters worse, some of the spectators mistakenly ran on to congratulate him when he reached 99 and the police dispersed them so heavy-handedly that a riot ensued, holding up play for 45 minutes. Pakistan ended the second day on 350 for five, with Geoff bowling 20 more overs for a further 54 runs.

> Haroon was a good player. He was one who tried to dictate how you bowled. Mudassar was boring, he just accumulated. On a pitch that gave you nothing. I didn't get my first wicket till the third day.

Wasim Raja stumped Taylor bowled Cope 24

> Wasim was a good player, and he was a lovely man, as good as anybody out there that I befriended. A more than useful leggie, and a good left-handed batter who played his shots. He came for me, I drifted it, and Bob did the rest. My first Test wicket.
>
> I remember thinking, "I've bowled all these overs and my first wicket is a stumping. And my first wicket for Yorkshire was a stumping. Are these batters just being sympathetic?"
>
> Bob Taylor was fabulous. The Second Test in Hyderabad he stood up to everybody in the whole match. That included Bob Willis. He was a very, very good keeper.

The game was moving on at last and, four overs later, Geoff was centre stage.

> I had Abdul Qadir l-b. Off he went. Sarfraz came in and, first ball, he tried to sweep-slog me, missed it and was bowled.
>
> Then in came Iqbal Qasim. We had five, six men around the bat: Brearley at slip, Roopy at second slip, Willis in the gully, somebody

156

round the corner. I can remember, clear as day, little Iqi took guard. A left-hander. It was a hat-trick ball, and we were all a bit tense.

For that day, that moment, that pitch, I bowled the ideal ball. I flighted it a bit more, gave it more of a loop. I'm not saying it turned, but it held. Just sufficient. Iqi pushed at it as you do; your first ball you're always a bit tentative. There was a little bit of bounce, it moved, and he nicked it. Brears dived to his left and caught it.

We all went up. The excitement. It was brilliant. The umpire gave it out. He'd never seen a hat-trick before. "Well bowled," he said. And Iqi nodded at me and set off. Everybody was running about. And I was right up there.

According to John Woodcock, 'Cope was jumping in the air in the style of a boxer who has just won a world title, and his colleagues were congratulating him as though they were his seconds.'

Abdul Qadir lbw bowled Cope 11
Sarfraz Nawaz bowled Cope 0
Iqbal Qasim caught Brearley bowled Cope 0

Not for 20 years, not since Peter Loader at Headingley in 1957, had an England bowler taken a Test hat-trick. And on debut, too. The statisticians were hard at work. A hat-trick on debut. Only Peter Petherick, a New Zealand off-spinner, had done it before – strangely, a year earlier on this very ground.

Then suddenly Brearley said, "I'm not sure that I caught it."

"Well, I can assure you you did. You caught it inches above the ground." He caught the ball and hit the ground with the fall. There was a bit of grazing on the back of the hand because it was gravel, not grass. Iqi was on his way, well on his way. And he said, "I think I'm going to bring him back for the future of the series."

"What are you on about? The umpire's happy, Iqi's happy, everybody's happy."

"I don't think I've caught it." And back came Iqi.

It wasn't long after that they declared. We came back in, and Kenny was straight to me, sat down with me. "Well done, lad, well done. Your first Test, you've bowled very, very well. It's hard work bowling eight-ball overs." He just understood.

Had it been one of those catches where the batsman stood, the two umpires conferred and at the end they said, "We're not sure, so it's not out," it would have been a different kettle of fish. But everybody was convinced. 'For the future of the series' – those famous words.

Geoff put a brave face on his disappointment when he spoke to the press. "I wouldn't have wanted a record completed with a suspicious catch," he told them. But forty years on, reflecting on his captain's words, he smiles when he recalls the umpiring in the Third Test at Karachi. Appeal after appeal was turned down when they fielded. Then in their own first innings:

> In the interests of the series six of us were given lbw.

'In all six instances,' Henry Blofeld observed in the *Guardian*, 'the umpire's fingers were up before the appeal had finished. I never think this is a good sign.'

At Karachi the lbws were two on each side. At Hyderabad there were none. So what was different at Karachi? One of the umpires was new, certainly. His name was Shakoor Rana – and among those given lbw (in both innings), making his Test debut, was Mike Gatting.

Events on the third day at Lahore soon put the disappointment out of Geoff's mind. Pakistan was under military rule, with General Zia having seized power in a coup from the elected government of Zulfikar Ali Bhutto. The former prime minister was under arrest, but his wife and daughter arrived at the Lahore ground that day and soon there were bottles and bricks flying, a fire was started, and the police were letting off tear gas.

> It was horrible. We had the sanctuary of the dressing room, the armed police around us, but we were edgy and nervous about what was going on. The tear gas was awful. As soon as you got near it, your eyes started watering and you were coughing. It was frightening. But the authorities were good. They kept us all together, and they looked after us.

It calmed down soon enough. Play continued, and England – thanks to an unbeaten 98 from Geoff Miller – saved the follow-on and drew the match. Geoff, alas, was out second ball.

> lbw Sarfraz 0. I remembered Leeds Schools, first innings, 0. Yorkshire Schools, first innings, 0. Yorkshire 2s, first innings, 0. Yorkshire, 2. The only one that broke the trend.
> It was a big shout. And off I went.

Next on the tour itinerary, on 23 December, was a one-day international at Sahiwal which Geoff did not play.

> I stayed in the hotel at Lahore. Kenny said, "You've had a long bowl, get your feet up, relax." Those of us left there had to hang up some Christmas decorations in the manager's flat.
> Suddenly the manager of the hotel came in: "Oh, Mr Cope, I didn't know you were here. You have had a phone call. From Mrs Cope."

I thought, 'What else can go wrong?' That was my first reaction. I said, "How important is it?" "Oh, she's going to call back." "Have I a chance of calling her?" "I'll do what I can." And off he went.

Sure enough, this call came through. "Hello."

"What are you doing ringing me when we've got a free call in two days?" The Yorkshireman speaking.

"Well, you've just had your first Test match, and I thought I'd congratulate you ... And, well, it's like this. You've got an early Christmas present."

"Go on."

"You're a dad."

"Go on."

"You've got a son."

Suddenly I was thinking, 'He shouldn't be here till February.'

"Is everything all right?"

"Yes, they say so."

We had a little discussion about my dad, and he became Andrew John Charles Cope. Blofeld said, "Are you trying to get in the honours list, a Yorkshireman with three initials?!"

Don Mosey was out with us. I knocked on his door, and I put my head round. "I'm a dad." I was armed with a bottle of Bristol Cream Sherry – all we had over there – and we celebrated the birth. He arranged for a girl at the BBC in London to ring the hospital half an hour before he was due to come through with his report each day. So I got a daily bulletin on how Andrew was doing.

Twelve months earlier, when his father had died, Geoff had flown home from India, losing his chance of playing in the First Test. This time the hospital decided to conceal from him the complications of the early birth.

I thought we'd had a premature baby who was doing well. If I'd have been at home, I'd have been told he only had a fifty per cent chance of survival. I'd have had a worrying 72 hours. But they chose not to tell me anything and to pray. He was a good weight – five pounds eight ounces – but he had a problem with his lungs. Now he's a strapping six foot one.

The tour went on. In his 12 years at Yorkshire Geoff had played little one-day cricket, a source of some irritation to him.

Boycs said he didn't want the one-day game to take away what I had in the three-day game. But you got match money for the one-day games. There weren't so many championship games as there had been so I was losing money.

In Pakistan, however, he was selected for two of England's three one-day internationals, in which he was the team's most economical bowler, conceding only 35 runs off 14 eight-ball overs. But it was his batting in these games of which he remains most proud.

> I had a magnificent strike rate for England in my one-day internationals: 100. I got one not out in one ball.

The tour schedule took them from Sialkot to Hyderabad, and their journey was delayed by a day. After a plane flight to Karachi, they had to endure a long drive north on the day before the Second Test.

> We travelled on the morning of New Year's Day, in two ten-seater combis. I looked at the gear stick, and there was a hole completely around it. We drove four hours across the Sind Desert with these birds of prey hovering and everybody coughing.
>
> When we got to Hyderabad, we went down a dusty road to this prefab hotel – cement and a little bit of stone. You went into the hotel, you went up a corridor, and you carried your bags one in front of you, one behind, because it was so narrow. You couldn't open the room door properly because it hit the second bed. The shower was a pipe down the corner of the wall and when you opened the back window, which was wooden slatters, the stench was unbelievable.
>
> We went for dinner, a room with burgundy walls and two 60-watt bulbs at each end. It was unbelievably dark. The chef was very helpful. We found out that tomato soup and croutons was his speciality.
>
> We convinced the guy that one of the great traditions of English culture is that you had bananas and custard to finish with. So he produced these bananas and custard. We told the head waiter that there was a tradition in England that the leader of the household, when taking his bananas, would dip the head in quickly and stand there with thumbs up. At that time there was a television programme *Magic R Morris*. We got this little fellow, he pushed Kenny's head in, and he said, "Magic R Morris". Bless him, Kenny saw the funny side of it, and it was funny. But we spent the least possible time in that hotel.
>
> We went in the afternoon to the nets, and on the pavilion there were two huge water tanks. And from those tanks they watered the ground. You walked out, and it was like walking on soft sand. You put your foot down, and the dust fell over your foot. Yet the next day it had all been watered, there'd been some sort of roller over it, and it was like tacky mud. By lunchtime it was drying off, and at the end of the day it

was dust again. They had to water it every day before we started. A flat track, slow and low. Bob Taylor stood up to every delivery.

Edmonds came into the team, in place of the injured Chris Old, and the match was drawn. Geoff had the best figures of the three spinners, but again it was his batting that stays more clearly in the memory. With the leg-spinner Abdul Qadir running through the England middle order, the score was 157 for nine, still 118 behind the Pakistani total, when he and Bob Willis came together. In the words of *Wisden* they 'managed a brave 34 in 68 minutes.'

I read Abdul Qadir like a blind man in a cave. I played him as a straight-on bowler. When he bowled a big leggie, I played down the line and I missed it completely. When he bowled the google, it hit the pad but mainly outside the line. And when it was straight, I was knocking it back.

There were no clocks on the ground. Bob Willis came in, and by this time we were in a battlefield. We'd been in together for a while, and I drove Qadir for four. And Bob came down: "Do you realise that's the last ball before tea?" You'd no idea of time.

After tea frustration started. They couldn't get Bob or me out. Wasim Bari started jabbering in Urdu. And the next time I played and missed, they all went up. Jabber again. Play and miss, they were all up. Then they started throwing gloves around, as if to say "He's cheating." So Bob said, "Don't worry, they're only cheating. I'll tell you if you're in or out." There was a big shout: "Not out. Stay there, Geoff." And this is how we batted as the last pair. Finally they brought Wasim Raja on. He did me round the corner with a google. I played well forward, bottom edge and it went to leg slip. And Bob said, "It's carried, Geoff. That's out. We'll leave now." And we walked off.

Cope caught Sadiq bowled Raja 22

Kenny said, "Well played."
I said, "They're cheating."
He said, "They've been like that all their life. It's part of your education." Which it was.
It was a pitch that was never going to be there for a result.

Between the Second and Third Tests, Mike Brearley had his left arm broken in a game against a Sind XI and returned home. It ended Geoff's brief experience of the Middlesex man's captaincy.

My first ball in Test cricket, he said, "I'd like men round the bat." I said, "All right. Slip, boot hill and son of boot hill", meaning silly point and forward short leg. "If you want, we'll put one round the corner, but it doesn't appear to be turning." He said, "Well, this guy plays very much with the open face. I think we should have gully rather than point." So I said, "I've never bowled to a gully before." I couldn't see why I needed a gully. But I said, "You're captain. We'll do it."

First ball, I got a bat-pad, and it went straight to silly point. Gully dived, and he was inches away from it. And Brears walked up to me. He said, "I'll never interfere again. All I will say to you is, Can we attack? And can we defend? And you set your field." And he left me to it. There's a lot in a captain who gives you that.

When I changed my field, Brearley said, "There's not a hint of an old left-armer in this, is there?" I said, "Yes." He said, "We'll have dinner and you can tell me more about it."

Johnny Wardle talked to me before I went on the tour. He wanted me to bowl with John Lever at mid-wicket and Derek Randall at mid-on. Because your left-handed fielder, Lever, can go wider at mid-wicket and cover more because his strength is his left hand. The batsman's got to wait till he's got it past John. Then on the other side it's the same when he sees the strong right arm of Randall. So what could be a three is a two. You're playing to your V – and that's where you've got your two strongest fielders. At dinner Brearley said, "Tell me more." And he said, "That's fascinating."

I thought he was a good captain, certainly a thinking captain. He did ask questions, and he tried to understand you. But he tended to look round at some of the players who were with him who were better players than he was. He was finding that part of it demanding.

The vice-captain Geoff Boycott would also let him have his field, but the conversation would have a different tone to it.

Boycs was "Your ability, my brain." That was fine, but I would say to him, "I want two there, I don't want anybody there, I'll have a slip." "What do you want a slip for? It's turning." "Because I'm bowling round the wicket. If one holds up slightly, it's a run down there, and slip will make them think twice." "Do it."

He generally let you have what you wanted, but it was very much that you were allowed to by him. You'd get a wicket and he'd say, "You see, I told you." When you went for four, it would be: "That's your fault."

For the final Test at Karachi Boycott was in charge, and immediately he was plunged into a crisis. Pakistan had flown in their three Packer recruits – Imran, Mushtaq and Zaheer – and were planning to play them.

We got to the hotel, and suddenly we were all hustled together in the manager's room. Boycs said there were strong rumours that Pakistan were going to play their Packer players. If so, how do we react? "Do we agree to play or not? I feel we shouldn't." Before you know it, you're in a political situation. Boycs and Kenny were on the phone to Doug Insole at Lord's, by which time Kenny was taken out of his normal bustling, comical personality. This was the serious side that Kenny wasn't suited to. There was a lot at stake. The phone calls were still going on. We had another meeting, and we said we weren't going to play.

You'd got one or two who thought, "Hang on, I've just got into the England set-up. If I'm going to strike, I'm going to be out of it very quickly." The word strike was something totally out of the context of anything in my previous life – or of most of the people in that room.

There was never a time when I felt we were threatening the TCCB. They were in a political situation which we were putting pressure on because we were at the coalface. It was all happening with a decision needed in 24 hours. The calls went on for so long, and there were so many points raised, so many points that came back. We might be playing; we might not. And what would happen in Pakistan? Would they have a go against the team? Were we secure there? There was all sorts that you couldn't answer.

It went on till the early hours of the morning before it was finally agreed that Pakistan would not select their Packer players.

The game that followed, though it was enlivened by the rash of lbws given against England, was another dull draw. This time Phil Edmonds was England's star, taking seven wickets in Pakistan's only innings, with Geoff having no happy memories of the match.

I was ill during the Test. I never wanted the toilet. I bowled through it, but I'd come back to the hotel and I had a pain that caused me to lay on the bed curled up. The pain would disappear, and the first thing I felt was that I was hungry. I'd get off the bed carefully, but in two strides I was on the floor in a heap, curled up again with this pain. I lost almost two stone in next to no time. I got on the plane to New Zealand holding my trousers up. If I'd just stood there, they'd have fallen down.

Geoff's other memory is of General Zia visiting them during the match.

We all got a medal presented by him. These five fighting helicopters landed, then he landed in the middle of them. They got out, and they'd all got these machine guns. Boycs had sent General Zia a magnum of champagne with the Pakistan colours on – in the land of prohibition.

The two teams with General Zia

And when we got lined up, this voice comes shouting out from Ian Botham: "We've come all this way, Boycs, to get shot because of you." That was typical 'Both'. A bubbly youth. I liked him. He was refreshing.

In the three Tests Geoff had bowled more overs than anybody in the England team, and his figures were reasonable: eight wickets and a decent economy rate. But, if the surfaces in Pakistan were not conducive to wicket-taking, the umpiring in New Zealand posed an even greater problem, one that became evident in his first three-day game against Central Districts at New Plymouth.

It was one of the most picturesque grounds I'd ever played on. Behind each end there were grass banks with ledges that looked like pyramids, and on each of the levels of the pyramids they had marquees. Geoff Miller and I bowled on the first evening, and we got hoarse with appealing for lbws. Eight-ball overs, when we were appealing five or six balls an over. David O'Sullivan was playing for them, I knew him from when he played for Hampshire. At the end of the day he said, "Geoff, you know what's going to happen tomorrow. They'll kick you for six balls and slog you for two. We play l-b different to you." They'd go half-cock, towards the off side, and kick it.

When we got back to the hotel Geoff Miller and I sought out Kenny Barrington. He was with John Woodcock and Alex Bannister, two senior and trusted journalists, and we explained our predicament.

"This isn't the first time this has happened in New Zealand," Alex said, and he went up to his room to look up some facts. He came back down, and he told us that New Zealand batsmen, when they were in England, were four times as likely to be given l-b as in New Zealand. In England the batsman's sideways movement across the crease was not treated as an attempt to play a shot, but in New Zealand it was.

Sure enough, the next day, I bowled a lot of overs, and I didn't get many wickets. Kenny had said he wanted me to play in the Test, but it forced a selection change.

Geoff Miller stayed in the team as a specialist batsman, not bowling a single over in the first two Tests, while Geoff's short Test career came to a halt. He joined the non-playing extras, offering support when required to his Yorkshire captain.

I was known as Boycs's Man. I did what I could to help Boycs. Sometimes I would say to the lads, "There's a blue moon coming up." That was my way of telling them to keep away from him. I was a sort of middle man. 'Both' used to say, "What are we doing now? What's your mate saying?"

For Boycott it was the moment he had long been waiting for, the chance to prove he was the right man to lead his country, but the series started calamitously at Wellington.

He was sending me out to look at the pitches. I said, "I think it's a put-them-in wicket." Kenny agreed. We did everything right. We were left 130-odd to win and got rolled over for 64.

It was the 48th Test between the two countries and the first that New Zealand had won. With little support, and with the wind getting grit behind his contact lenses, Boycott batted for nearly 7½ hours in the first innings, scoring 77. The strain of this and the subsequent defeat took its toll on his mood.

At one big dinner, with the Prime Minister there, he got up in his egg-and-bacon blazer: "After so many weeks in Pakistan, to come to this country with its rich, green grass, to look at this magnificent buffet over there ..." He was flying away with his compliments. We were thinking, 'Who's written this for him?' Then he said: "And now we're here, how do you expect a world-class batsman like me to play on the shit heaps that have been provided?" Kenny had to jump up and say something about Yorkshire humour.

We went to a Cricket Lovers Society in Christchurch, down by a river. A beautiful spot. He came in late: "Tonic water, ice and lemon, please." "I'm sorry, we've run out of that." "You've got f--- all in this country." Bernard Thomas took him away.

He let himself down badly at times. Things like this you see, but they don't always come out. It annoys fellow players, and I was a bit caught up in it all because they saw me as a Boycs man.

On the first morning of the Second Test at Christchurch Boycott again sent Geoff out to advise him on the pitch.

I came back, saying, "There'll be something in it early doors. If you can get five wickets by lunch, it's worth putting them in. But if you bat, you've got to graft because it will come good."

Mark Burgess was the New Zealand captain, a super guy. He came in. "Can we toss up, Geoffrey, if you don't mind?"

"I'm not ready."

He came back: "Geoffrey, there's twenty minutes to go."

Boycs had asked everybody what he should do. All the batters had said bowl, and all the bowlers had said bat. I said to him, "For Christ's sake, be your own man."

Off he went. He came back, and John Lever said, "What are we doing, Boycs?" There was this silence. "Who's playing?" And he started to put his pads on. We got a scorecard to find out who was in the team.

Then he got out, lbw. He sat in the corner with his hands on his knees, pads still on. Two hours later he was still there.

England were soon 26 for three, but Botham, in only his second Test overseas, hit a thrilling hundred, then took five wickets. By the fourth afternoon they were well on top, with a first innings lead of 183.

We were left with two and a half hours' batting. We said we've got to get 100, 110. The last day you're half an hour short. You're one-nil down in a three-match series, and you're in prime position. You've got to give yourself as much time as possible. Boycs was thinking, "I don't want to be seen as the England captain who loses twice to this lot." He got 26 in two hours, and 'Both' ran him out.

Even then, with a lead of 280 in a shortened day, he wanted to bat on for half an hour to make it safe. In the end somebody else in the team made the declaration. Bob Willis bowled out of his skin. Mark Burgess got hit on the elbow and was carted off, and they were 25 for five. We won the game during the afternoon.

Boycs came in and said, "I only said what I said to get you bowlers fired up."

The final match at Auckland was drawn. Asked at the match's conclusion if he wanted to continue at the helm, Boycott replied, "I like the taste of it. I'm very pleased and delighted with the way things have gone technically since I took over as captain and I'm happy with the job I've done."

Geoff returned to England, his brief international career over. He had not had the best of luck. A double hernia cut short his trip to South Africa; his father's death deprived him of a Test in India; lingering doubts about his bowling action ruled him out in Australia; and unorthodox umpiring lost him his Test place in New Zealand. Only in Pakistan had he played – three Tests and two one-day internationals – and even there his greatest glory, a Test match hat-trick, lasted only a few moments.

> Although it was a very short international career, I visited a lot of places and I made some good friends. A lot of good pals. That's what's been to me the magic of it. I've toured everywhere bar the West Indies.

On Leeds railway station he finally caught up with his 11-week-old son Andrew. "I was jumping up and down waiting to see the baby," he told the *Daily Mail*. "But, despite my enthusiasm, he just lay there half-awake amid all the fuss."

An England cricketer and a father, he had fulfilled his dreams.

June, Andrew and Geoff

14

You play for England – and then wallop

1978-1980

On Friday 14 July 1978, when Yorkshire beat Surrey at the Oval, they moved up to third place in the championship table, challenging Kent and Essex for a title they had not won for ten years. The early weeks of the season had been wet, the pitches more suited to seam than spin, but Geoff had played his part in the successes, his 31 first-class wickets for the county second only to Steve Oldham. He was enjoying his cricket.

How fast all that changed! They travelled from the Oval to Northampton where tensions in the team erupted in an extraordinary way on the Monday afternoon. With each team's first innings limited to 100 overs, the vice-captain John Hampshire was so angry with Geoff Boycott's slow batting that he made almost no attempt to score in the closing ten overs of the innings, encouraging his uncapped partner Colin Johnson to do likewise. With seven wickets in hand, they scored just 11 runs in 10 overs, sacrificing the chance of a further bonus point and a healthy lead. Once more, the fault lines in the team had surfaced.

Boycott, after the triumph of his 100th hundred the previous year, was not having a good summer. After a run of poor scores in May he bruised his thumb badly in an England one-day game and was out of action for a month. In that time Hampshire, enjoying the best form of his career, led the team to several victories, one of them over Leicestershire whose captain Ray Illingworth had already been appointed as Yorkshire's cricket manager for the following year. What was Illingworth planning for the captaincy? Rumours and speculation were rife, with Boycott moved to send a letter to *The Times*, insisting that he intended to continue playing for Yorkshire.

Despite the problems created by Don Brennan's advocacy of Geoff as captain the previous autumn, Geoff was still the man Boycott turned to for advice.

> Boycs questioned me at Northampton whether he should send Hamps and Johnson home. I said, "No, I don't think so. They're both strong Yorkshire people. If you're going to do anything, you've got to go back and report the situation." That allowed Hamps to have his say, rather than going to the press. At the inquest Hamps was quite forceful, saying "We've put up with it for years." It was an unpleasant time.

By Saturday, however, it was not Hampshire and Boycott who were the main story in the newspapers but Geoff himself. Unbeknown to him, his bowling action had been reported by three umpires, and he had been filmed at the Oval the previous week. At home on Friday evening, the night before he was due to play the New Zealanders at Headingley, he was rung by Joe Lister. The TCCB had suspended him from bowling 'for the remainder of this season or until such time as his basic bowling action is corrected and approved.'

> The years from 1974 to 1977 were years when I felt I'd been forgiven. It was my happiest time in cricket. I felt relaxed, I felt part of the game, part of the team. I was going out with a smile, able to enjoy the game that I loved. And then all this came up again.
>
> You play for England, you come home, and it all comes back – Bang! And you think, "Why did they say it was all right?" There was the Gubby Allen thing – "You don't pick him in Australia" – but I still went on the following tour. I thought, "I must be all right." And then, wallop.
>
> I was thinking, 'Have they used me?' Peter Parfitt, bless him, he admitted he was on the throwing committee. Parf said, "You should have been banned for life, or you should have played fifty Test matches for England because you were the best spinner." Those were words that stayed with me because I respected Parf.
>
> You just go negative, and I didn't want to do that. I was 31. I was looking that I had at least five more years to play a decent level of cricket. Then all of a sudden the whole thing turned on its head, and I started feeling, "This is tiring."

"I'll be back," he told the *Yorkshire Post*. "I'm a Yorkshireman, and I know how to fight. I've overcome problems like this before." And once more he was off to see Johnny Wardle at the Ponderosa Club.

As before, there was no invitation to Lord's to watch the film of his bowling and to be told what was wrong. Instead, he had to listen to all the different explanations and to find his own way through.

Wardle told the press that the problem lay with his not having bowled enough that summer, an explanation which Geoff seemed prepared to accept: "It's been such a stop-go season, I haven't really got into a flow. Perhaps I have been trying too hard, and that has led to the problem."

Some thought that he was getting too chest-on, some that he was kicking his front leg too high. Then there were those that doubted whether he was gaining any advantage from whatever it was that he was doing wrong. When the ball left his hand, it was going upwards, not firing at speed at the stumps. And in any case, one local umpire wrote, the little straightening of his arm was occurring too far back in the delivery to affect the flight of the ball.

A rare, grainy sequence of Geoff bowling in club cricket in August 1978, photographed by the Yorkshire Evening Press

One correspondent to the *Bradford Telegraph and Argus* quoted Percy Holmes, the great Yorkshire batsman of the 1920s, who was asked 'Did they ever chuck them in your day?': "Aye, happen they did. But tha' knaws, they could nobbut chuck 'em one at a time."

"It is sickening," Geoff Boycott said. "It's a dreadful business for Geoff, and it obviously affects Yorkshire's chances in the championship."

The regulations were strange. Geoff was banned from the first-class game till the end of the season, but there was nothing to stop him playing – as he did in late August – for the second eleven. Then the next summer he would be free to start again. By then Ray Illingworth would be in post as manager, and it was not clear that, as a fellow off-spinner, he had full confidence in Geoff's action.

In his autobiography Pat Pocock recalled a Surrey/Yorkshire game in which Geoff was bowling: 'Illy approached me in our dressing room. "How can you let him get away with that?" he said. "He's chucking every ball. It's terrible, that is. You'll have to report him."'

Geoff spent a full twelve months in the wilderness: working with Johnny Wardle, driving through the heavy snows of winter to the Headingley nets, even going down to Lord's to get help from his old spin partner Don Wilson, now MCC's head coach. At one stage he was the subject of a lengthy feature on BBC's *Nationwide* programme.

> For a fortnight they came. I spoke at a dinner, I presented cups, I did a prize presentation at a boxing tournament, and they took me to see Wils at Lord's. They filmed me bowling with various cameras, and afterwards Wils and I sat looking at every frame of each ball. The only time we came up with anything that looked strange was from directly behind. It was different from the others. If you turn a door lock, watch the elbow from behind. It's not bending but it moves.
>
> Sue Lawley was presenting the feature, and she was marvellous. "That's perfect television," she said. "Now I'm going to let you into a

secret. You only discussed one ball. We've had five cameras. And four are saying it's perfect."

A professor at Leeds University said half of it could be camera angle. He put six cameras on top of each other and filmed me driving a golf ball. In two of them the club was bent. A bent club and a straight club, cameras in a row all taking the same shot.

It was the worst of winters, for Geoff and for the country, and it was not helped by a rash of public-sector strikes that affected hospitals and schools and left rubbish uncollected for weeks.

Geoff started the summer of 1979 with three matches for the second eleven, in one of which he took 9/27 in the Northamptonshire first innings. Yet his winter's work was not to the liking of Yorkshire's newly appointed manager. At a meeting of the Cricket Committee on 22 May 'Mr Raymond Illingworth said he was still not happy with Geoff Cope's action.' In the light of this, a decision was taken to re-register the manager as a player. He was a fortnight from his 47th birthday, but the previous year he had finished second in the Leicestershire bowling averages and scored a first-class century.

Another can of film – this time with Billy Sutcliffe and Johnny Wardle
'He's been filmed more times than Michael Caine,' one journalist wrote.
'He's watched more slow motion playbacks than Jimmy Hill.'

Illy wasn't too supportive of my situation. I felt all along that he wanted to play again.

Geoff's place in the first team had been taken by Peter Whiteley, a chemistry graduate whose father was director of a paper mill in Pool. He had made a promising start in the final games of 1978, when the pitches were hard and dry, but by mid-July in 1979 he had taken only 10 expensive wickets in 11 appearances. Yorkshire had won only one of those 11 matches.

Out of the blue Geoff got a phone call, telling him to report to Worksop for the next first-team match, the first of four they were giving him. "When he gets into a rhythm we will be happy to have him filmed again," Illingworth told the *Yorkshire Post*. "We owe that to the game and to the lad himself; he simply has to know where he stands – and sooner rather than later."

"It's a bit disappointing," Geoff quipped on his first day back. "Illy didn't even introduce me round the team this morning."

They fielded first, and he was soon in action. "Pitch 'em up, chucker," bellowed a harsh voice from the crowd when he was hit for his first four, but he persevered with his reformed action for 23 overs.

"I'm like one of those cars that's had a Mark One version, a Mark Two, a Mark Three and so on," he said. "I can't even remember what my first action was like, except that it was right-handed, and sometimes I doubt that."

It was not an easy day. Though he kept line and length, he finished with no wickets for 77 runs. Then, after Notts had declared, he went in as nightwatchman and was caught at slip for a duck.

He played the last nine matches of the summer, with little success, but he did have one golden game, a game that still glows in his memory, at Hove.

> A magic day, one of my best days ever. The Sussex batsmen set off like tracers. They must have had 70 or 80 on the board in not many overs, and I came on as a last resort. At the sea end, up the hill. I got Mendis lbw, and in came Javed Miandad – 'Me-mam-and-dad', as I called him. We used to have a bit of banter. He gave it away that he was coming down the wicket, and I bowled it wider. He was well stranded.

Javed Miandad stumped Bairstow bowled Cope 0

> I bowled at Phillipson for 65 minutes, and he didn't get a run. Then he got an edgy single. I just looked at Fergie, and he knew I wanted him back at my end. He pushed his mid-on and mid-off back for the last two balls; Phillipson pushed for one and he was back at my end. He holed out the next over. And he'd scored two. I said to Fergie, "That's *our* wicket." That's how we did it.

Phillipson caught Lumb bowled Cope 2

172

I bowled 35 overs, six for 37, something like that. It was ridiculous, after the way they'd set off at eight an over. There was a big crowd. It was a sunny day. The deck chairs were full. Probably the crowd were two-thirds Yorkies, and they all clapped me off.

For Peter Snape in the *Yorkshire Post* 'the sight of the members in the Hove pavilion – Sussex and Yorkshire alike – rising on Saturday evening to acclaim Geoff Cope was one of the most moving this summer. Nobody with an ounce of sentiment could quibble with his reception. Not only had Cope taken 6-37 in 34.3 overs of consistently accurate off-spin, he had made the hours of physical toil and mental tribulation correcting his bowling action worthwhile.'

"As I came in, I dared not look up," Geoff told Snape. "There was a lump in my throat. Yorkshire are followed by so many people all over the country, and they appreciate what this day means to me. I was doing it almost as much for them as for myself. ... Since I returned to the side at Worksop last month I have been very tense. For the first time I felt relaxed and the rhythm returned. ... The pressure is something I have got to put with. A day like this is like putting a lifebelt on."

I didn't play in the Sunday game. But Burt Rhodes, his wife Flora and daughter Alison of the Yorkshire Southern Members Group were there, and they brought a hamper. I sat upstairs on the balcony with them. There were a couple of girls to the right. They were having a bit of a party, and they offered me a glass of wine. I went back to the hotel absolutely fine, right as a bobbin. I'd had a right good day.

When I woke up next morning, I felt well. But when I walked out of the hotel, the brightness of the day really hit me. I thought, "Gee, what's this?" I was staring at the pavement as I was walking along. But I was thinking, "We're 15 for one. I won't be needed."

I got in the dressing room. Mollie Staines brought me some Alka-Seltzers. I got them down me, and I went to relax. Then, before I knew it, I had my pads on. Geoff Arnold had taken six for six. And I was going in some three or four hours before I expected.

I walked in. I pulled my cap down, and I stared at the grass. I was thinking, "Gee, it's bright out here." Pigott was bowling. First ball he hit me straight in the groin. I took the box out. Knocked it back.

It was 69 for eight when he went in, joining Richard Lumb who had opened the innings. Resolutely, in the words of Peter Snape, 'he shrugged off a sickening blow in the groin to get his forward defensive stroke into full working order.'

I was just trying to hang in there, get some vision.

At 120 Lumb was out, bringing Steve Oldham – highest first-class score 19 – to the crease. 'At first Cope tried to push singles to keep Oldham away from the bowling. Gradually, incredibly the number 11 became the dominant partner.'

> They bowled Cheatle, the left-armer, down the hill, and the shorter boundary was to the pavilion. And Oldham kept slogging him over there. I'll never forget it. I kept saying to him, "Come on, come on, play. You've never had a fifty. Play sensible." "I'm all right. I'm winning." And finally he got this fifty. I went down, and we shook hands. "Right," I said. "Well played, pal. Now play for me, and let me get mine." "Bollocks to you." And he smacked it straight up in the air.

Oldham caught Cheatle bowled Phillipson 50
Cope not out 39

All out for 198, the Yorkshire innings had lasted 89 overs.

> Well, it would do. I blocked 50 of them.

Geoff was back in the team, and in the long months of winter, when they went their separate ways, he organised their football side, playing charity matches around the county. They had several good players – Arnie Sidebottom had turned out for Manchester United, David Bairstow for Bradford City, not to mention Brian Close, once of Arsenal; they were fit, and they were fiercely competitive, never more than in the two games when they took on the Leeds United Ex-Players XI.

In the first of the matches the cricketers were 5-4 up in the closing moments when, according to Geoff, the referee decided that the reputation of the ex-players was more important than an exact application of the game's laws.

> We were 4-2 up at half-time, and they made five substitutions, including Lorimer, Gray and Hunter. We were hanging on for grim death at the end, and a shot hit David Bairstow on the chest. There was the mark of this great muddy ball on his shirt, and the referee gave a penalty. "They haven't been beaten," he said when we protested. It ended up 5-5.

A butcher in Steeton was so impressed by the whole-heartedness of the two teams and the quality of the names on show that he set up a second match at Malsis School, raising funds for the kidney unit at Leeds Hospital. This time it was no ten-goal extravaganza but a hard-fought 2-1 victory for the footballers which ended with one of the Yorkshire team – Bernard Ellison, a Bradford League cricketer who worked at Bradford City – being stretchered off after a wild challenge from the Scottish international Bobby Collins.

Geoff, John Charles, Cyril Partridge (Leeds United trainer), Ray Illingworth, Brian Close

Bernard had run round the back, with a chance of scoring, and Bobby took him out by the hip, feet straight in. They had to bring out the stretcher. And all Collins said was, "We haven't lost." That was the competitiveness. We got Bernard off, and the ref blew for full time.

Amid all this burning desire to win, there was one moment of unhurried magic in the first game that stands out in Geoff's memory. It was a moment when he witnessed something of the glory of the great John Charles, who by now was in his late forties.

Their keeper threw it to Big John who was in the centre circle. He'd got Arnie Sidebottom at one side of him, Steve Oldham who played at Stocksbridge on the other. Both big lads. Big John called "Eddie" to Eddie Gray who was on the touch line, he just went 'boom', and the ball dropped at Eddie's feet. With his soft Welsh accent Big John said, "Hold it, son," and he ambled down to the D.

We had Rocker Robinson in goal. He played for Northallerton Town. "When you're ready," Big John said. The ball came over, we were all round him, and this great neck came out. He hit the ball with his head, and Rocker never moved. Nobody moved. We just stood with open jaws, looking at this man-mountain.

I was about five yards away, and he winked at me.

I said, "Never mind winking. I'm just pleased I were here."

He said, "You should have seen me in my pomp."

It was a glimpse of a legend, and Geoff had another special moment with a legend the following June when Yorkshire were playing at Southampton.

It was John Arlott's last summer before he went to Alderney, and he invited us all to supper. It was very disappointing. The only person who wanted to go was Ted Lester. So it was just Ted and me.

We went to the Old Sun pub in Alresford, which he'd bought. He'd converted the upstairs, and he had all his wine in the cellar. He'd married his housekeeper and adopted her son. And we sat at this long table. Mrs Arlott at one end, with the son there. The white wine was poured out. "Come on, get it down you," he said. "Then we can get on to the Real McCoy."

"Hang on, John, I'm driving back."

"The sheets are already pulled back." He was expecting us to stay.

A bit of fish, then steak. Then the red wine came out, John's eyes shut, and he starting talking about Yorkshire and about all its players down the years. And while he talked, with his eyes shut, his hand would go out, and he never missed the bottle, he never missed the glass. Then his son would get up and replace the bottle.

He talked of Len Hutton and Herbert Sutcliffe, then he talked of Wally Hammond, and it was just as if everything was yesterday and they were in the next room. He was magnificent with words and with feelings. The evening was wonderful. We tried to talk to his wife. But she said, "Leave it. He's in his element. He's happy."

The summer of 1980 was Arlott's last as a commentator and, as it turned out, it was also Geoff's last as a player. Banned in the middle of 1978, he had returned to the team for the final weeks of 1979, during which he was filmed while bowling at Cheltenham. It was more than three months – the end of November – before the Adjudication Committee viewed the footage, at which point they declared themselves unsatisfied with the latest version of his action.

For years he had put up with the cheap jokes, like the men in the pub who would say, "I'll pass you your drink, lad, save you bending your arm." In getting through it all, he had relied on the good humour he learned from his father, but now the accumulation of setbacks was sapping his spirit.

"All my life I've simply wanted to play cricket," he told a reporter. "Suddenly this latest blow has hit my enthusiasm. I feel like a boxer who's been knocked down three times. You brush off the first one, the second one tingles a little, but the third one hurts."

> I became tired of it all, getting less and less support. I was someone who responded to an arm around, and there was no arm at this stage. Fred had put his arm around me, Closey had helped, and Wardle, but now there was nobody. Illy made a statement, "I don't want to clog the second team up with 32-year-old spinners, to try again to satisfy the authorities."

Yet, in this bizarre process, the verdict from Lord's – because it came after the season had ended – did not constitute a ban, and he was free to start again the next year. It was the worst of times and, with so much uncertainty about his long-term future, he was talked into accepting a joint benefit with Barrie Leadbeater, whose contract had not been renewed.

> Illy made me the offer one Saturday night. Barrie, he said, would probably not play after '79, and he was getting '80 as his benefit. He said no decision had been made for me. If I played in '80, I could have 81 as my benefit. But if I didn't finish up playing, it might not be awarded at all. So I had to choose between half a benefit in '80 and the chance of no benefit at all, and he needed the answer first thing on Sunday morning.
>
> Afterwards I had two phone calls from members of the committee, saying they thought I had more oil in my lamp than to accept a joint one when I could have had one on my own. And to this day I don't know who I believe.

The return of Ray Illingworth had not worked out well for Geoff.

> When Illy came, I thought, "That's a good appointment. I like that." I saw him as a cricketer – a fabulous tactician, a very good bowler. Shrewd, knowledgeable. But as a manager I felt he still wanted to be playing.
>
> We would be struggling at five or six down, needing to get our heads down, and Illy would say, "We were in a situation like this at Leicester, and Birky and I went out and got some runs. That was always the advantage of having somebody like him in the lower order." He said it not once but fairly regularly. "What I did at Leicester was …"
>
> It rubbed. "Illy, you're not at Leicester. You're at Yorkshire, and we need a bit of advice."

Illingworth's biggest decision, taken as soon as he took up post, was to take the captaincy away from Boycott – and to appoint in his place John Hampshire, the man at the centre of the go-slow bust-up at Northampton. With Boycott's supporters now mobilising, it created much bad feeling in the club, and some of that bad feeling has come to involve Geoff's role in the episode.

'Let me put this on record,' Illingworth said in *Yorkshire and Back*, the autobiography he wrote with Don Mosey after the first summer of Hampshire's captaincy. 'Because I was still not officially the cricket manager of Yorkshire, I asked the senior capped player, Geoff Cope, to check with his colleagues. Three players had already gone to Australia (to play club cricket) – Bill Athey, Jimmy Love and Kevin Sharp – but as they were not capped players they did not come within the scope of Geoff Cope's check-up. He spoke to all the capped players and gave me the answer: *not one of them is against the change of captaincy.*'

Geoff was not, in fact, the senior capped player but, otherwise, this account is entirely consistent with Geoff's own memory of the affair.

> I'd gone back to work, and I was at work when I was called by Illy. "I've got something for you to do for me. You are the players' representative. I want to know if the players want Boycs as captain."
>
> I said, "I don't think that's fair, Raymond."
>
> He said, "Well, don't you worry about it. You're the representative, you're doing something for me. I'll deal with it from then on. But I want to know where I stand."
>
> He was taking up the post, and he was going to fire the bullets.
>
> I rang every player bar those who were abroad. I said to everybody that I didn't like what I was doing, but it wouldn't go any further.
>
> I rang Illy back, and I said to him, "The vast majority are in favour of a change of captain, but it's not unanimous because of abstentions." There were four abstentions – David Bairstow, Phil Carrick, Graham Stevenson and one other. I don't know about Hamps. 13 for a change, 4 for an abstain. "I'm still not happy, Raymond," I said, "but this is what you asked me for."
>
> He said, "Thanks. I'll deal with the rest."

But this version is not consistent with what appeared in print in 1987 in another book by Ray Illingworth, this one called *The Tempestuous Years* and written with Steve Whiting of the *Sun*. Now he was telling the story as follows: 'Even though I was still in my last season at Leicester and a good few miles down the M1, I would have needed to be a polar bear living on an ice floe not to have known that Boycott's captaincy was causing a fair amount of unrest at Yorkshire, particularly amongst the players. I knew it was a problem that would have to be sorted out one day – one way or another. But what I then heard on the cricket grapevine told me that things had gone as far as could be tolerated. What I heard was that off-spinner Geoff Cope – a nice, decent, family lad who wanted little more than to be able to enjoy his cricket in a congenial atmosphere – had conducted a round robin amongst the Yorkshire players to ask whether they wanted Geoffrey as captain. It has been suggested in some places – and by now you may well be able to guess where – that in some way I instigated this poll. Well, that is totally untrue. I didn't even hear of it until it had already taken place.'

> When I read that, it hurt me more than anything. I mentioned it to Raymond once in front of some people, and he laughed it off. He said, "It'll be a mistake with printers."

The summer of 1979, with a new captain, saw no great progress – though Boycott, for the second time in the decade, averaged 100 with the bat. For Geoff, returning to the team in the last nine matches, there was just that one good day at Hove and another negative report from Lord's.

He started again in 1980, missing only two championship matches, but he never found his best form. Worse, when Yorkshire's Cricket Committee met the week after the season ended, they had to digest another letter from Lord's, this one reporting that over the course of the summer they had received six 'adverse comments' on his bowling action. The minute of the item concluded: 'It was clear that Cope's future in first-class cricket was now over.'

Geoff was offered a one-match-at-a-time contract for 1981, paid when he played and nothing more, but he decided to call it a day. He had two children now – Nicola had been born in November 1979 – and he had been offered a good job setting up a distribution network, from Birmingham to Scotland, for Hovat, a subsidiary of Wiggins Teape, who manufactured computer labels and were based in Kent.

> I had that in the back of my mind when I went to see Yorkshire. They offered me this match-by-match arrangement. At this stage Andrew was three, Nicola was one, and basically I could be playing on Tuesday morning, then there could be a phone call from Lord's on Tuesday afternoon, and that would be the end of my career. I'd have nowhere to go. I couldn't afford that.
>
> I was tired. I was weak. I'd been knocked down. Could I get up again?
>
> I'm not saying it was the easiest way out. It was the hardest. Because it was taking away something that I loved. But you can only stand so much. June was the only one who'd been there all the time. She's the one who got me through all that.

179

We will never know now quite how it came to this, but there were more than a few who looked at other actions on the circuit, particularly those of a couple of fast bowlers, and wondered how it was only Geoff taking the flak. In mid-August in that last summer the Yorkshire team went down to the Oval to play a Gillette Cup semi-final against Surrey and found themselves batting on a newly laid pitch in poor light against the West Indian Sylvester Clarke.

It was a very wet day, and unfortunately our supporters were there in force, demanding some action. We had a second day to play it, and the umpires came up with this stupid idea to play one innings one day, one the next. Whoever won the toss won the match, and we lost it.

They put us in. Boycs was on the back foot – and when Boycs is on the back foot and he's hitting just behind square, there's not many better players. Well, he whacked this one, it went past backward point, and it slowed up in the wet. It went about twenty yards. Next morning that was a four.

It was at the time when the West Indians went round the wicket to Boycs. Whatever you feel about the fella, he could play – but I've never seen anyone pin Boycs like Clarke pinned him that day. He hit him twice, and Hamps turned round to me in the dressing room. "I feel for you," he said. "You've been handed all these bans, and this fella's just blatantly chucking it."

Sylvester Clarke was dangerous, no ifs and buts, and in my opinion he threw it. We reported him, and we got two comments back. One said it would cause trouble with international relations. The second said the BBC film was not clear.

I'm no wiser today than I was in 1978. The committee make the decision and go off, and you're left on your own. Over the years I tried to seek answers, but the answers and the clarification are hidden from you. I could get absolutely bitter and twisted about this, and it would make me ill. At the end of the day I've tried to stay above that.

On Tuesday 5 September 1980, at Scarborough's North Marine Road ground, Geoff left the fields of county cricket for the last time, his final victim his one-time England spin partner Geoff Miller. The following week his departure was announced, with Terry Brindle of the *Yorkshire Post* reflecting on what he called 'the abrupt and messy execution of his cricket career':

'The laws which prevent throwing were designed, primarily at least, to protect batsmen against physical injury from renegade fast bowlers rather than to weed out spinners whose action is less than perfect ... There are at least two fast – very fast – bowlers in county cricket, their names regularly whispered on the circuit, who are regarded as "chuckers". It is, of course, purely coincidental that they are overseas players and an entirely unworthy suggestion that they escape because their exposure might create a so-called "international incident".'

He went on to quote Geoff: "I haven't had much time to think hard about the future, but the game still means an awful lot to me. In a daft sort of way I'm looking forward to going back to where they play the game for fun – to the league and club cricket, long grass and that sort of thing ... County cricket hasn't been all fun to me for a few years now but I know I shall miss it."

Brindle concluded: 'If it is any consolation to a marvellous, dedicated man who always put more into the game than he took out, professional cricket will miss him more. There is no doubt whose loss is the greater.'

For Geoff, the most sociable of cricketers, it cut him off not just from the cameraderie of the professional game but from the many folk beyond the boundary whom he had come to know up and down the country – people such as 'Auntie' Betty and her husband Mike, Yorkshire supporters who lived in Cornwall.

Geoff with 'Auntie' Betty, Weston-super-Mare, August 1980

Mike was a photographer down in St Ives. They were at all the games in the south of England, right up to Edgbaston. Every year she used to send a cheque to the captain for drinks. We adopted her as 'Auntie' Betty.

June and I went down to Cornwall for a holiday once. We didn't have their address, but we went into St Ives and we found them – and the welcome we got was just over the top. It was wonderful.

Geoff received offers, some inviting him to play as a professional in the Lancashire League, but in December he announced that he would be turning out next summer for Yeadon, a club that was at rock bottom in the Bradford League. It was a decision that owed much to the advice of his great pal Lawrie McMenemy, the manager of Southampton Football Club.

He said, "You've offers from the Lancashire League which means money and pressure. You're in the other half of God's Country, and you'll be on your own. At some time during the season Yorkshire will be at Lord's or wherever. You'll be stood at slip, and something will whack you on the middle of the chest – a cricket ball that you should have caught. But you were down at Lord's with the lads, wondering how they were getting on, thinking 'I should be there.' How important is the money? If I were you, I'd get a few mates around you and go and enjoy your cricket."

15

It's amazing what can be achieved

The years after cricket

"I want you to have something behind you in case cricket doesn't work," Geoff's mother had told him when he was 16. It was advice that he had long come to appreciate but now, at the age of 33, with his years as a professional sportsman over, the words seemed wiser than ever. His income from the benefit he shared with Barrie Leadbeater was just under £17,000 and, with the strong recommendation of his bank manager, he bought a house in Tranmere Park, Guiseley, the house where he and June would bring up Andrew and Nicola and in which they would live till the spring of 2017. The move stretched the household finances to the limit, but Geoff had the security of a responsible job in the paper trade where he had built up a good reputation.

Without his mother's prompting, Geoff might have been in the same situation as his great friend David Mills, the Middlesbrough footballer whose transfer to West Bromwich in 1979 had made him Britain's first half-million-pound player.

David loved his cricket, played for Thornaby, a good standard, and all his life he'd played football. Very sadly, towards the end of his career, he was involved in a car crash in the Tyne tunnel; to this day nobody knows how it happened. His father was killed in the passenger seat, and the boys in the back – his son and a couple of his friends – were very seriously injured. David was battered, there were no ifs and buts about it. Straightaway I went up to see him in intensive care, and I walked past both him and his son because I didn't recognise them.

That put an end to his football career, and one of his friends offered him a job selling print – Thomas Hill, printers in Bishop Auckland who did the Middlesbrough programme. He'd known them over the years. He rang me up and I said, "It's a good trade. What you've got as an advantage is locally you're David Mills the footballer and everybody knows you. If you're going in for quotes, people might give you the chance. It's up to you then to get it done properly by people who know what they're doing. In the meantime you've got to get something behind you."

So at 36, 37, David started going to night school with 16-year-old apprentices, to learn about print. And he said to me, "They've only offered me so much." I said, "You're very lucky." He said, "You're joking." He was so caught up in his football that he hadn't seen the reality of life outside. It was a major culture shock, to start with 16-year-old apprentices learning the trade.

David did well for them, and in time he got back into football. He's now chief scout at Leicester City. He brought Vardy in, he brought Mahrez in, he brought Kanté. But at that time he was where I would have been if I'd not gone out and got a job when I was young.

Away from the first-class game, Geoff continued to play cricket. For four summers, from 1981 to 1984, he turned out for Lincolnshire, following in the footsteps of a string of county cricketers who had enjoyed a second life with the minor county.

Wils had played for Lincs; Ramadhin, Vic Wilson, Johnny Lawrence, Jimmy Binks; Brian Evans from Glamorgan. The key for me was Geoff Robinson, a lad who opened the batting for Lincs and got a lot of runs. He was one of those players where you could say, 'Forget county cricket.' He wasn't the right make-up. But for the 50 overs or the T20, he'd have been a belter. He didn't half give it a smack.

It was he who rang me: "Do you want to come and play?"

"I'd like to, if I can fit it in workwise."

The good news was that their fixtures were played Sundays and Mondays. They were a good bunch of lads. Rick Burton, opening bowler, a Steady Eddie type. Young David Marshall, left-arm spinner. They played around Lincolnshire, a big county. I'd leave league cricket on a Saturday night and drive to Sleaford or Stamford or, for away games, Wisbech or Norwich. Some fair drives. But I was fit enough.

There were some lovely grounds. At Stamford you played in Burghley Park which was beautiful. Lincoln was nice; it turned square there. And you always got a good game at Grimsby.

I could still play a decent level. And I could enjoy myself.

It was good to get away from the politics of Yorkshire County Cricket Club, though there was still politics in Lincolnshire, with tension between the north and the south of the county. In all, across the four years, Geoff played in 36 two-day championship matches and took 140 wickets. In 1983 he renewed his contact with the first-class game when, in the first round of the NatWest Bank Trophy, Lincolnshire were drawn to play Surrey, the cup holders.

For a time, in the 60-over match at Sleaford, a shock seemed on the cards with Roger Knight's Surrey struggling to 137 for six. But a late blaze of runs by their keeper Jack Richards, including 26 off the last five balls, took the contest out of reach of Lincolnshire. Amid the flurry of runs Geoff's bowling figures stood out, though he retains a 34-year-old irritation that they should have been better.

I ended up with 12 overs, nought for 12. And in the twelfth over Rod Estwick, our West Indian pro, let a four through his legs. At square point. Otherwise it would have been nought for 8. Roger Knight was playing. I put him in my pocket and he hardly scored a run. They played it as you'd expect. They blocked me out. Then at the death we thought Rick Burton was good to bowl, and he went for a lot.

In 1985, no longer playing for Lincolnshire, Geoff played one last three-day match: at Swansea for MCC against Wales and, though 38 years old, he showed no sign of decline. Captained by Roger Knight, he bowled 53 overs in the two innings and took four wickets for 80 runs. At the other end the slow-left-armer Nick Cook, who had played for England the previous summer, took one wicket for 83 runs in 29 overs.

But it is not the details of the cricket that dominate Geoff's memory of the trip into Wales but the shock of the news he heard on the way down. Johnny Wardle had died.

I'd just gone over the Severn Bridge when I heard the news on the radio. I was all for turning back there and then. I remember sitting in a layby, not knowing what to do. I rang the house, and Gerald answered. "I'm supposed to be playing in Wales. I'm more than happy to turn round and come back."

"Hold on," he said. "I'll just have a word with my mum." He came back. He said, "I've got to be polite to you. But I think you'd have copped it if you'd been here. Mum says, Johnny would have wanted you to play the game."

The funeral was on the third day. "I'll have to come back." "No, you don't." "What about flowers?" "Just a minute. ... Mum said, it's family flowers only, but you're family."

I got to the hotel, met up with Knighty. I explained it all to him. "We're friends," he said. "We'll look after you." That was typical of Roger. He's somebody I've a lot of time and respect for. He said, "We'll be all right, you and me." We went out for meals together each evening. He never allowed me to be on my own.

I sent a message with the flowers: 'Dear Dad, without you I would not have achieved my wildest dreams – and we shared those dreams together. Thank you for all you have done. Geoff.'

I'd spoken with him earlier in the year at Baildon Cricket Club. It was typical Wardle. He started talking and he mentioned something – how, when the fielders on the offside used to walk in, they looked towards him, the bowler. Somebody said, "What about the batter?"

He stopped in his tracks, and he said, "No, look, I've got three men in the covers, I'm bowling here. If they're coming in to the batter and they see a ball there, if it's going to be driven, they've got to turn to go there. But if they're walking to me, the ball will be driven, and they're on the way. It's that split second. This man could go a bit deeper ..." He just turned it into a coaching session.

He must have done an hour, walking round the room, and everybody was listening. He told stories. He mentioned Ken Taylor – "one of the finest cover fielders, his anticipation ... if he saw the batsman looking to drive, he put his weight on his left foot to push him off to the right; equally if he saw him go on the back foot, the weight was on the right foot because he was going to cut and he'd go to his left." When he finished, everybody stood up. The roar was unbelievable. He sat down and he said to me, "I'm tired, lad." It was late February, early March.

It was the first time I'd seen him for a while. "Are you all right?" "I'm just tired, Geoff, I'm tired." "What can I do?" "Have you got your car with you? ... Will you lead me through Bradford? I'm not sure where I'm going." "Shall I get you onto the 62, or do you want me to get you onto the A1?" "I think I'll be all right if I get to the 62." I drove in front, and he flashed me. "Can you take me a bit further?" He flashed me near Leeds, and he came off at Rothwell. He said, "I'm all right. I know where I am. The A1's just a bit further down. It's been a good night, hasn't it?"

I said to him, "The last thing I want to do, John, is stick here on the side of the road, chatting away." He just wanted to get his breath and have a little break. And he went. I rang up next morning. "Ay, I'm all right, lad, don't worry." He had a brain tumour, but I knew nothing.

It was the saddest time. He was about to become a bowling consultant at Yorkshire, and the players would have gained so much from that. It would have bridged the gap of what had been missing for so many years.

Geoff's main cricket in these years was at Yeadon, playing in the Bradford League, another world from the grounds of his county days.

We played at Hanging Heaton, who'd got Ronnie Hudson, one of the biggest hitters in the league. I came up to bowl – whack. I thought, "That's it, that's out." I turned round, mid-on was on the boundary, 27 yards away, and the ball came down directly behind him. Six runs. I bowled him the same ball at Yeadon, and he blocked it. He smiled at me: "Big ground this, Geoff."

Yeadon were at rock bottom in 1980. Last in the lower division, their record of six draws and 20 defeats was as bad as any club in the 68-year history of the league, and for the second year in succession they had to apply for re-election.

> They were in a mess. They'd spent the summer going down the High Street, saying to the butcher "Can I borrow your apprentice?", just to make the side up. They played a lot of the games one and two short.
>
> The Chairman was a chap called Michael Handley. He used to do a song-and-dance act, dressing up, at the White Swan, and he followed Yorkshire all over the place. The Secretary was the Yorkshire Bank manager in Yeadon, John Rafferty. I met these two.
>
> The state of the club was dire – not just the team but the ground and the pavilion.

The challenge appealed to Geoff, and soon there was a whole group of them bringing fresh life to the club. The driving force was John Harker.

> I'd played with John at Otley; it was his father I'd rung up when I'd played for the third eleven. And there were about six lads who joined from the Wharfedale Ramblers, a good Sunday side.

The transformation on the field was immediate. In the first summer Yeadon won the second division, thanks in no small part to Geoff, whose 65 wickets at under nine runs each won him the division's bowling award. The following summer, in the top flight, they finished third, the club's highest position since a young Brian Close had played for them back in the 1940s. Again Geoff won the bowling award for the division, this time with 72 wickets.

It was not only on the field that the club was moving forward.

> We started getting juniors together, and we ended up with a good second team. Playing wise, we did well. But we didn't have any money, and the ground was in a bad way.
>
> We had to raise £6,000 a year, and every year we raised £6,000 and a penny. And we just survived with the costs of the club – new balls and everything. We managed to pay a groundsman, and gradually the wicket and the outfield became better.

Yeadon's White Swan ground had a great history. Back in Victorian times the Australian tourists had played there, as had WG Grace. A triumphant local had bowled the great doctor for a duck, only to be told off for spoiling the large midweek crowd's afternoon. It was a big field, and the two-storey pavilion had an old-fashioned grandeur in keeping with the ground's past. Unfortunately, with so little money, it was in a terrible state.

Yeadon 1981
Chris Farrell, Chris Smith, Clive Kelsey, Pat Fordham, Clarrie Samuel, Peter Hardcastle
Robert Slater, Les Wood, John Harker, Geoff Cope, John Bridgman

If you could imagine the pavilion you wanted, this was it. The dressing rooms were either side at the top with windows. Downstairs was a tea room. It was a super-looking building. But there were splinters and all sorts. You always wore flip-flops to walk round, you daren't go on your bare feet.

It had a metal frame with timber round it. At the first floor level you had a beam across joining the two parts. When I was still playing, I became Chairman, and we stripped down one side – "What have we got here?" – and there was just this metal that was bent.

I went to Bass, the brewery who owned the ground. The lease had run out two years previously. I made this appointment to see the guy, and he said, "What are you wanting?" "We need to play." "Well, carry on playing." "There's a lot needs doing. We've got to get ourselves a lease. Ideally 21 years." That was the minimum for getting grants. "What do you need grants for?" "We need a new pavilion for a start. And we can't get the funding without the lease."

"Come back and see me in a month," he said.

A month passed, and he cancelled the meeting. Eventually he sat me down. "What do you really want?" "I want Yeadon Cricket Club, which is now on its feet, to go forward. I want a new pavilion, and I want a bar, which we've never had."

As you go through the gates, there's a pub on the corner of the ground. Bass owned the pub. He said, "You've got the back room of the pub which is a cricket lounge. We did an extension for you." "No, that's the music lounge where the landlady performs every Saturday and Sunday. When we go in, it's 'Will you go in the small room at the back?' We're really not welcome. We need our own clubhouse. We need a bar."

He said, "You don't want much, do you? What have you got towards it?" I said, "Half a crown." He looked at me and he said, "I think you'd better leave it with me."

It was a pipedream, perhaps, and the months went by. Meeting after meeting was cancelled, with rumours rife that Bass were going to build a new hotel on the site, catering for the fast-expanding Leeds-Bradford Airport less than half a mile down the road.

Geoff continued to take wickets – 371 in the six summers to 1986 – and at one point he was bowling in tandem with a young left-armer, Richard Illingworth, whom he tried in vain to persuade Yorkshire to take onto the county staff, finding no way through the manager/coach partnership of Ray Illingworth and Doug Padgett.

I rang Padge up. "Padge, have you seen Richard Illingworth?" "Ay, I have." "What do you think?" "He were all right." I said, "I don't recommend too many, but I think this kid can go all the way." "Oh, you'll have to speak to Illy." So I got hold of Illy. "It's not my decision," he said. "It's up to Padge." "Well, hold on, Padge is saying it's up to you." "He's left arm. We've got Carrick." "But who else have you got?" "We're all right. We don't want two left-armers." "But at Leicester you had two off-spinners and two left-armers." "Well, how good is he?" "I think for his age he's a pretty good player." "Well, have a word with Padge." So I went back to Padge. "What's Illy said?" He went back for a word with Illy, and he rang me back. "Right," he said. "Illy's going to have a word with you." And Illy said, "Keep an eye on him, and let me know."

Before long, Basil D'Oliveira, the Worcestershire coach, was turning up at the Yeadon ground.

I picked up the phone. "Illy, Dolly's been here. They've watched him every week for a month. They're very keen." "Well, if it gives him a chance," he said. "I'll have a word with Padge." Padge rang me back: "What's Dolly been there for?" "He's a good bowler." "Oh well, it's up to Illy." And we heard nothing after that.

Richard said, "What should I do? I want to play for Yorkshire. Am I going to get a chance?"

Soon enough the youngster was in the Worcestershire first team, going on to a long career in which he played nine Tests for England, seven of them when the Chairman of Selectors was Raymond Illingworth.

It was just indecision. I've not rung up about many.

By the end of 1986 Geoff's shoulder was aching from Saturday night to Tuesday or Wednesday of the next week. He went to see a consultant, Ian Adams. He was the Leeds United club doctor, and he ran a sports clinic with some of his students every Monday morning at St James's Hospital.

The purpose of the clinic was two-fold. Any amateur sportsman who had been injured over the weekend could call in for advice and treatment, while the students gained experience of sporting injuries.

He offered me the same operation as David Gower had on his shoulder. "Come in here at the end of March, and I'll open it up," he said. "And you can play through the summer. Then at the end of the summer it will just go back. The following year I can open it up again. But every time I open it up, the gate's open and arthritis walks in." I said, "What you're saying is, I pack in."

After that I played one year just as captain, and that took the fun out of everything. You saw things on the field that you knew you could do and you couldn't do a thing about it.

What Geoff did do, though, was to see through the negotiations with Bass. The brewery had opened their hotel at Apperley Manor, and out of the blue Geoff was summoned to a meeting with the properties manager at their head office in Headingley.

I went in. The carpet was this thick, it was absolutely beautiful.

"Right," he said. "What did you say you wanted?"

I said this, this, this and this.

"You don't want much, do you?"

"You asked me what my dream is, and I've told you."

"I'll tell you this, Geoff," he said. "You joined Yeadon after you finished playing with Yorkshire. They were at the bottom, and now you're running four junior sides, three teams on a Saturday, one on a Sunday. The number of people there is quite amazing. Have you got any money?" "I told you, we've got half a crown." "Right, well, I want you to meet me as soon as you can. Tomorrow, this afternoon." "Now?" He picked the phone up and he said to this guy, "Are you available? ... Right, meet me at the main entrance."

We went up to the ground, he brought with him an architect, and this chap went in the front door of the pavilion. He came out, he looked round the side, he went to his car, he brought some rods, put the rods in and he put a red-and-white tape round. "It will be dismantled tomorrow."

I said, "It's March. We've a cricket season coming."

"It's not safe. It's a public liability. I'll provide you with portakabins. I'll get you two for dressing rooms and a shower unit."

"But we'll have these portakabins for a year. What are we going to do then?"

He said, "Do you want a brandy or a coffee?"

"I don't know. It depends what you're about to say. Are you going to tell me you're about to take the ground away from us?"

"No, I'm not. We're going to give you a pavilion and new dressing rooms, and the pavilion will include a bar."

They had checked Geoff's story about the cricketers' room in the pub, and it was true. So Yeadon Cricket Club finished up with a brand new pavilion, costing £250,000, with a bar that was soon selling four times as much beer as the brewery had estimated.

So I went back to them and I said, "Can we have the interior done now?" We'd got breeze block on the inside and plastic chairs and tables. It was basic.

He said, "How are you going to pay for it?"

"Barrellage, what we've already spent."

"And what have you got towards it?"

"Half a crown, and we've spent it."

Bless him, they did the whole of the inside.

The pavilion was officially opened in July 1988 with a match between Geoff's Yeadon XI, including three of his old Lincolnshire team-mates, Geoff Robinson, Rick Burton and David Marshall, and a team of young cricketers got up by Don Wilson, now MCC's Head Coach. Geoff had persuaded the entertainer Leslie Crowther to accept the presidency of the club, and he drove up from Bath for the day.

The opening of the Yeadon pavilion
Don Wilson, Geoff Cope, Leslie Crowther, Phil Sharpe

Leslie arrived in his Roller, and he went round everybody, shaking their hands, He was typical Leslie. Full of fun. Afterwards we had a magnificent buffet in the pavilion, and we invited the hierarchy at Bass. "You know," Leslie said, "I tell people I've come from Baaath, but up here they tell me it's Bath. Now you lot, are you working for Bass or Baaass?"

"You've done a fabulous job," he said, "but there's one thing you've left out. From the main entrance, coming down here on a dark night, it's all rough, there's no road or car park."

This guy from the brewery turned to me, "How much is that?"

"Forty grand."

"You'll have one."

We got everything.

It was one of the great achievements of Geoff's life, but his contribution was not unanimously appreciated in the club, with one AGM spilling into acrimony when a member opposed his re-election as Chairman on the grounds that he was not doing a shift behind the bar.

I said, "You've known me long enough. A brandy and lemonade, and that's me for life. I don't know one pint from another. I've never pulled a pint in my life."

Then John Rigg, the vice-chairman, had a go at this chap. "Let's put it differently. I'll be able to talk Geoff into going behind the bar, I'll go

192

with him and show him what to do, if through the day you go to the 115 meetings he's been to. He's probably put his job at risk at times. He was there when he should have been elsewhere. Will you do that?"

"Well, I haven't time to do that."

"Well, be grateful for somebody who has. And don't talk such rubbish."

"I'm not talking rubbish. I propose we have a steward."

I said, "I'll let the finance man reply. Can we afford a steward?"

"Why not? What's the surplus from the bar?"

It just became a farce.

I thought I can't do any more. So I stood down. Leslie Crowther had died, and they said they'd like me to be President: "If we can call on you ..." Two years later there was a function and, when I got there, somebody said, "Oh, you're not President now, Geoff. David Wild's President." Nobody had told me.

Another way Geoff kept in touch with cricket in these years was through Radio Leeds. Back in the 1970s, as a result of his friendship with John Helm, he had recorded a 15-minute slot that went out each Sunday morning in summer. It was called *Cope's Corner* with its own cheerful theme tune, *The Push Bike Song*:

> *A-round, round, wheels goin' round, round, round*
> *Down up pedals, down up down.*

In winter the footballer Jack Charlton took the same Sunday slot with *Jack's Tracks*, and he ventured into wider realms – an abattoir, a glass-blowing factory – but Geoff stuck to sporting subjects.

I started by recording interviews in the studio. One of the first was with June Moorhouse, a cricketer with Yorkshire Ladies. I asked her about twelve questions, and all she would say was yes, no, no, yes. So we went down the pub, I got her a bit more loose-tongued, and we started again.

I interviewed pals from football and rugby league – and, of course, Johnny Wardle. That one was very special. And I started to take the tape recorder out to matches with me. I played at Oxford, and I got two programmes in no time because Michael Parkinson and John Alderton turned up. Parky had just done George Best's autobiography so I sat him down and off he went. That was a half-hour programme. A belter.

John Alderton was brill, too. "John," I started. "I've got one question that I've got to ask. You claim to be a Yorkshireman. But during the war your mother was in Hull and, when you were delivered, you had

193

to go across the Humber to be born." "Nobody has ever questioned me about that," he said. And the banter started. That was another half-hour programme.

You'd go to the ground for a Sunday afternoon game, and people would say, "I heard you this morning, Geoff. Who have you got next week?" It created a bit of a buzz, and it was a lot of fun.

Geoff returned to Radio Leeds after he had given up playing club cricket, spending Sunday afternoons as the summariser at Yorkshire's 40-over matches. The commentator was the young Kevin Howells.

I like Kevin, he's an honest lad. "Geoff, I don't know the game of cricket, you teach me."

I remember an enthralling finish at Scarborough. He said, "What I can't understand, Geoff, is why all the people are pouring out of the ground." "It's six o'clock," I said. "They're going for their teas in the boarding houses." I was as professional as I could be, but we added a bit of humour, a bit of fun.

We were doing the Sunday League at Lord's. Quite early in the afternoon a cloud came over and the rain started. He wrote on this bit of paper, "Don't forget, we've got to do till seven." He introduced topics, just the two of us. I wrote down, "Burt Rhodes is here." He wrote, "Who?"

I went and grabbed Burt. He was a Guiseley man who had lived in London for years. MCC member, straw hat. He'd helped form the Yorkshire Southern Group, and I'd got to know him well.

"You're due down at Lord's," he said one time to me. "Would you have dinner on Saturday night?" We got in a taxi, and next thing I knew we were at the stage door of the Talk of the Town. It turned out he'd been the musical director there for 25 years, and he'd never mentioned it. He was just a genuine, soft-spoken gentleman. He had a meal with us at a table in front of the stage. Then he said, "I must go, I've got work to do."

I brought Burt into the commentary box at Lord's. I talked about the Southern Group. Then I moved on to other topics. Kevin wrote: "Can you do five minutes?" Then he crossed it out: "Can you do ten?" Then: "I'm going for a cup of tea." He left us to it.

With Burt being a professional man, he nattered away. "Did you see Hutton?" "I actually saw Sutcliffe." He was wonderful. Then music. "Who have you most enjoyed working with?" "Oh, without a doubt, Garland and Sinatra. Judy was marvellous. She came over and said

'Darling' to me. We were in love from the first moment she spoke. I would have moved mountains for her."

He talked and talked. Then Kevin came back. He said, "They've been playing two overs."

Geoff provided a good go-between when local cricket clubs wanted big-name guest speakers for their dinners. One year he arranged for Michael Parkinson to come up to the Otley club, only for Parkinson's wife Mary to ring in the afternoon to say he was poorly. Tony Nicholson filled in for him, but the next year, when they ate their way through the meal and there was no sign of the speaker Fred Trueman, Geoff's stock plummeted.

"First it's Parky, Geoff. Now it's Fred. What's going on with you?"

Oh dearie me! The soup went by, the main course, and suddenly the door swung open. Boom. Fred had a violin in his hand. He walked up, and he said, "Do you know? The divorce came through today, and it's cost me a fortune. I've been busking in market square while you lot have been enjoying yourselves in here." The whole place erupted.

"I'm very sorry," he said when he got up to speak. "With this divorce, I've been waylaid a little in my thinking. I haven't prepared anything so I'm just going to take you round the world, playing cricket." And he spoke for an hour. He didn't swear once. It was pure cricket, it was pure fun. The ovation he got was fabulous. They were stood up, and they were stamping.

Within three weeks we went over to St Helens to a sportsman's dinner. There was Alan Rudkin the boxer, Bill Shankly, Joe Mercer and Fred. It was a tribute to Shanks mainly. This fellow Rudkin got up: "Err ... umm ... err." Fred was next, and he thanked the Queen's Ambassador to the English Language. Then he proceeded to eff-and-blind his way through forty-two dirty tales. Not one bit of cricket. That was the other Fred.

He did a dinner for me at the Parkway in my benefit year, he and Leslie Crowther. Crowther said, "There's only one thing in Yorkshire. I go before Fred." So Crowther got up, a bottle of red wine in one hand, a fag in the other, and he was marvellous. He had people sobbing with tears. Then he said, "There's nothing greater than sharing a table with Fred. He doesn't have a surname because everybody knows him as Fred. Get up, lad, and give 'em it." Fred stood up and started telling his dirty tales, and people shouted "Cricket". Crowther got back up, only he could have done it, and he said, "Fred, did you hear that? They want to hear cricket." And Fred switched just like that. He talked cricket, and he was brilliant.

I think he let himself down badly by doing the working men's clubs.

Geoff had a strong bond with Otley Cricket Club. June was an Otley girl, and Geoff had enjoyed occasional games there till Yorkshire told him he had to play at a higher standard. During his time at the club he had formed a friendship with their wicket-keeper-batsman Mick Wood.

> Mick was a Pool lad. He was born there, he lived there all his life, and he worked as an electrician at Whiteleys Paper Mill in Pool. He knew everybody in the village and, if he could help them, he would. He was that sort of chap.
>
> After a game we'd always have a drink in the bar. Then he'd say, "Well, lad, I'll have to get down valley." Down valley was his trip home to Pool. "I've got a dream," he'd say, "that Pool becomes a league club and does well."
>
> Pool were a family club. They played friendlies Saturday and Sunday. I played there for the Yorkshire Owls and the Wharfedale Ramblers. Good fixtures. The competitiveness was there. Then Mick joined them in the late '70s, and he threw himself into the club.

Pool was a village of fewer than 2,000 people, but Mick Wood knew them all – and he surprised many of them by combining his enthusiasm with great organisational skills. He captained the team, insisting on punctuality and smartness; he organised winter nets, he established an annual dinner in the village hall, and in 1984 he fulfilled the dream by leading them into the Leeds and District Cricket League.

> Then, in their first year in the league, playing against Leeds Police, he squatted down behind the stumps, rolled over and died. It was very sad; he was only 47.
>
> He'd fulfilled his ambition, but more importantly he'd got people around him and he'd got an infrastructure in place. After he died, Pool Cricket Club grew and grew. Now they've got three teams on a Saturday, they've got junior teams for all the age groups, and the facilities are outstanding.
>
> My involvement was nothing except Mick talked to me about it. He asked me if I'd finish my days at Pool. My first intention was to go down there after Yeadon, but it never happened because my shoulder went.

Geoff had always had an affection for Pool, right back to the time when in a Boxing Day fixture at Alwoodley he had opened the batting with their previous captain John Metcalfe, a GP in Otley.

> John being the senior said, "I'll take first ball while you have a look at what it's doing." After four overs I'd yet to face a delivery. So, as the

pro, I thought I should have a word with him. I said, "It's like batting with Boycott." And his reply was, "Is it my forward defence or the way I work it off my legs?"

He typified what was so lovely about Yorkshire village cricket.

Geoff is now Pool's Honorary Vice President, and he talks with as much enthusiasm about their success as he does about the revival of the county club.

Mick's son John had been a page boy at our wedding; his daughter Susan a bridesmaid. After Mick died, John said to me, "Will you do us a favour? You always came to the dinner with my dad. Will you come with me?" From that day I think I've only missed two dinners.

They get 120 into the village hall, and there's never a spare seat. I take David Ryder, Bobby Ham and Helmy, and I always get a welcome. You go to the dinner, and you walk away with a warmth inside you.

They've done tremendously well. It just shows. If you have an ambition to do something and you set your stall out, it's amazing what can be achieved.

16

Well, you're going blind

Retinitis pigmentosa

The sudden shock of having to wear thick-lensed spectacles as a teenager was behind Geoff by the time he started playing cricket for Yorkshire. He wore safety lenses, though that did not prevent him from getting fragments of plastic in one eye when a ball hit him in the face on the last day of Yorkshire's tour of Bermuda.

> I was taken to the hospital. It was a Sunday, and we had to wait for ages for the consultant to finish his game of tennis. He flushed out the eye, but that night, back in the hotel, I had a throbbing pain, I didn't sleep. So, when I got home, I went straight to my optician in Leeds, he sent me to the hospital, and they flushed out some more plastic. They assured me it would knit and cover over, which it did.

The next step for Geoff was to follow the example of his captain, Geoff Boycott, and play his cricket in contact lenses.

> At that stage there were only hard lenses. I went over to see a chap called Mike Clapham in Wakefield whom Geoffrey used. He was very thorough. He said, "We'll spend the winter getting used to them." It was quite amazing the difference. It's hard to describe. Your sight becomes clearer, more magnified. But I couldn't wear them for more than three hours. I said, "If I can't wear them all day, they're no good to me." I'd put them in, he'd send me off walking round Wakefield. I'd be fine, and you could set a clock. 2¾ hours, 2 hours 50, OOH! By the time it got to three hours, my eyes were red. And Mike said, "It's no good; it won't happen."
>
> Eighteen months later I got a call to say they'd brought out these new lenses that were gas-permeable; they allowed air through. That was an improvement, but still not the answer. Then they brought in soft lenses.
>
> It was 1974, Boycs' benefit year. He had a match one Sunday that Colin Graves had arranged at Carlton Towers near Selby. Colin's father had owned the strawberry fields opposite. I went over to Wakefield that morning, and I put in these soft lenses. Everything looked huge. I went for a drink, a lime juice and soda in a half-pint glass, and I put both hands out to pick the glass up because it looked like a pint glass.

Road signs, everything was spot on. So Mike said, "You go and give them a try."

I drove to Carlton Towers. When I got there, the lads said, "What's happened?" I said, "I've had a bit of a bump on the way, smashed my glasses." I went out to bat, and there was this football being bowled at me. The ball was enormous, and I got some runs. "Well, you're better off without glasses," they said. "Are you playing from memory?" But when it came to bowl, I was lost. Every time I moved my head, this big picture moved up with me.

I went back to Mike next day, and he said, "We'll start gradually building it up." So I started playing in lenses, and I never looked back. I played the rest of my cricket with lenses.

Ten years later he developed a fresh problem.

All of a sudden, at the age of 37, I kept saying, "There's something that's not right." It was as if the lens was moving, which of course distorts your vision. I went to see a specialist at the eye hospital, and he said, "We're going to have to do some tests." He didn't warn me about anything, just made an appointment.

So I drove down to St James's, parked up and went in. One of the tests was a chessboard on the wall with a red dot in the centre. And in my head were 27 needles going back to a computer. They moved the chessboard right to left, then up and down, then diagonally, and all the time I had to focus on the red dot in the middle.

I had a break, then they put the disco flashing lights on, and that was horrible. It all took about 2½ hours and, when the needles came out, my head was throbbing. This guy said to me, "I'll get the results, and I'll call you to my rooms in Harrogate."

I went out, and I couldn't see. I had to sit on the kerb by my car for the next three hours – until the eyes came round to a point when I could drive home.

I got the call to go to his rooms. I drove over there for a 12 o'clock appointment, and he called me in at about twenty-five past. He opened the door, and his words basically were: "I'm sorry I've kept you waiting. I do apologise. Don't sit down. You've got retinitis pigmentosa. Unfortunately there's nothing we can do. So don't go off to America or Australia where they think they've got a cure; they haven't." And he opened the far door as if to say, "Go out."

I used my words very carefully. I said, "Excuse me, you just swore at me." He said, "I've never sworn at a patient in my life."

"Well, what did you say? Reti– what did you say?"

He said, "Do you want me to write it down?"

"Yes, please."

So he wrote down 'retinitis pigmentosa'.

I said, "What the deuce is that?"

"Well, you're going blind."

And that was the end of the conversation.

I came out. I got in the car and drove from Harrogate to North Rigton. It was near North Rigton that it suddenly banged me between the eyes. 'I'm going blind!' I drove into North Rigton where our friends Jane and Martin Hunt lived. Martin was at work, but Jane was home. I knocked on the door, and all I can remember was I walked straight past her and said, "I'm going blind, Jane." I sat in the kitchen, and the shock had really got to me by then. I don't drink tea, but she made me a very strong cup of tea with plenty of sugar in it. She was offering to run me home, and I said, "No, no, I'm fine." Because I'd been able to talk to her, I could settle down a bit.

I drove to Otley where June's mum lived. Then I managed to get home. By which time I'd rung Mike Clapham, told him that I'd been to see this consultant. Mike said, "Stop worrying. At the worst, it's mild." He had a look and said, "I can't see anything. But clearly we'll keep an eye on it. You've just got to lead your normal life."

For five years Geoff managed to keep it at the back of his thoughts. Work was going well, and he was busy with Yeadon Cricket Club.

Then, when I was 42, I got conjunctivitis. It's an impurity that gets into the eye, and it stings like billio. I got it at two in the morning so I rang my GP. "Get a cucumber, boil a flannel, and bathe the eyes as much as you can. Do you think you'll survive till the morning?" I said, "I'll do my best." Seven o'clock he rang me: "How are you?" "My eyes are shut, and I know there's a lot there. But it's better than it was." "Right," he said. "I've rung a pal of mine. If you can get to the Nuffield at Horsforth for eight o'clock, he'll see you."

Bruce Noble, a consultant. He was about six foot ten, and he came out of this room, looking down at me. "There are a few things not going for me, Geoff," he said. "One, I went to school with Graham Roope. Two, I'm a public school boy. Three, I'm a southerner. But I do like cricket." And that broke the ice. We went in, and we chatted cricket. "Oh," he said, "I'd better have a look at you." Yes, it was conjunctivitis. "Don't put your lenses in, throw them away, I'll get you some more. Take these drops." Then he said, "Before you go, do you mind if I have a look at your other problem?" He put the helmet on and was very thorough. "Would you do the test again? I'll pick you up, drop you there and take you back." This is a different breed of man, I thought. He was the arm round the shoulder.

I went and had the tests done. He said, "Bring June down with you." He started drawing pictures on postcards. Explaining retinitis.

He asked, "Can you recall mum and dad?" I said, "All I can remember with mum is that during the day she didn't wear glasses but at night when she was tired she'd wear them to read or to thread a needle. But nothing serious. Dad wore glasses all the time, but they weren't thick lenses like mine."

George Stephens, our optician, had retired by then, but Bruce got in touch with him, and he said he'd not seen anything that related to my dad in any way. So really we were at scratch. Bruce said, "Generally it's hereditary."

You think of your children. If they're born with RP, they can be blind by late teens, twenty. But if you don't get it till later, it becomes milder. And I'd been 37, which was late. Bruce spent time with the children, and he couldn't find anything. We didn't tell them about it till later.

"Get on with your life, Geoff," he said. "It's mild, and I'm here. But I think by 55 you may be losing your car. Sister will explain about the counselling."

So began the regular check-ups, with Geoff often having to report for the results at the opticians where he is seen by the straight-talking Denise.

I do the width test, as I call it: sky blue dots on white, and you've got a buzzer. You've to press when you see a dot. Over time you see it getting worse. They take pictures of my eyes, and they send them through to Denise.

In my language, what I see are black lumps, black sections around the outer part of the eye. They are where the vision is spoilt, and gradually those black bits around the outer join together. Once they've joined together, they work inwards – and the centre of the eye is only a millimetre or a millimetre and a half.

Sometimes I get down in the dumps; I think my eyes are worse. I go and look at these pictures, and Denise will say, "What are you worrying about? Don't give me this business, 'I can't see'. Come on. What's the difference between that, that and that?"

"Well, not a lot really."

"Well, what are you moaning at? You just think, I'll see Denise and get a cup of tea."

And that's what I love.

In 1988 Geoff left Wiggins Teape to work for Gerald Judd Paper, a national firm with a small branch in Leeds.

> Murray Judd was the finest guy I met in the paper trade. My interview with him was a meal in a Harrogate hotel that started at seven o'clock in the evening and finished at a quarter past one. "You work for the biggest paper merchant, and I want you to work for the smallest," he said.
>
> A few days later I met him at their Birmingham branch. He walked in, and this big West Indian guy called down from a balcony, "Hi, Murray, how are you, man?" Murray asked him about his five children, and he knew all their names. I'd never met such a gentleman.
>
> He was Mark Nicholas's godfather. He did a lot for him when Mark's father died. I used to say, "I don't work for Gerald Judd Paper, I work for Murray."

They were happy years, but an international takeover changed the culture and in 1993, at the age of 46, Geoff was head-hunted by the paper merchants MoDo to revive their underperforming Leeds branch. He was a great success, increasing the monthly profit from £16,000 to £75,000, but, with his eyesight deteriorating, he started to wonder what the future held for him.

> Gradually it hit me that I was going to lose my car before too long. I was a sales director, I was doing 30,000-plus miles a year. I was in charge of a branch selling and distributing paper, and I also had responsibility for the night trunker going down to Birmingham to pick up the paper and bring it back for distribution to printers around Yorkshire. I had twelve key accounts and four or five reps under me. I'd an office staff, I was to make sure the warehouse was working, and I had to go down for meetings. How was I going to cope without a car?

At the start of 1998 Geoff and June went to Barbados, their first holiday without the children, and it was clear that his peripheral vision was now so poor that he had become a risk on the roads. He lost his driving licence and for a while he battled on, doing his sales work by public transport. But it was not a happy experience.

> I was taking the train from Guiseley to Shipley, then changing at Shipley to go to Keighley. I'd be walking round four printers in Keighley, and it would be absolutely piddling down with rain. By ten o'clock your underpants were wet, you'd got a briefcase in your hand, and you're thinking, "What am I doing here?" Before you know it, you're not just worried about your eyes. You're worried about the job. You're worried about the financial outcome.

Don't take this as a moan, please. I played cricket, and I would not have changed my life for that at all. But the only pension Yorkshire gave you was a lump sum at 40, and I got £2,000 – a good holiday in Majorca and it was gone. So I'd no pension from cricket. My pension from Wiggins was four-twelfths or five-twelfths, depending how many months you'd worked in a year, and some of it didn't qualify because I was part-time. All of a sudden you start adding your sixtieths up, and you're thinking, "What's going to happen to me?"

I was just at the point when I was starting to put a little extra in, all I could afford, in an effort to make up a decent pension. But when I was told my car was gone and I couldn't do the job, I knew what was coming.

It did not help that his firm had been taken over and that he was not dealing with the people he had come to know over the years.

Gradually the word depression came in. I was at home for a while. I couldn't have a conversation with somebody for more than five minutes before I lost interest or couldn't take it in. My home was my castle. I'd go out with Helmy, I'd go out with June, and after that I didn't want to know.

I was off sick with this problem, and my immediate boss wanted to see me one day, not long into the sickness. We met down at the Marriott. We chatted. "Geoff, you're not well are you? Have you understood what I've said?" "Not really." He went away. "Look after yourself", etcetera.

Then he wanted to see me again. Would I go for lunch? This time he came with his boss, and he started using the words: "Do you want to retire?" I said, "No." "Well, when are you coming back?" "I don't know. That's down to my doctor." And this guy just came up with pension plans, pay-offs. It ended up being awkward, but I knew where I stood – which made it worse.

I took battle and, when I left, he gave me basically what I fought for. But a lump sum looks nice till you have to spread it out over the years.

The children were moving on in their lives, both at university, and Geoff, the most sociable of characters, was left at home with no sense of purpose. Looking back now, he struggles to put that time into words.

I could go and play golf with John Helm. Hit the first ball, chat about football, chat about all sorts, have a fabulous time. But he'd drop me back home, and I was straight back where I was before I'd gone out.

I went to see a psychologist at Yeadon. I talked to him. I could tell him how I felt and what needed doing, but I couldn't do it. June went with me more than once.

I had a few friends – Colin Graves, Murray Judd – and they helped. But it was a long period and I wasn't good to live with. June would say to me, "We've got each other." But it's like memories. When you go to the butchers, you don't get much for your memories.

A year after losing his car, Geoff was elected to the committee of Yorkshire County Cricket Club, and that – like his golf with John Helm – got him out of the house. But all the while his field of vision was growing narrower, and soon he was carrying a white stick.

When you've had the life I've had, playing sport, there's a lot of pride, and suddenly to have one of these white sticks you're thinking, 'This isn't me. I was a sportsman. Sportsmen don't go like this. Get your back straight, get up and go.' That was all playing on my mind.

The worst times were when I had to get a train into Leeds. When you get off, everybody's getting off, and they're coming at you from all angles. You just stand, like a rabbit in the headlights. You're frightened, but you daren't move because you can't plot a route. You tend to stand to one side and let everybody go. People still barge into you, though, and you always have the feeling it's your fault.

Retinitis pigmentosa, RP, is a condition that affects about 25,000 people in the UK. It is caused by a genetic disorder that damages the light-sensitive lining at the back of the eye. Most commonly the first symptoms are night blindness, difficulty seeing in dim light. This is followed by a loss of peripheral vision. Ultimately it can lead to blindness. There is currently no treatment that will halt the progress of RP or reverse its effects.

I go in a restaurant, and nine times out of ten I stand in the doorway because I can't see a thing. It's just black. If I stand there, after a while images start coming. Ah, there's the gap, that's where I go.

You sit at a table, then you get up and knock over a chair you haven't seen. So when you get up, you have to plot your journey before you set off. But still you don't see people on the sides.

When you get to the door and you open it, suddenly brightness hits you and it's a reversal – a quicker reversal; dark to light is easier to adjust.

Light to dark is a nightmare. Possibly the best way of describing it is that it's like when you go to the cinema. You go in and you know where the seats are, but you can't see them. Then very quickly you adjust. But with me it could take five or ten minutes..

At Headingley one day Geoff ran into Alison Parker. Some years earlier she had worked for a while for the county club; now she was employed as a senior fund-raiser for the Guide Dogs for the Blind Association.

I said, "Is there anything I can do? I'd love to help." So she started getting me involved. That gave me something else to do.

I met people there, and they suggested I should have a guide dog. I said, "No, I can see. There's others need it more." Then I got more involved with Guide Dogs, and I realised the width of their service. Only about five per cent of dog owners are totally blind. The other 95 per cent are partially sighted.

Soon enough Geoff became involved in raising money for the Association. He has organised fund-raising days at Pannal Golf Club; he runs an annual evening at his local Chinese restaurant, with a raffle and an auction; he worked with David Armitage, owner of Sellers Engineering, to stage a brass-band concert for guide dogs in Huddersfield Town Hall. In total, Geoff has now raised over £200,000 for the Guide Dogs for the Blind Association.

The Guide Dogs for the Blind Association relies on the dedication of many volunteers, but it is an expensive business. There are currently 5,000 working guide dogs in the UK, each of which costs £55,000 in the course of its lifetime: breeding, training, placing and supporting. The annual budget of the Association is between 50 and 60 million pounds, all of which comes from donations.

Their promotional leaflet spells out 'The Facts':
- 43 per cent of people who lose their sight suffer from depression.
- 180,000 people with sight loss rarely leave home alone.
- Almost 50 per cent of people with sight loss feel cut off from the people and things around them.
- Only one in three people with sight loss (of working age) is employed.

As Geoff became involved in raising money for the Association, the suggestion was put to him again that he should have a dog, and in 2006 he agreed. It turned out to be a life-changing decision.

I got Kemp, and all of a sudden I had to go out because he wanted exercise. I wasn't sitting at home so much. When I went out with the stick, June used to worry whether I would get back. But with a dog she knew I'd be coming back. It meant a lot to her.

To date, Geoff has had three dogs: Kemp, whom he had for seven years; then Queenie, for three; and now Lester. Each time he has to go through a lengthy process of being matched and bonded with the dog.

You go on a two-week residential to a hotel at Wetherby. It's very exhausting emotionally. You're watching the dog with everything it does. You go to bed at night shattered.

Geoff and Kemp

You do a fortnight of that, then you come home. At that point you're not insured to use the harness so you take it out on the lead. The trainer comes every day for half-days. We do the local walks round Guiseley, then we catch the train to Ilkley.

At some stage the trainer will do a test. You're not supposed to know it's going on. They make sure the dog is responding to you, that you're walking at the right pace, and so on. Then from that moment, when you pass the test, you've got the harness and it's your dog.

The intelligence of the dogs is extraordinary. Geoff can leave the house and say to his dog, "Bank, building society, Morrisons, office", and it will take him in turn to the bank, the building society, Morrisons and ... the wine bar!

When Yorkshire had its 150th anniversary, we were invited down to the House of Commons for drinky-poos. We got there at a quarter to twelve, went through security and ended up after a long walk in a room adjacent to the river. At a quarter past three it was time to go. I was with Colin Dent, and we hadn't a clue where we were. I said, "Don't worry ... Kempie, we need the front door." He turned around and set off. And within 30 yards this security lady came up: "Can I help? Are you all right?" Colin said, "We're all right, but we're aiming for the front door." She said, "I'm going that way. I'll walk with you." He said, "Do you mind if you walk behind the dog? My friend says the dog will get us out of here."

We went through the big hall, up a lift, across a corridor, down another lift, up three floors, down two floors. Then she said, "Well, I must leave you here." Colin said, "Hang on, where's the door?" She said, "There." The dog was sat by the front door.

Colin turned to me and grinned. "Can I borrow him when I go to the pub on an evening?"

On another visit to London Geoff set off with Kemp, aiming to cross Marylebone Road for a walk in Regents Park.

I pressed the pedestrian button on the traffic lights. The lights changed. Kempie looked at me. I said, "Go forward." The next thing I knew I was flat on my back on the pavement, and he was licking my face. I thought, "Where did that come from?"

Then there was a bus driver at the side of me: "Are you all right?"

I said, "Have I committed the cardinal?"

"No," he said. There were two lanes. He was in the outside one, and this woman came up on the inside and went straight through the red light. He said, "It's a good job you've got your mate."

I rang Janet at Guide Dogs, and she said, "He's trained to do that."

I worked out it was five years, three months since we'd done the training of my saying "Forward" and him over-riding my instruction because he saw danger. "They never forget, Geoff. They never forget."

Unfortunately the problems Geoff has are mainly with people.

When I got the dog, I had people saying, "What's he got a dog for? He's not blind." Or "Well, I'm not moving there because he's only training it." People don't understand. I've been called a fraud numerous times, and it hurts.

One of the hardest times is when I walk down to Guiseley with the dog. You come back through the schoolkids. The junior school children stand aside to let me through, I say "Thank you" and they say, "It's a pleasure. Can we help?" But the older ones drive you potty.

They're coming down four a breast. Even if you stop, which you're not encouraged to do by the Guide Dogs, they say, "Well, he can see" or "What have we got to move for him for?" They don't have the manners.

Some people will say, "I'll stroke your dog as you're only training, aren't you?" Then: "Why have you got a dog?" "Because I can't see." "Well, you can see me." "Yes, I'm sorry. I can see you. But have you somebody with you?" "Of course I have. There's my daughter here." "Well, I can't see her." And they look at me as if to say, "You're making that up."

For Geoff, his situation has been best summed up by an article written by a fellow RP sufferer Annalisa D'Innella. It appeared in the *Guardian* in November 2016 and begins as follows:

Two young men are in my way. Their laughter echoes off the houses opposite as I move quickly to skirt around them on the narrow pavement. As I pass, they fall silent. I am a few inches away now, my white cane skimming the uneven paving stones, when one of them shouts to the other. His voice is confused, angry. He is shouting: "She's not blind."

You can't be a bit dead. It's a binary thing. You either are or you aren't – same goes for pregnancy. But what about blindness? Can you be a bit blind? Is that allowed? And how does that work? What does it look like?

It looks like a woman seeing two men in front of her and using her cane to navigate around them. It looks like a man folding up his cane outside the cinema and going in to enjoy a movie. It looks like a girl on a train reading a newspaper while her guide dog rests his chin on her lap.

… Blindness is not binary. It is a rich and fascinating spectrum. Visually impaired people come in many different variations. Some of us have central vision but no periphery. Some have periphery but no central. Some see the world through a window stained with blobs. For others, it is all a blur. We could form a zombie army. But we will probably just quietly get in your way on staircases.

Year by year Geoff's peripheral vision is declining. If he watches cricket side-on, it is like watching tennis, moving his head from bowler to batsman – and, if the ball is hit towards the boundary, he has to have his wits about him, to remember where the fielders are. From end on, it is easier, but even that is getting harder.

With l-bs I used to think, "That's out." Now it hits him, and I'm thinking, "I don't know. It's close." It's getting worse, but it's all gradual.

No two days are the same. You have days where you think, "I can't see." Then next day you look out and you think, "I can see." And tomorrow it could be a fog or a mist.

They found it by mistake at 37. If I have a bit of luck, then I'll still have some vision to my last day. But if I do live long, there's a danger that it will go. It will never get better. I'm a lot worse than I was at 55. But I go to the hospital every three months, and they say "Geoff, you're 70 now."

Geoff draws inspiration from what David Blunkett as a blind man has achieved, but as a sportsman it is the blind golfers who have most moved him. Each year they stage a three-day match between England and Scotland and, by the cruellest of coincidences, knowing nothing of Geoff's problems, they invited him to be their speaker on the very day his consultant had registered him as officially blind.

> "Would you speak at our dinner? On the Tuesday. It's our practice day. You could have a round." The English Blind Golf Association.
>
> My first reaction was, Who's taking the Michael here? "I've just come back from the hospital. I've been registered blind."
>
> "I'm sorry," he said. "I had no idea."

Geoff's own golf is mostly with John Helm.

> I see the ball in front of me, I whack it, and I've no idea where it's gone. You've to be told where it's gone, then you've to do it again. If we go round in 120, we go round in 120 and we have a chat. If we go round in 90, well, we've missed a bit of chat. It gives me some exercise.

On one occasion Geoff and John Helm teamed up with the former Leeds footballers Eddie Gray and Trevor Cherry for a day with the blind golfers.

> Eddie is a good golfer. His handicap is 4, I think. He plays at Pannal four days a week, at seven in the morning. He was going round the course with this blind golfer, and he turned to me. "I'm not going to get round, kid."
>
> "Why? What have you done?"
>
> "I've never felt so humble in my life. This fellow, he can't see his nose end but his wife sets him up, and he brays his ball thirty yards past mine. Then we get on the green. She walks him from his ball to the hole, then walks him back, "Slightly uphill, bit left to right", and every time he's within three inches of the hole. I'm on 4, and I can't play like that. I've never ever felt so humble."
>
> John Helm was chatting to his carer. "Are you with him all year?"
>
> "Oh, no, we only play the golf for six months."
>
> "What do you do for the other six months?"
>
> "Well, you know he's the world champion snowboarder."
>
> And this guy's blind.

17

A solicitor, an accountant, one with brass and one without

The restructuring of the county club

The years after cricket are often hard for former professionals, and in Geoff's case they were all the harder for the nature of his departure: the suddenness of the news that he faced a third ban from bowling, the finality of the committee's decision to dispense with his services. Yorkshire cricket was at the centre of his life, and he was not ready to part company with it.

The years that followed were not good ones for the county. The top-six finish of Geoff's last summer, 1980, would not be repeated till 1996, and the intervening years were marked by great upheavals on the committee.

> The first few years I found it difficult to go and watch. There was a lot of unrest, and the side wasn't a good one. When I saw what was happening on the field, I felt I could contribute, and therefore it was hard for me emotionally. And it was made harder because the Yorkshire public are special people, they make you welcome when you go, they say things you like to hear. "Eeeh, lad, tha' should be out there. Tha'd have bowled this lot out." I think a lot of them meant it in their own way, but perhaps they were things I didn't want to hear at that point.

Geoff considered standing for the Yorkshire committee in the spring of 1982, but the regional system meant that there was only one place for his district of Wharfedale and he was persuaded to let Bryan Stott, the opening batsman of the late 1950s and early '60s, take the place.

> Jack Harker, the Chairman at Otley, came to see me. "I don't think it's a good idea of yours to stand," he said. "I think you need a break." With hindsight it was very sound advice. There was a lot in that period that happened; the Boycott issue got very nasty. I look back now and I think, "Well, I'm glad I wasn't there."

Through the 1980s Geoff threw his cricketing energies into the Yeadon club but in 1991 another opportunity to serve Yorkshire arose. Joe Lister, the county's long-standing Secretary, died suddenly, and the committee reshaped its administrative structure. David Ryder, the Assistant Secretary, took the reins temporarily, and an advertisement appeared for the new role of Chief Executive.

There were several envelopes containing the advert that were dropped through my letter box, all in their different ways saying, "I hope you've seen this."

Being Secretary, or Chief Executive, of Yorkshire had always been among Geoff's ambitions, even to the point of once upsetting Joe Lister.

> Towards the end of my time as a player I went across to speak to the Wombwell Cricket Lovers. One of the questions afterwards was: "If you weren't playing cricket, what would you like to do?" And I said, "Without a doubt I'd love to be Secretary of Yorkshire. It's a wonderful job." It was just a simple answer to a question, "What would you like to do?", nothing more. But when I got home, there was this message: "You've got to ring Mr Lister, whatever hour you get in."
> "What's this, you want my job?"

Lister was only the fourth Secretary of Yorkshire since 1864, and after his initial explosion he calmed down.

> Joe was a good administrator, he was his own man, but you never knew where you were with him. At the end of the telephone call he said to me, "Pop in and see me some time. I'll talk to you about it."
> We sat down in his office. "How serious are you?" he asked. So I told him it was an ambition if anything cropped up. We probably spent an hour and a half chatting. He told me everything that was involved in the job. He was a good man trying to help me.
> Then the next time you'd go in, he'd have the racing paper in front of him, and it would be "Yes? ... What? ... No." You never knew what you were going into when you knocked on the door.

Geoff duly applied for the position, but he lost out to Chris Hassell, who had been Secretary of Lancashire for the last twelve years.

> I'd seen him at Joe's memorial service. He'd had words with Sheila, Joe's wife, and she told me that he was interested.
> "You will apply, won't you, Geoff?" she said to me. "Joe always knew you were interested."
> I chatted to David Ryder for a couple of nights. For the interview for the job I drew a family tree of what I wanted, with David as my number two.
> Lawrence Byford, the President, chaired the panel. He asked me the question, "How will you deal with Geoffrey Boycott?" I said, "He's one of the committee. I'll give him the respect I'll give all

211

the committee." They didn't ask me, "How will you deal with the Chairman of Finance?" They only asked me about Boycs.

Was the club still crippled by the animosity engendered by the Boycott rebellion?

> To some degree, it still is in 2017. The heights were the early '80s, when it was really bad. You got these people who were clearly blinkered. They couldn't see outside what Geoffrey was saying.
> I was hoping that my feelings for Yorkshire cricket would help to unite the factions. It would have been difficult. You had a force that was in decline, but it was still very militant.

A restructuring of the committee into four regions, with only one ex-player allowed among the three members for each region, meant that the Wharfedale district was amalgamated with Bradford, among whose representatives was Brian Close.

> And nobody was going to challenge Closey.

Close stepped down in 1998, and the following year Geoff stood successfully for election. It was 19 years since he had left Yorkshire as a player and, if he had been on the committee earlier, he would probably not have been able to change much of what happened in those years. But he would have fought hard against two decisions.

The first involved the staging of Test matches:

> There were three grounds that were given Test match cricket every year: Lord's, the Oval and Headingley. With the other three, two got a Test and one didn't, and it rotated. The Chairman, Reg Kirk, a leading light in the Boycott affair, went down to Lord's, and he didn't think the arrangement was fair. So he withdrew Yorkshire's privilege of having a permanent Test match.

The second was the decision to let the players' badge – the white rose that Lord Hawke had designed – be used commercially by the club.

> I'd have fought that tooth and nail. Immediately it took everything away from you as a player. The rose with eleven petals, one petal for each of the first team. It was on the cap and the blazer.
> The losing of the rose meant so much to so many, and the people on the committee making the decision didn't understand that. A lot of them were like nodding ducks. They were told how to vote.
> They let it go, and now you sit there and see a member of the public – twenty stone, totally out of everything – with a Yorkshire sweater

on because he's bought it from the shop. And you think, "I've given blood, sweat and tears for that, and he just walks round in it." It hurts.

Geoff feels much the same about the more recent decision to allow non-players to wear the blazer that Lord Hawke had created.

> An Oxford blue blazer, with Cambridge blue and gold stripes. It was brought it out in 1979 for the players. Illy wore it quite a bit as manager, and Hamps as captain wore his on occasion. I only wore mine for the press shoot. I thought, "What's this? We'll be going to Henley next."
>
> Then a few years ago they got some similar cloth, and all of a sudden all the vice-presidents and their ilk were allowed to buy one. You see it, and you think, "What is the player left with?"
>
> The only thing now that is exclusive to a player is the capped player's tie, with the Hawke badge on and his number underneath in silver.

Geoff's arrival on the Yorkshire committee came at a time when the county's playing fortunes were experiencing an upturn. They had an outstanding set of fast and medium-fast bowlers, five of whom played for England: Darren Gough, Matthew Hoggard, Chris Silverwood, Craig White and Gavin Hamilton. Having finally put aside their Yorkshire-only principles, they had an outstanding overseas player in the Australian Darren Lehmann. They had the emerging talent of Michael Vaughan and a strong, no-nonsense captain in David Byas. Once more the county were a force in the land.

Geoff was put on the Cricket Committee under the chairmanship of his former second-eleven captain Bob Platt, and he quickly struck up a relationship with David Byas. In the spring of 2000, his second year on the committee, Geoff was appointed manager for a pre-season trip to Western Australia where they played against sides got up by the former Australian captain Kim Hughes and Geoff's great pal Dennis Lillee. Though Geoff's role was primarily administrative, he was soon in the thick of the cricket, working alongside Martyn Moxon, Yorkshire's Director of Coaching. He had a special interest in the slow bowlers: off-spinner James Middlebrook and left-armer Ian Fisher.

> Martyn asked me if I'd help in the nets, and I really enjoyed that. On one occasion I said, "I'm going to bowl Fisher for six balls, then Middlebrook for six balls. We'll tell the batter what the field placings are. I'll decide whether it's a four or not."
>
> David went in first, and he came up to me afterwards: "What have you done that for?" I said, "I think if you have different bowlers every ball, you don't focus." "Brilliant. I've enjoyed that. I've learnt something."

Then back at the hotel I was in my room, and there was a knock on the door. It was Fish and Midders. They said, "We're going back to the nets. Would you like to come with us? Just the three of us." That meant a lot to me. I felt a part of the cricket again.

After almost twenty years away from the first-class game, Geoff was invigorated by this involvement. Especially he loved it when he was able to suggest things to David Byas, one memorable moment coming in a match at Headingley when, near the close of play, James Middlebrook was bowling at a batsman who was approaching his century.

I was on the balcony, signalling 'Four' with four fingers. David had two round the bat, and he brought in a third to backward short-leg. I signalled 'Four' again, and he shrugged his shoulders. So I pointed to backward point, and he brought him in to silly point. Almost immediately the batsman played a shot and was out.

One of the committee was standing next to me on the balcony. He said, "Does that add to your first-class wickets, Geoff?"

David came to see me afterwards: "What was all that about? The lad was playing well."

"He was getting near 100. So he was either going to play a bit rashly to get there tonight, or he was going to block. If you put men round the bat, you make him think and he might make a mistake." You learn every day, don't you? "Well done," he'd say.

Sometimes he'd say, "I'm not sure about that one." But it didn't matter because you were talking.

That was one of the roles of being on the committee I enjoyed most – being close to David, being close to the playing side. I didn't interfere every match, but I was a sounding board.

In 2001 Yorkshire were champions once more, for the first time since 1968. Such was their dominance that the title was sealed at Scarborough on 24 August, the earliest date since the 1970s. It was a great collective success but, for Geoff, the two crucial figures were the captain and the overseas player.

I like David Byas a lot. He didn't stand nonsense. He was a farmer. It was: "Roll your sleeves up and get stuck in or you're on your bike." You knew where you stood. He had a big influence on discipline and the dressing room.

I never played with someone like Lehmann. Gee whizz, what a difference he made. He would have walked into the dressing room of 1966, with Fred, and he'd have been one of them. A pint in one hand, a fag in the other, and let's talk cricket. That was Lehmann. He gave

*David Byas leaves the field to applause after scoring a century
in the match that won the championship at Scarborough*

a lot of time talking to members. He gave a lot of time talking to the players, helping them, and his batting was immense. I remember the 190-odd in a 40-over match at Scarborough, coming in in the fifth over. Eleven sixes. And he didn't bother running. It was fabulous.

Then there was the innings against Lancashire – and the 339 against Durham when he nearly beat George Hirst's record. I'm convinced he gave himself up because, when he came out, the first thing he said was: "The record belongs to a Yorkshireman, not to me." That was the type of bloke he was.

Before you know it, you've somebody with discipline, you've somebody who can make people laugh, and you can get the best out of people. All of a sudden you've got a side that can play a bit, that's knitted together, and they performed all season. The day at Scarborough when we won the title: caught Byas, bowled Lehmann, it was just so appropriate. And the raindrops were starting to fall.

The leading bowler in the campaign was Steven Kirby, a Leicestershire reject whose debut in mid-match against Kent was the stuff of fairy tales. It was not, however, a stroke of genius by the Cricket Committee, more an accident of fate.

He'd written to us several times through the winter: "Can I have a trial?" He'd had three years of back trouble at Leicester, and we had a battery of seven quicks. Was it fair to say "Come and see us" and he'd be number eight? Then he suddenly turned up pre-season. We sent him off with the Academy, and they had to take him out of the net after ten minutes; he was too quick for them.

Kirby was given two second-team games, in which he took 12 wickets. But there was still no thought of registering him for first-team action. Then in the sixth championship match, at home to Kent, Matthew Hoggard was called away by England after the first day's play. Kent had already batted once, and Geoff found himself with the task of identifying a like-for-like replacement.

David Byas said to me, "What have we got?"
We went through who was injured, who was with the second team, and I said I'd ring Arnie Sidebottom.
Arnie said, "What about this fellow Kirby? It's one innings. What have we got to lose?" I rang Platty, and he said, "Go for it."
I said to David, "I've sorted it."
"Right, who have I got?"
"Kirby."
"Who?"
"Kirby."
"What the hell does he do?"
"He's this fellow who's a bit quick."

The 'fellow who was a bit quick' took seven wickets in the Kent second innings and ended the season as Yorkshire's leading wicket-taker, a vital component of the championship triumph. His raw on-field aggression has become the subject of many an after-dinner tale, not least his confrontation in that first match with Matthew Fleming, Old Etonian and one-time officer in the Royal Green Jackets. It is a tale that Geoff enjoys telling.

He was bowling from the rugby end. The non-striker was their captain: Matthew Fleming of Fleming Investment Bankers.
First ball goes whistling through. Next ball he's warned for running on the pitch – not at the delivery end but at the other end where he's gone down to give the batter some verbal. On his way back he allegedly says to Fleming, "What you looking at?"

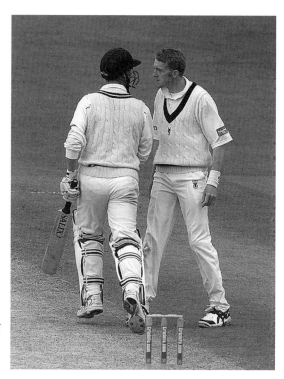

*Matthew Fleming
and Steven Kirby*

Next ball is a bouncer. The fourth is into the rib cage, and he's snarling away again. Has another go at Fleming: "I've asked you, what you looking at?"

The last ball is delivered. The crowd are clapping. He stands and looks at Fleming. "I've asked you three times. What are you looking at?"

Fleming takes his hat off, leans on his bat and crosses his legs. "Dear boy, I was thinking, 'Did we go to the same school?'" As only Flem could. It was brilliant.

I loved the lad, but he was barking mad. He was never out. He'd play an immaculate forward defensive and be given lbw. And he'd scratch his head. "I must be doing something wrong. I never get given them. Have we got some video?" "Don't bother, Steve."

He was just a lovely, lovely lad.

It was a golden summer for Yorkshire, and the icing on the cake was a Headingley Test against Australia when a large fifth-day crowd saw England hit a remarkable 315 for four to win the match. It seemed that all was well once more in the White Rose county.

Alas, it was not. Within months the club was plunged into a crisis as deep as any in its history. Geoff was not a member of the Finance Sub-Committee and did not see the full figures, but he knew that money was tight when, in the winter of 2000/01, the Director of Coaching Martyn Moxon resigned. He had accepted an invitation to join the coaching team for England's tour of Pakistan and New Zealand and was told by Chris Hassell, the Chief Executive, and Keith Moss, the Chairman, that as a result a deduction would be made from his salary.

> That had never happened with any county. Martyn got agitated with Chris Hassell. Then Keith came in and was quite blunt. Martyn said, "That's it, I'm off, I'm going."
> Platty was not consulted as Chairman of Cricket. He rang me, "Have you heard?" I rang Martyn, but it was clear the damage had been done.
> "Geoff, you're too late," he said. So he went to Durham.

The loss was not felt that year. By video-link they interviewed the Western Australian Wayne Clark, who had never set foot on English soil. He arrived in the spring, and he took them to the championship.

> He was a one-off. Very laid back, more motivational than technical coaching. Totally different from what we'd had before.
> But you don't measure a title by what the side does in that one season but by its composition, where it's come from, and a lot of that was down to Martyn.

Even in the immediate aftermath of the championship triumph at Scarborough there were problems. Darren Lehmann headed back to Australia, and David Byas was not given the team he wanted for the final games, both of which were lost. Then the Cricket Committee, to the great disappointment of Geoff, decided to take the captaincy away from David Byas.

> I was a great admirer of David, and I can't remember now how that decision got made. David was 38 years old, and Lehmann was such an impressive character; perhaps people felt it was time to give him the captaincy. In many ways that made sense. But what would it mean for David? He'd just won us the championship.

Byas, hurt by the decision, promptly retired from the game.

> After the dust had settled, David rang me. He said, "I've got a problem. Lancashire have rung me."
> I said, "What's the probem, David? You've given everything for Yorkshire. Why don't you think of yourself for once? What have you got to lose?"
> "But do you think people will think ... ?"
> "It doesn't matter what people think. Go and enjoy yourself."

Jack Simmons was Chairman at Lancashire. At the end of the summer he said to me, "I wish we'd had him ten years ago. He's made such an impact in the dressing room."

For Yorkshire the magic of 2001 was lost. For the only time in the competition's history, the champion county finished the following summer in last place.

Much more worrying, however, was the state of the finances. At the annual meeting in March 2002 Peter Townend, the Treasurer, told members that, despite the championship title and the Ashes Test, the club had made a heavy loss. Attention at this stage focused on the failings of the marketing department and, in particular, on the collapse of the profits of the club shop. The police were called in to investigate the loss of £100,000 in stock and takings but, with little to inspect in the way of detailed book-keeping, nothing worse than inefficiency and bad decision-making was unearthed.

By midsummer the marketing director, only one year into post, had disappeared on sick leave, and the Chief Executive, Chris Hassell, had agreed to retire.

There was great press coverage of this, but far worse was to come. The club had embarked on an ambitious redevelopment of Headingley, and costs had spiralled alarmingly, with the club borrowing way beyond its agreed limit at the bank. The members of the Finance Sub-Committee were the only members of the committee to see the full details, and this frustrated Geoff.

The Chairman's verbal reports of the finances were not over-good. But, if you weren't on Finance, you didn't get to see the thick A4 book they produced. There'd be a Finance meeting in the morning, the General Committee in the afternoon. The Chairman would give a finance report to the General Committee. He'd turn to the Treasurer and say, "I think I've covered it, haven't I?" You never quite knew where you were.

Sport England and Leeds City Council had put money into the redevelopment, but it was not covering the escalating costs and Geoff arranged for three of them – Chairman, Treasurer and Geoff himself – to meet his old friend Colin Graves, Chairman of the Costcutter supermarket group. He was often at Headingley, watching the matches as a member of the Executive Club, and had chaired Darren Gough's benefit committee the previous summer.

I met Colin for the first time in '73 when I spoke at Carlton Towers Cricket Club dinner, a small club near Selby. He was there with his friend Stuart Watson. At the time he was an area manager for Spar, the grocery group. He worked for a subsidiary out at Hull, based in Morley. Stuart Watson had one of the largest Spar shops in York. They were pals, and the three of us got on like a house on fire. Plenty of laughing. After the dinner he asked, "What are the chances of getting Yorkshire to play here? I'll cover all expenses." "It's not easy," I said. "If we do one, we'll have to go all over the place." "Well, keep in touch."

He rang me not long afterwards and said, "What are you doing for lunch?" We started meeting each other after work. His wife and June got pally, and a family friendship developed. I said to Boycs, "Can we go to Carlton Towers?" "No, we can't go this year, but you can put it down as one of my benefit matches next year." That was the game when I played in contact lenses.

They had children before us. It was a great friendship.

I was with Colin when Costcutter was born. He told me a lot about Costcutter, things that were private.

The arranged meeting between the Costcutter chief and the Yorkshire trio did not go well. Geoff sat quietly through the conversation as his friend told them that they had an unsustainable business model, with no assets and wholly inadequate income streams. It was 'a runaway train' that they did not know how to manage. The only way forward was to buy the ground. It was not what Keith Moss wanted to hear, and they left with nothing.

When the vacant post of Chief Executive was advertised, Colin Graves let it be known that he could do it part-time for them.

I said to him, "How can you be Chairman of Costcutter and Chief Executive of Yorkshire?"

"Of course I can. I've got a good ship at Costcutter. It can run. I'll come down and sort you lot out."

"I'll have to interview him," Mossy said. "But there's no way he'll get the job. Over my dead body."

He wouldn't have him near, and Colin knew.

In the event he did not apply, and in late July the position was offered to Alex Keay from the Manchester Rugby Union Club. Within a week of the appointment, however, the crisis had intensified – and Keith Moss, who had done so much to drive forward the ground development plan, was feeling the strain.

It was a fast-flowing stream.

There was a meeting of the General Committee that was to deal with the finances. Before the meeting I asked the Chairman, "Could I have a look at the full figures so I know what we're talking about?"

David Welch, the Chairman of the Finance Committee, was there. He said, "With respect, Chairman, there's a lot to discuss financially.

Geoff's been asking for nearly a year for these. I think you should consider that he be allowed to look."

Keith ummed and aahed: "Well, go and get them."

"Where do I go?"

"See Ryder." By this time he was quite wound up.

I was at the cricket centre, and I walked across to the offices.

David Ryder said, "I'm not allowed to give you them."

"I'll tell you what," I said. "You make four copies and bring them across to the Chairman."

I went back. "Have you got them?"

"David's bringing them."

They arrived, and Keith threw them across the table, knocking some water over.

The meeting started, and by this time I was opening the book up, trying to read it. Half, three quarters of an hour. "Right, move on."

"Just a minute, Chairman."

"What now?"

"Page three."

"We've passed that."

I said, "One of the things I've noticed is that there were two championship dinners. I've got it in the back of my mind that we got 90-odd thousand from those dinners. Here it's saying we made ..."

"There's expenses."

"But the expenses are here, they're shown."

"Well, speakers."

"If you can get me a speaking engagement for 75 grand ..."

"I don't want you being flippant."

There was nothing in the figures suggesting wrong-doing. It just wasn't clear.

David said, "He's right. I'll look into it."

Then I saw something else.

"We've got to move on."

I came home and looked at the figures. I probably made a dozen notes with question marks. I thought, "What can I do?"

There were so many issues: the failures of the marketing department, the inadequate records of their activities and now, amid all this, the overspend on the development work. Geoff, deeply troubled, decided to break with confidentiality. He rang Colin Graves, who drove over to his house. In the dining room they sat together, Geoff staying quiet as his friend turned the pages of the document, then repeated what he had said when they had come to see him.

He was somebody with a brain you could bounce something off, and you knew it wouldn't go any further. He just looked at me. "You're in the mire. Totally. The only way out is to buy the ground."

"Buy the ground? There's no money."

Robin Smith was President. I rang him to say I wasn't happy with what I'd seen. "No good ringing me. I haven't got the report."

"Well, where are you now?"

"I'm in Portugal."

"Well, when are you back? ... Right, I'll drop a book through your letter box, and I'll mark up pages. Will you ring me back when you get home?"

I stuck yellow post-it notes in various places in the document and put it through Robin's door.

Then I got the call. "This is frightening."

Keith Moss had scheduled a further meeting, to discuss ways of saving money, but Robin Smith knew that the problem had gone well beyond the sums of money such economies would generate. They were talking about a shortfall of two million, not two hundred thousand.

"Right," Robin said, "Geoff and I are going to see the bank tomorrow."

Keith said, "I'd better come." "I'm sorry, Keith, that won't be necessary."

It was a brutal business, but Robin Smith, head of a solicitor's practice, had decided that the committee, good men though they were, did not have the calibre of people or the experience to deal with such a financially dangerous situation. Many of them saw themselves primarily as district representatives, looking after the interests of their members. Some had come on originally as Boycott supporters. When a vote was taken, according to Geoff, there was one elderly member "you had to nudge him to wake him up."

The bank was HSBC; the manager of their account was Wayne Bowser.

Wayne had put his job at risk. He said, "Really you should be in administration. But it's Yorkshire County Cricket Club. I'm a big fan, I've tried to do all sorts." He told us our account was going to be taken over by head office at Canary Wharf. No sentiment.

Robin said to Wayne, "How long have we got?"

He rang Canary Wharf, and the guy said, "I'm coming up to see you tomorrow." We'd literally 24 hours, if that.

Wayne was very professional, very honest and very upset.

Robin and I came away. I told him about Colin Graves, how I'd broken confidentiality. "No, Geoff, you've not broken anything. You've gone to one of the likeliest lads in Yorkshire."

It turned out that Costcutter also banked at HSBC.

> I spoke to Colin. He said, "Don't worry. If the bank threatens administration, get Wayne Bowser to ring me straightaway. Don't listen to the bloke from Canary Wharf till he's spoken to me."
>
> Colin is straightforward. There are no corners.
>
> I rang Robin that night. He'd rung Brian Bouttell from KPMG. I'd only met Brian once. He'd driven me down in his Jag to a game at Taunton the previous summer.
>
> Robin and I went back to the bank the following morning. Wayne informed us that the guy from Canary Wharf was on his way up. He was due very shortly. "I'll be straight with you. If there's nothing in your pockets, it will happen."
>
> "Are you saying administration?" "Yes."
>
> "Well, before we go any further, would you ring Colin Graves?"
>
> His words were "Our Colin?"
>
> Robin and I gave Wayne permission to speak to Colin. I rang him and passed the phone to Wayne. Then all I heard was "Wayne Bowser ... yes ... yes ... yes ... Is that Costcutter or personal? ... Both ... Right." He put the phone down. "I'm instructed by Colin to say that whatever you say, Geoff, he will support you one hundred per cent. The debt is covered."

The next morning they all assembled at Headingley. Robin Smith, taking the lead, went with Geoff into the committee while Wayne Bowser, Colin Graves and Brian Bouttell waited outside. He explained the situation that the overdraft limit was being raised, and in return the bank were insisting on the resignation of the committee. Then he brought in Wayne Bowser, and he confirmed what had been said. In place of the committee there would be a four-man board made up of Robin Smith, Brian Bouttell, Colin Graves and Geoff Cope – or, as Geoff likes to put it, "a solicitor, an accountant, one with brass and one without." If the committee refused to resign, the club would be put into administration and the same four men would be the administrators.

> There was a lot of shock. One or two members asked, "Is my house at risk?" It didn't dawn on me till then that we were in that position, but there was a lot of nervousness, a lot of anxiety. It was not pleasant. Robin brought in Colin and Brian and introduced them.
>
> Keith said, "I've got to go then." And he went out.
>
> That was the breaking up of the committee.

It was a fundamental change to the traditional democratic structure of the club, with an extraordinary general meeting in late August approving the new

The four-man board: Brian Bouttell, Robin Smith, Geoff Cope, Colin Graves

order. "I'm clearly a scapegoat," Keith Moss told the press. "I feel I have been badly let down, especially by the marketing side which has failed abysmally."

> Keith had come onto the committee at a difficult time. He'd given eleven years of service, four as Chairman, and he'd thrown everything into it. He'd led the ground development project but, even with his business expertise, he couldn't control the runaway costs.

Things moved fast from this point. The overdraft limit was raised from five to ten million pounds. The appointment of Alex Keay as Chief Executive was cancelled, and Colin Graves stood in on a part-time basis. Robin Smith and Brian Bouttell spent long weeks in the old pavilion, wading through the paperwork of invoices, paid and unpaid. It was fire-fighting, they were constantly on the edge of further crises, but eventually they got on top of things.

For a brief period Geoff was the club's Chairman. Then he took on the role of Director of Cricket, travelling with the team to games.

His first task was to replace Wayne Clark, the coach, who was only prepared to come over to England for the six months of summer. It was not what Yorkshire needed, and Geoff's first thought was to go back to Martyn Moxon.

I spoke to Martyn three or four times. He said, "I left Yorkshire at a time when I was building, and the building was looking good and I wasn't able to fulfil. Now I'm exactly at the stage at Durham that I was with Yorkshire. I don't want to walk away a second time. I want to see it through. But Yorkshire cricket is Yorkshire cricket."

I could see that it was a difficult decision for him. His love of Yorkshire was without doubt. So I said, "I'm going to do something, Martyn, that might help you. I'm going to say it because I think I understand. But if I'm wrong, tell me. I'm going to withdraw the offer."

He said, "Thank you."

There was relief in his face, but there was also sadness.

I admire Martyn. I've always admired him.

In 2004 David Byas returned as Director of Cricket, and Geoff became Director of Operations. It was not an easy time for him. His eyesight was getting worse, and his approachability was not always an advantage when members were looking for a grumble.

I used to get all sorts. "Why have we only got Izal toilet paper when there's Andrex in the pavilion?" The paper towels were always running out. People were coming out with great wads of them in their pockets.

The big decision, to purchase the ground, was made. Most of the negotiations with the owner, Paul Caddick of Leeds Rugby, were conducted by Colin Graves, but it was Geoff and Brian Bouttell who were there on the final day, 31 December 2005, when Caddick sprang a last-minute surprise.

We'd signed the majority of the deal on the 30th, and we'd got to lunchtime the next day to tell Lord's we'd bought the ground.

Colin was in the West Indies, Robin was in South Africa, so Brian and I went to Caddick's solicitors on the morning of the 31st. Our solicitors were with us. We walked in, and Caddick said, "Oh, there's one last thing. We need a catering agreement, otherwise the whole thing's off."

We were absolutely stitched, but what could we do about it? Failure to comply would have cost us our agreement with the ECB for staging international cricket.

We had to sign a 15-year deal on the catering. The barrellage at Headingley is second to the university in Leeds. It's a huge amount of liquid that goes through rugby, cricket and hospitality. On top of that there is food.

Yorkshire get paid a fixed sum: about £110,000. When the deal comes to an end in 2018, that £110,000 will become over £1m to us.

There were also deals done with the ECB for the advertising hoardings. To help our cash flow, they gave us a lump sum at the beginning, and in return we gave them the power to do the selling. That deal ends soon as well. Then we'll get the power to sell. That will be another income stream.

It has been a long, hard journey, and it is far from being over. Yet Geoff is optimistic. When the rugby stand is redeveloped, there will be another 4,000 seats, generating extra income at the big matches. With the money from the catering and the advertising boards, he thinks the club will finally make the annual profits that will not only service the interest on the debt but in time pay it off.

We came in at rock bottom. Things had to be totally reorganised with the budget. Gradually we got to the point where we were making a bit of money, but the interest on what we'd borrowed took everything away. The plan was right. You can't look at the interest until you've got things running properly. It's taken a long time to get the ship steady, but we're getting to that point now.

For four years, till Stewart Regan was appointed Chief Executive, the four-man board took the reins. In 2007 Geoff stood down as Director of Operations but, ten years on, he is still there on every match day – in a role for which he is ideally suited: looking after the guests in the Hawke Suite. Whoever they are, cricketers of yesteryear or leading politicians, he livens their day with his stories and his banter.

No moment has been more poignant than Michael Holding calling in to say goodbye to Brian Close when the old man was nearing the end – and no guest gets a warmer welcome from Geoff than Doctor Ingrid Roscoe, the Lord Lieutenant of West Yorkshire.

She's not a big cricket fan, but she's a special lady. She did an interview when she said how much she looks forward to the Test match: "to my bacon sandwich on arrival, to meet Geoff Cope, with his dog, and Dickie. I just love the atmosphere and the place."

In 2014 and 2015, with a largely home-grown side, there was the joy of winning the championship. The second of these titles, by the most emphatic margin since 1979, was achieved in a summer in which the Ashes were won and the county gave six players to England.

For many, many years a strong Yorkshire was a strong England. History demanded that we produced players, and now we're getting back up there. Yorkshire are at the top, and so are England.

18

There's plenty you want doing, isn't there?

Improvements at Headingley and Scarborough

As late as 1996 Yorkshire were spreading their programme around six grounds: Leeds, Scarborough, Bradford, Sheffield, Middlesbrough and Harrogate. Yet the championship had shrunk to 17 four-day matches, meaning that there were only eight or nine home fixtures to share around the six grounds. As a consequence, in 1995, when they did not host a Test match, Headingley staged only two championship fixtures.

> I loved going to the outgrounds: Harrogate, where you got some good cricket, the pitch turning square on the last day, the marquees above the terracing; Bradford was a good cricket pitch. But you were moving on. Bradford had a dressing room where the masseur used the big table in the middle. At Harrogate the umpires had to use the players' showers, and the floors had splinters. The TCCB were saying the physio must have a room on his own, treatment must be done under Health and Safety, a clean environment; umpires should have their own room.
>
> At most of the grounds those facilities would have had to be put in, and the improvements were the responsibility of the clubs. But if you've got 120 grand to give to six grounds, that's 20,000 each, and you're hardly touching the surface of what has to be done. So it was far more sensible to put all the money into Headingley.

Unfortunately there were great problems at Headingley as well.

> The ground was tired. I was a great lover of Headingley, but it wasn't fit for Test match cricket. We were very concerned about the facilities, the overall look, and the pitches themselves had not been good. We'd had a couple of years when we'd been reported as below average for the wicket for Tests.

Geoff had long been fascinated by pitches, and by this time he thought he had a good understanding of them. But does anybody ever understand pitches fully? In his role as a trustee of the Professional Cricketers' Association's Benevolent Fund, Geoff had once been to the house of Tommy Mitchell, the coalminer who bowled leg-spin for Derbyshire and England in the 1930s. Among his many victims were the Australian captain Bill Woodfull, twice in the Fourth Test of the Bodyline series, and Jack Hobbs, twice in a county match at the Oval.

He asked Geoff, "How do you know it's going to turn?", and Geoff launched into an explanation of what he knew: about the solidity of the surface, the amount of grass, the moisture, the length of the match.

> Tommy looked at me and he said, "You're all wrong. You just go out, lick your thumb and if there's a bit of dust on it, it will turn."
>
> I started to say I didn't think it was as simple as that, and he went across to this sideboard where he had three cricket balls on display. He took the first one, and he said, "Groundsman said it wouldn't turn, I said it would. And I did Jack twice in day."

The Headingley groundsman was Andy Fogarty, brought across from Old Trafford by Chris Hassell in 1996, and his first five years were hard ones. Yorkshire's average pitch score across those summers, in both the four-day and the one-day tables the ECB issued, was the worst of all the 18 counties.

Despite this, the England team liked playing at Headingley:

> The players always said that Headingley was their only home game; the support was magnificent. But equally they said that, if somebody takes us for 100 and he's played well, the Yorkie crowd will give him his due desert for his innings. They understand cricket. I used to stick my chest out and think, "That's my county, that's my club." But it was at a critical stage. Something had to be done.

Matters came to a head when the 2000 match against West Indies ended in two days, the first time since 1921 that a Test in England had not reached a third day – and in 1921 they were three-day, not five-day matches. Inevitably the ECB wanted an inquest on the pitch, and it fell to Geoff, as a member of the Cricket Committee, to deal with the matter.

> I said to Fog, "We've got to go down to Lord's."
>
> "Oh, I can't do that. I can't talk."
>
> "Well, will you feed me?"
>
> I sat down with him and went into it. I rang Paul Hudson the BBC weatherman, and he came back to me with the previous three weeks' water levels, what had dropped at Headingley. There wasn't one day when we didn't have some rain: some a full day, some a couple of hours. I worked out the number of times during the preparation when we could take the covers off. When we did take them off, there was this green mass that seamed and turned. So we went down, just Andy and me, and we explained the hours, the rain, the drying, the rolling. At the end of the day Lord's said, you were unlucky but you've done everything you could have done.

Andy Fogarty

On the way back, we talked about the future. We were starting to get pitches with uneven bounce and cracks; they were becoming dangerous. Andy said, "There's only one way. We've got to dig the square up."

We sat down together, and I learned more about pitches than I've ever learned. I said, "We'll do pitches 1,2,3. Then 4,5,6."

"You can't," he said. "You've got to play." He was brilliant.

Headingley is not a big square: 15 pitches at most. The middle five are TV pitches – for Test matches, quarter- and semi-finals, one-day internationals – and five pitches don't go far for television. Equally you can't play on pitch 6 one match, pitch 7 the next, because you might run across it.

One of the Test pitches had to be done in the first batch. You'd do it in September, leave it proud by an inch through the winter. Next year you'd roll it pre-season but not play on it. The following year you might just play a one-day match in late August. It's the third year before you're thinking of playing a longer game on it, and then you don't play a Test. Before you know it, within three years, you've got six pitches out of commission.

Andy would come to my office, and he'd stand at the door. "Come in, pal." "No, I'm all right here." So I thought I'm going to change this. "Right," I said, "I'll meet you at your place."

"Do you want a brew?" he'd ask. I'd sit down, and I'd be in his environment. He'd talk, and I would listen.

He showed me the hole he'd dug. I've never seen anything so different from what I'd anticipated. It was about two foot down, and all you had was this rainbow of different colours. You looked at the rainbow, and you could name the layers: Humberside Silt, Ongar Loam, Ongar Mix, and so on. All the top dressings over the years were there.

The grass was growing in its first topsoil, then it was hitting the next soil and going sideways. If you cut the grass to prepare the pitch, you were pulling the root out. There was no growth, no nothing. We dug this all out. We laid a bit of stone, a bit of dust. Then we started laying in the soil, using all the same soil to the top. And all of a sudden, when you seeded it, the roots grew deep. You could use a pitch again in three weeks.

For some years Harry Brind, the former Oval groundsman, had been in charge of pitches throughout the country, and everywhere he had advocated the Ongar Loam that had worked so well for him at the Oval. It was not a universally popular prescription, as Geoff discovered when he met up with Steve Rouse, the groundsman at Edgbaston.

Rousy said to me, "Look at this. I've half a square." You could see a line with two shades of green. The top end he'd done what he'd always done, used the local soil. The bottom end was Ongar Loam. It was patchy; he couldn't get growth. "I'll have to dig the lot up."

If you ran a survey of every groundsman, you'd get a different answer every time. But what you would get from them all is, "I know my area, I know what works here." At Headingley we relied on Andy and, from the day those pitches were dug up, we've had good marks.

Such has been the improvement that Yorkshire can now be found at the top of the ECB's Pitch Merit tables, and three times Andy Fogarty has won the Groundsman of the Year award.

The groundsman is the key. There was one game when we got rained off about half past five one day. This cloudburst came. From the rugby end of the Western Terrace, all across to the top end of the East Stand, just missing the square, it was a great pond.

A wag came in at half past ten next morning: "I presume we're starting on time." And we did. Andy had made sure the drains were working, he'd got rid of the water that was there, got the water hog on, and everybody turned up as if it was just another day.

I said to Andy, "What's the situ?" All he said was, "We'll start on time." No "I've done this … I've done that."

"When did you get in?" "I came in about three."

They are a breed. They love their jobs, they love their grounds.

Before Geoff joined the committee, Yorkshire had approved a plan to leave Headingley for a new site near Wakefield, only to find that the terms of their lease at Headingley made this financially prohibitive. So, with most of the outgrounds abandoned, they set about a major redevelopment of their headquarters. A Ground Development Sub-Committee was formed under the chairmanship of Keith Moss, and Geoff became a member of it.

No disrespect to Lancashire, but they'd said 'We need a stand' and they built a stand. Then they said they needed another one, and they built another one. And before you knew it, you had all these stands with different designs.

At Headingley we drew up a horseshoe plan before we started, and we got the whole drawing to form a jigsaw. The Western Terrace – a notorious, noisy, troublesome area – was the first stage. We knocked it down, and we found all sorts there: shale, ashes, it was horrible. We redid that from the bottom end next to the rugby stand, all the way round to where the old scoreboard was.

We then moved to the Cricket School as the second development. We had help from Leeds City Council for that.

The third stage was the East Stand: the Long Room, the indoor school underneath, the terraces and the offices where the museum is now. The hotel was built at the same time.

The indoor school had two classrooms, one with computers. We had a teacher given to us by Education Leeds, and it was partly sponsored by Leeds Rugby. The schools come for a day and split into two groups. Group 1 use the classrooms for the morning; Group 2 use the indoor school and/or the outfield. There's lunch in the East Stand, when somebody pops in, and they reverse for the afternoon.

Then Stage 4: the North-East Enclosure, knocking down the 1960s pavilion, where the new scoreboard is.

Then finally the Carnegie Pavilion. Robin Smith came up with this statement: "It's got to be an iconic building." I'm just glad I sit in it, and I don't have to look at it.

There is major work scheduled for the rugby end of the ground, but already Geoff can see the benefits of the progress.

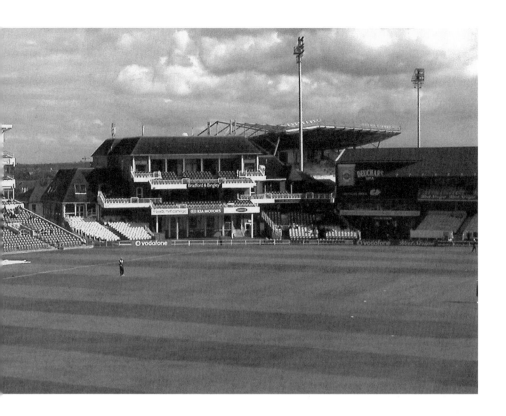

I look back with a lot of pride, a lot of pleasure. There are people now drifting back to Headingley who stopped coming in the '90s when you got your feet soaked in the toilet, mud everywhere on a dry day. It was awful. What they have now is a stadium that everyone can be proud of.

The county club has come a long way in the last few years, both at Headingley and at Scarborough, where Geoff is a trustee.

I'm immensely proud of Scarborough. I get great joy and pride when I walk round and see the people who have made the pilgrimage. The marquee, the flowers laid out, it's a fabulous sight.

I'm proud of the outground, but now I'm equally proud of the headquarters. From the bad pitches, the decaying stands, the talk of a supermarket on the ground, to where we are now, it's been a fabulous journey. And in three years Yorkshire should be in an even stronger position.

You'll never get it right for everybody, but we've given it our all. And if you do get anything wrong, it's Yorkshire. The people will let you know.

I was just one of a team, a small part of it. My greatest contribution was knowing Colin at the time we needed him. If it hadn't been for Colin, I shudder to think what would have happened. It was a situation that needed an answer, and he gave an answer. He's given a lot of years of saying "I will". His marriage to Yorkshire cricket has been strong. He's kept his word, and he's gone beyond it. Whatever Colin gets out of it, he deserves everything because he sat down and did it.

The tribute that Geoff treasures above all others came from the great Australian fast bowler Dennis Lillee, a veteran of the great 1981 Test at Headingley when he famously put ten pounds on England at 500/1 and won his bet.

He stood at the top of the balcony near the Hawke Suite, and he looked out. Then he turned to me and he said, "Copey, it's a bit different, and it's different for the good. But there's still an air in the nostrils that tells me it's Yorkshire. And that's good."

They're lovely words.

The redevelopment of Headingley, begun by Keith Moss's committee and seen through by the board, has been the principal focus of the Yorkshire club for nearly two decades, but there have also been great changes at Scarborough during this time, changes in which Geoff has played a significant part.

As at Headingley there were problems with the pitch. In 2000, when Yorkshire were challenging for the title, their main rivals Surrey, captained by Adam Hollioake, came to Scarborough at the end of August, and Geoff found himself in the thick of an unpleasant sequence of events. It started with a phone call from the Yorkshire batsman Michael Vaughan, who at the time was playing for England at the Oval, and finished with a ruling by the pitch inspector Mike Denness that cost the Yorkshire club £50,000.

We'd been having problems with the Scarborough pitch. It had become slow and low. We'd got to do something. Andy was advising: "If we leave a bit of grass on, we'll get more pace." We tried it in club cricket, and it worked. You have a maximum and a minimum cut you're allowed so we left near the maximum. There was grass on the pitch.

I got a call from Michael Vaughan: "Be careful because Hollioake's on his way up. He'll have a look at the pitch and he'll throw Denness at you."

"Right. We've nothing to fear. We haven't done anything."

"I'm just warning you, Geoff."

I was at Scarborough on the day before the match. It was more than a sea drizzle, it was raining. Hollioake arrived. "I want to look at the pitch. Now." Nothing polite.

"I'm sorry," I said. "You can't. We're not prepared to take the covers off."

"I'm telling you, I want to look."

"I'll tell you what we will do. We'll take the end cover off. You can get underneath and look from there."

"Right, I want to do that."

He came out. "I want every blade of grass on that pitch taken off."

I said, "That is cut within the rules."

"I'm telling you, Denness is on his way, and he'll do you."

On the day of the match we took the covers off, and it was no different from any of the previous years. At the end of the first day Surrey had scored 330 for eight. People were going through the gate saying, "What a great day's cricket."

Denness arrived at half past eleven that morning. He wandered around, spoke to the groundsman. Then suddenly we got this message that there was going to be a meeting after the day's play. We went in the offices near the gate. The two umpires spoke, Denness, the two captains. David Byas said, "What are we doing here? This is a great cricket wicket. The carry to the keeper is up here. It's no different from other years."

At half past eleven at night I took a call from Denness saying, "We're doing you eight points." I said, "I think there'll be trouble."

You could appeal any decision, but you had to lay down a deposit. Several grand. And we couldn't afford it. It cost us second place.

It was the third time that summer that Denness, the fiercest of the pitch inspectors, had docked a county eight points. Some time after the Scarborough match Geoff sat on the appeals panel that removed one of his penalties.

Because of fixtures at Lord's Middlesex had to play two games on the trot at Southgate. During the first match it rained a lot, and they only had enough covers for one pitch. So they used blankets for the second pitch, and it was very damp. I said to the judge chairing the panel, "I've a lot of sympathy." We allowed the appeal to stand, but we issued a directive that, unless there is sufficient covering, outgrounds should not have two games on the trot.

The Scarborough story has a happy outcome, however, and as at Headingley it has been down to the dedication of a skilled groundsman.

Scarborough recruited John Dodds, and he's been superb. He lives for Scarborough cricket, and his wife does the cakes and teas.

He's won the outground award four times in five years. He's got more pace back in it. It's probably the quickest pitch in the country now. The outfield is redone. The drainage. He's done the lot. The lads love going to Scarborough.

John's small and rotund, Andy's taller and thinner, but they've both got red faces. It's this healthy life they live on the land they love.

The ground belongs to the Scarborough club so that Geoff's work there has always been in co-operation with Bill Mustoe, the club chairman. Together, on one occasion, they did a favour for an elderly lady called Mrs Grace, to whom Geoff – being Geoff – always stopped to speak.

She was an invalid. She drove one of those motorised chairs. She was a lovely lady, and she loved her cricket. She never missed a game at Headingley or Scarborough. One day she collared me at Scarborough. "Geoff, do you think it would be possible to have a yellow line drawn next to the railings of the members' enclosure so I could park here as I can't get into the enclosure?"

As you walked in front of Yorkshire's dressing room, there was a ledge with a step up. There was another one further on, then you were on the level. "If I could, I could sit there with the members. I'd love that."

I had a word with Bill, and he got it sorted. The next game I walked down with her. She drove round, and she looked. "Where am I going to park?"

Bill said, "Has that machine got reverse? Back it up, and follow me." He'd had the two ridges turned into a ramp. He got her to drive up the ramp, then he turned right and there was a space that she could park by the brick wall, opposite the walkway where the players came down.

And she sat there with tears streaming down her face.

Such small improvements created good feeling but they did not go far in addressing the shortcomings of the ground. Without question it had seen better times, a point hammered home in a match report by David Hopps that appeared in the *Guardian* in 2009.

This was one of those days when cricket at Scarborough seemed in terminal decline. It was not the size of the crowd, which was healthy enough to provide a slow handclap at a decent volume whenever a sullen, drizzly day forced the players from the field. It is the sheer lack of pride: the rubbish strewn outside the back entrance, the blocked drain that gushed soapy water across the concourse behind the pavilion, the squalor of fag ends and assorted rubbish, the toilets that did not flush last year and predictably did not flush this.

Scarborough has it easy. Everybody rocks up happily, quoting for the umpteenth time JM Kilburn's famous phrase about it being 'county cricket on holiday'. It is a wonderful, natural amphitheatre where the sound of bat on ball competes with the squawk of gulls. But in a year where summer holidays in England are meant to make a comeback, North Marine Road's shortcomings remind us why this might be short-lived.

It hurt at the time, but he wrote it because he cared about Scarborough. And it was an awakening for everyone. We got a NatWest Cricket Force together the next spring. 350 people turned up with paint brushes and goodness knows what. They did a super job in sprucing up the place.

Mike Gatting and Jimmy Anderson at the Cricket Force day

Volunteers came from far and wide: not just the Scarborough club members but some of the greats of English cricket: Jimmy Anderson, Mike Gatting, Matthew Hoggard, David Byas and Dickie Bird.

And, when we finished, we paid tribute to Hoppsy. We put a sign on the press loo door – The Hopps Inn.

"It's an ongoing project," Bill Mustoe told reporters. "A bit like the Forth Bridge, it never ends."

The work of the volunteers gave the ground a fresh look, but the greater structural problems remained – until one day, out of the blue, another source of help appeared.

At the time Tony Gibson, a butcher in Scarborough, was a vice-chairman of the club, and he got this phone call: "I think you and I used to go to the same school. Can I come up and look at the Scarborough ground?"

"Yes, sure."

"Can I meet you at half past eight in the morning?"

I was over at Scarborough, helping Bill, and this guy turned up. He'd come over from Ampleforth. "I've brought some friends," he said, and he had these six henchmen with him. "I'm just wondering if there's anything that needs doing."

Tony said, "Geoff's got quite a list. For instance, the toilet here, the roof needs sorting."

"Make a note of that."

We walked right round the ground, and we pointed out everything. At the finish he said to the people with him, "What have you got for me?" These lads had i-pads, and they made 3-d drawings of what they could do. "There's plenty you want doing, isn't there? Leave it with me."

I said, "What? We haven't said hello."

They left, and we had the impression that they'd pick one from all the items we'd shown them. Then Tony got another phone call: "We'll do the lot. Everything we discussed." It turned out he was from Tesco. They were looking to build a big store in the town, and they made it their number one community project of the year. Two million pounds they spent on the ground. There's a lift in the pavilion, everything.

Then came the revelation that made sense of it all.

His name was Kevin Grace. He was the son of Mrs Grace.

"I just want to say thank you on behalf of my mother," he said. "Your help meant the world to her, and I know that Geoff always speaks to her. All I ask is that at the finish you put up a little plaque with her name on."

Though Mrs Grace has died now, her memory lives on at Scarborough on a plaque on the balcony of the offices, overlooking the ground she loved so much.

Scarborough Cricket Ground after its renewal
A 5,000-strong crowd watch Yorkshire play Somerset in a 50-over match on Wednesday 5 August 2015. Two days later there were 5,300 there for the first day of Yorkshire's match against Durham, the largest crowd to watch a day of championship cricket at any ground in the country in 2015.

19

He's having me on, he says you played for England

Family and friends

Geoff's time as a Yorkshire cricketer came to an end in the autumn of 1980, when his son Andrew was approaching his third birthday, his daughter Nicola her first. For them, growing up in the family home at Guiseley, Geoff was a dad who came home from a day's work in the paper trade and for a few summers in the 1980s, like so many men, went off to play cricket on a Saturday. There was no talk at home about his glory days with Yorkshire and England.

As a young boy Andrew showed no great aptitude for, or interest in, sport. He attended Tranmere Park Junior School, where the deputy head was Ray Beadle, a hard-hitting batsman at the Otley club.

> When Andrew was nine, he came home one night, and he said, "Mr Beadle has been having a go at me. He says he can't wait for me to get a bit bigger and, if you're like your dad with your football and cricket, we'll have a good side next year."
>
> Ray had obviously seen that Andrew hadn't quite got this. So he said, "Your dad used to play football and cricket, you know."
>
> "Did he?"
>
> "He played cricket for England."
>
> He said to me, "He's having me on. He says you played for England."
>
> I said, "Well, come up with me." We went upstairs, and I got out the cap and sweater. I put the sweater on him, down to his knees. The cap went round on his head. "Go look in front of that mirror then."
>
> "Well, they're like what they wear."
>
> He wasn't quite convinced.

Nicola, by contrast, was sporting from the outset. As a teenager she broke her school's records for the 1500 metres and the triple jump, and she was a good cross-country runner, coming second in the Yorkshire Championships.

> When she was doing the long-distance running, I'd be there at the start, then I'd cut across to appropriate places. When it came to the last 400 metres, I'd say the magic words – "Pink Panther" – and off she'd sprint. She was nimble, like June. She would come in first or second; she was always up there.

In his teens Andrew began to follow football.

He became interested through Fantasy Football in the paper. We each had a team, and we followed it every week. It got to the point where he was meeting me at the door, telling me who'd moved from Seria A to Seria B. We played 'Football Manager' together on the computer.

As a boy he never seemed to have much co-ordination with a ball, but he started playing five-a-side football when he was at university. I went and watched him, and he put himself about. He was quite a sound defender. Then he started work and had a family.

Andrew's only two forays onto the cricket field, at the age of 12 or 13, remain part of the family folklore.

Rachel O'Connor, who was Secretary at Yeadon, rang. "We're short with the juniors. Does Andrew want to play?"

I said, "He's never played in his life."

I stayed for a bit. He was down on the third man boundary, one foot in front of the other, arms behind his back. Stood there. So I walked round. "You're supposed to walk in to meet the ball, in case it comes your way."

"What for? It comes quick enough, doesn't it?"

I came back at the end and I said, "How have you done?"

"They think I'm great."

"How do you mean?"

"I got minus 24."

It was that cricket where the team starts with 200, and you lose eight runs each time you're out.

The second time he played, I left him. When I went back he was there in the bar with his Coke. "How have you got on?"

"I'm not sure I can do with this."

"How do you mean?"

"I can't do with all this kissing and hugging."

"What have you been doing?"

"Well, you know that batting. You said I was to have two Vs down the handle and I've to point my elbow. Well, the first three, I never hit it. So I held it like a baseball bat, and I got 20."

"Well done. But what about the kissing?"

"Well, we were fielding, and it got to the last over. The teacher said, 'Somebody hasn't bowled two overs.' So I put my hand up. 'Come on, Andrew, bowl the last over.'"

The opposition were leading by six runs, and the batsman didn't score off the first five balls. Then he missed the last ball, and it bowled him.

"They all ran up to me. Kisses and hugs. What's all that about?"

I said, "You've won the game for them. Because minus six becomes plus two."

"Not sure about that." He'd no concept of it at all.

Andrew and Nicola have worked hard and done well in their careers. Andrew, a Computer Science graduate, is Senior Technology Manager at Morrison Supermarkets. Nicola, a Biomedical Science graduate, is Chief Operating Officer at Berkshire and Surrey Pathology Services. Between them they have seven children, with only Andrew's youngest, the second-born of twins, a boy.

Andrew is a wonderful hands-on father. Ballet, gymnastics, football, swimming, he takes the children everywhere.

Nicola's sporting days ended in her early 20s when, working in the laboratory at Harrogate Hospital, she picked up an 'atypical' bacterial infection, caused by mycoplasma pneumoniae, that attacked her nervous system.

Because she was young, she survived. A month in hospital, then nine months in rehab. She couldn't walk, she was paralysed. She said she'd walk by Christmas. And on Christmas Eve she did this two-minute walk; it took her 25 minutes. She refused help. The sister was in tears. Then she came home, and slowly she got better.

When she delivered her first child she was on a high, but within a few hours she couldn't get out of bed. The only thing was to sleep and rest.

It's only on odd occasions it comes back. She's 95 per cent. I can dance with her perfectly because she's got little feeling in her feet.

She met her husband Russ, a company director who played a leading role in the risk assessment for the London Olympics, when they were both in South Africa watching the England cricket team.

She loves her cricket. In her cottage there's a display cabinet, and in it are my three caps: Yorkshire, England, MCC.

There are no such sporting mementoes on display in Andrew's house. In February 2001 a special dinner was laid on for the 70th birthdays of Fred Trueman and Brian Close, and Geoff had to say a few words. With June not well, he persuaded Andrew to come with him.

I said, "You know Fred Trueman?" "I've heard of him." "And Brian Close?" "No." "Well, if I put it politely, he's probably the hardest man I ever played with."

David Jones, the Chief Executive of Next, was there. He'd rung me up. "What's this about Fred selling his memorabilia? Has he got hard

Andrew and Kathryn on their wedding day
Their children: (top right) Bethany, Millie,
Abigail, Oliver and (middle right) Sophie

Florence,
Nicola,
Russ and
Matilda

times?" But it wasn't that. There'd been three attempts at a robbery at Fred's house, and none of the children wanted it.

"Well, what was his favourite bit?"

"I don't know. When he got his 300 wickets, Yorkshire got him a tea service."

"Right, where is it?"

"Sotheby's."

So he rang Sotheby's, paid over the going rate and presented Fred with this tea service.

Fred said, "I don't think wife will be too pleased about this, David. Duraglit's cost us a fortune, and now you're giving it to me back."

"I'm sorry, Fred, I thought this was appropriate."

"Appropriate? Yorkshire gave me this thing, and they hadn't even done the engraving."

Then I got to speak. I did Frederick Sewards Trueman. Then Brian. I told Arthur Milton's story about his time at Arsenal: how they got him to practise heading the ball down and in the next match he headed the ball so far down it bounced over the top of the goal. Then how he was a legend with Yorkshire. "We used to look at the fixtures, and we'd say, 'Somerset, that's two wins for us.' Then he went down there, and suddenly two wins weren't taken for granted." I went on a bit.

When I sat down, Andrew said to me, "I thought you said he was hard. He's been crying through most of your speech."

Geoff enjoys speaking, and he is good at it. Whether it be the funeral of John Hampshire or the annual Guide Dogs fund-raiser at the Zen Rendezvous Chinese restaurant, he knows the right note to strike and he strikes it with warmth and with humour. His speaking even pops up in a published poem, *Scarborough Cricket Club Players' Dinner 1981*, written by the schoolmaster Bill Foord, who opened the bowling for Yorkshire in the early 1950s.

> *We listened hard to Geoffrey Cope*
> *Expressing well his fervent hope*
> *That out of Yorkshire's cricket weeds*
> *Would flourish strong and healthy seeds*
> *To root and sprout and quickly grow*
> *Into that fine white rose we know!*
>
> *Of course he told a joke or two*
> *To help to get his message through.*
> *Some little anecdote he'd tell*
> *And praised our club for doing well.*

John Helm interviewing Geoff at Harden Cricket Club near Bingley

Family and friends are important to Geoff, and he has no closer friend than John Helm, the young reporter who turned up on his doorstep on that fateful day in 1968 when his bowling action was first called into question. John is a Vice President of Bradford Park Avenue Football Club and, when Geoff was at a low ebb after he lost his job, he arranged for him to do some fund-raising work for the club.

Trips to local football with John became part of Geoff's life each winter, and none proved more significant than the game at Park Avenue on the evening of Monday 24 January 2011. It was a filthy night, Halifax were the visitors, and the two of them arrived later than they intended. Instead of queuing up for their pie and peas before the match, they decided to wait till the interval.

> Five minutes before half time, John said to me, "Let's go and get those pie and peas now." There was already a queue of eight or ten people, with children in it, and all of a sudden these two guys – bouncers that the chairman Blackburn had brought in – walked in and went straight to the front of the queue.

John said, "Excuse me, there's a queue here."

"And who might you be?"

I said, "He's the Vice President of the club."

John was explaining to them that it was a family club and that he'd speak to the Chairman. Then, when we'd got our food, we went to sit at a table. I was holding Kemp in one hand, my pie and peas in the other, and John suddenly had these two guys on each side of him: "Were you talking to us?"

I thought, "There's going to be a problem here."

Then suddenly they said, "Are you with him?"

They knocked John's pie and peas out of his hand onto the floor. Then they got hold of mine and smashed it straight into my face. I was a right mess. John said, "I'm going to Blackburn."

We went in the portakabin with the directors, and in there were David Bosomworth and Bobby Ham from Halifax Town. I knew Bobby well, and he was straight out of his seat: "Have you fallen?" Sharon, the match-day secretary, came out with a cloth and started to clean me up.

I told Bobby what had happened, and he was really upset. He said, "I'm not staying here." We went back to our seats, and Bobby and David disappeared. John said to me, "Do you want to go?" So I said, "Yes, let's go." We went after about 65 minutes. I have a great affection for Park Avenue. But this shook me up.

Blackburn promised the minders would never appear again. Then Bobby rang John. They had a conversation. And Bobby rang me. "Would you like to be the Vice President of Halifax?"

I said, "Well, I haven't any money, Bobby."

"I don't want that. Come when you want to come, and just be yourself."

It was in the programme: 'Vice President: Geoff Cope.' Then a few matches later, someone said, "I see we've got a new Vice President." And, when I looked, it said: 'Vice Presidents: Geoff Cope and Kemp.'

The old Halifax Town club had gone bankrupt in 2008, with debts of two million pounds. The replacement club, FC Halifax Town, was relegated three levels to the Northern Premier League Division One North where, instead of playing Aldershot Town and Exeter City, they were now up against Woodley Sports and Harrogate Railway Athletic.

It was a slow climb back, with the new directors determined to keep a firm control of the finances, but by the night of the Park Avenue game in January 2011 they were heading for a second successive promotion, a promotion that owed much to the goals scored by a lad they had picked up from Stocksbridge Park Steels in Sheffield. He had had his run-ins with the law, and he was persuaded to sign by Bobby Ham's assurance that they would take care of him.

At the end of the season they sold him on to Fleetwood Town, with clauses that would generate further payments for Halifax in the event of high goal-scoring, future transfers and even, improbably, England caps. After one year Fleetwood sold him to Leicester for a million pounds, the first non-league footballer to fetch such a fee, and in time he turned into a household name: Jamie Vardy. Three years later Halifax had a second success, selling another prolific goal-scorer, Lee Gregory, to Millwall.

> Every non-league club hopes to find a good player. It's where the cash flow comes from. And if you do well, as we've done, you start to get a reputation where scouts come regularly.

A third promotion took them up to the National League, the level they were at before bankruptcy, but, still a semi-professional club, they lacked the resources of most of their opponents and, after three seasons, were relegated. In 2016/17, at the first attempt and staying true to their values, they won their way back up. In the play-off final, in front of a crowd of almost 8,000 at their own Shay Stadium, they beat Chorley 2-1 after extra time.

> After the goal in extra time, every minute was like five. Then at the final whistle you looked round, and you saw the relief of the people involved in the club. The joy of the supporters. What's the difference between them and the Arsenal fans at Wembley winning the Cup Final? It's just the same.

It's a long way from the Premier League, and for Geoff the gap is too wide.

> It's one of the sad parts of sport. The Premier League talk monies that are unbelievable. Yet, if some of that money was spread around, clubs like Halifax would be able to do so much more. We could have our own training facilities, go full-time and become more involved with the community: going into schools and running coaching schemes.

For all that, he enjoys it as it is.

> I'm proud to take friends. There's not a club at that level that do it better than Halifax do. They put on a lovely spread prior to the game. The directors sit with the people, as against being in a room on their own. There's a buzz about the place.
>
> I get a lot of pleasure from watching the game and seeing lads who are part-time professionals. Jamie Vardy is the golden story, but there's

also Lee Gregory at Millwall, Marc Roberts at Barnsley, Matty Pearson at Accrington. Lads who have gone on to pro football, you get a lot of satisfaction from that. The general player, the part-timer, comes in, trains twice a week, gives his all on Saturday and on Tuesday night if there is a game. Then crack of dawn next morning he's back at work. He's just enjoying his game.

The directors would love to go back into the Football League, but they'll do it by working the budget right. Their vow when they bought the club was that they would never put it at risk.

Halifax is something for me to look forward to in the winter. It's not Leeds United. We're light years away from being with Liverpool and Manchester United. It's a journey and, if that journey were to go a little further, we'd be delighted.

To me, most of all, it's a family club. It's somewhere I enjoy going.

The programme now reads:

Vice Presidents: Geoff Cope and Lester.
Honorary Vice Presidents: Kemp and Queenie.

Geoff has endured more than his share of adversity, and at times he has been knocked down by the setbacks. But, with the help of family and friends, he has picked himself up 'like a true Yorkshireman', and he has used his infectious humour to spread good cheer and to help others.

His latest evening at the Zen Rendezous restaurant was attended for the first time by Ingrid Roscoe, the Lord Lieutenant of West Yorkshire. He was moved by the letter he received from her afterwards:

It is clear how very much everyone you know admires you, and I am not surprised. You are so friendly and laugh with great ease. Of course we admire the way you have coped with blindness for you are dignified, there is absolutely no self-pity and yours has been a most distinguished career.

£200,000 is an amazing sum to have raised for Guide Dogs. How much help that will have given to a number of people. You are a star.

According to his Yorkshire team-mate John Hampshire, there was 'probably never a more genial or better-liked player ever to come into the dressing room than Geoff Cope', and to this day Geoff relishes the company of cricketers, whether they be the opponents of yesteryear that he entertains in the Hawke Suite or the team-mates he meets at the reunions of the Yorkshire Players' Association, an organisation that he was a key figure in setting up in 2005.

From a very young age sport was so important in my life. The initial eyesight problem made me focus on one sport. But that sport, cricket, has given me over the period of time a lifetime experience that I wouldn't change for anything. I've travelled the world because of the game of cricket. Financially I'd never have been able to do that.

Cricket has given me some wonderful memories. They say memories don't pay the butcher's bill. But that doesn't matter. Because I'd do it all over again in the same circumstances. I've had a tremendous life.

Geoff is not one who decries the modern game.

It's a different game today, but it's not. It's still a battle between bat and ball. As time goes on, as technology develops, things change, and invariably they change for the better. If I'd have bowled at the time I did bowl, and I'd have had the lads who are fielding today, I might have gone for a lot less runs in my career. The fielding is so different today from yesteryear. I wouldn't be considered today.

The game has continued to improve, but possibly some of the memories today's players will have will be different types of memories from mine. They will be based more on what they did as a team, collectively and individually. They'll talk about the friendships with the lads they played with – but how many will talk about those they played against?

That end of the day, when we chatted in the bar with the other team and with the members, that's gone. Now the ground's empty in five minutes, and the players go their own way.

Above everything, sport is about friendship. It's about the people who play and the people who support. I've been blessed because I've made friends among both groups. And when you put the two together, the players and the supporters, all it boils down to is that we're just ordinary people – and as ordinary people we can share with each other the pleasures we have. If I've been able to play a small part for somebody not as fortunate as me, then I'm grateful that that person has got that little bit of pleasure.

I sit here now at 70 years of age, and I think, "Was there a better way to have a living?"

A BRIEF STATISTICAL DIGEST

BOWLING IN FIRST-CLASS CRICKET

HOME

Year	Overs	M	Runs	Wkts	Best	Ave	5wi	10wm
1966	36	16	98	-				
1967	277.4	129	553	40	5-23	13.82	2	
1968	114.3	36	284	20	7-42	14.20	2	1
1969	484.3	174	1171	43	5-49	27.23	1	
1970	880.5	284	2111	83	7-36	25.43	4	1
1971	477.3	158	1147	38	5-95	30.18	1	
1972	221.5	97	407	23	6-40	17.69	1	
1973	110.1	19	338	7	3-92	48.28		
1974	743.5	260	1681	77	7-101	21.83	5	1
1975	624.3	201	1509	69	8-73	21.86	6	1
1976	916.4	288	2245	93	6-37	24.13	7	1
1977	653.1	224	1357	56	6-29	24.23	4	1
1978	342.3	114	784	32	4-34	24.50		
1979	191.3	58	490	13	6-37	37.69	1	
1980	584.3	175	1558	42	4-69	37.09		
Total	**6659.4**	**2233**	**15733**	**636**	**8-73**	**24.73**	**34**	**6**

OVERSEAS

8-ball overs in India, Sri Lanka, Pakistan and New Zealand, 6-ball in South Africa

1975/6 (SA)	104	27	254	10	4-61	25.40		
1976/7 (I/SL)	203.2	96	506	26	6-41	19.46	1	
1977/8 (P/NZ)	161	40	455	14	3-102	32.50		
Total	**468.2**	**163**	**1215**	**50**	**6-41**	**24.30**	**1**	
Total	**7128**	**2396**	**16948**	**686**	**8-73**	**24.70**	**35**	**6**

BOWLING IN TEST CRICKET

8-ball overs

1977/78 (P)	108	29	278	8	3-102	34.62
Total	**108**	**29**	**278**	**8**	**3-102**	**34.62**

SEVEN OR MORE WICKETS IN AN INNINGS

42.2 - 18 - 73 - 8	Yorkshire v Gloucestershire	Bristol	1975
18.1 - 8 - 36 - 7 *(including hat-trick)*	Yorkshire v Essex	Colchester	1970
19 - 4 - 42 - 7	Yorkshire v Glamorgan	Cardiff	1968
33 - 9 - 101 - 7	Yorkshire v Middlesex	Middlesbrough	1974

TWELVE OR MORE WICKETS IN A MATCH

53 - 16 - 116 - 12	Yorkshire v Glamorgan	Cardiff	1968

FIRST-CLASS BOWLING RECORD ON YORKSHIRE GROUNDS

	M	Wkts	Ave
Park Avenue, Bradford	25	73	23.09
North Marine Road, Scarborough	25	55	30.87
Headingley, Leeds	25	35	31.97
Bramall Lane, Sheffield	16	39	25.12
Abbeydale Park, Sheffield	16	41	17.65
Acklam Park, Middlesbrough	9	29	21.27
St George's Road, Harrogate	9	48	14.06
The Circle, Hull	3	5	29.80

BATTING AND FIELDING IN FIRST-CLASS CRICKET

	M	I	NO	Runs	HS	Ave	100	50	Ct
Home	231	250	89	2264	78	14.06	-	5	67
Overseas	15	11	4	119	27*	17.00	-	-	4
Total	**246**	**261**	**93**	**2383**	**78**	**14.18**	**-**	**5**	**71**

BATTING AND FIELDING IN TEST CRICKET

	M	I	NO	Runs	HS	Ave	100	50	Ct
1977/8 *(P)*	3	3	-	40	22	13.33	-	-	1
Total	**3**	**3**	**-**	**40**	**22**	**13.33**	**-**	**-**	**1**

GUIDE DOGS FOR THE BLIND ASSOCIATION

£5 supports a working guide dog for a day
£20 pays for one hour's training of a dog
£25 buys a guide dog harness
£95 buys a Training School Kit for a trainer
£140 buys a Starter Kit for a new dog owner

If you would like to make a donation, please send a cheque to:
Guide Dogs for the Blind Association, Shire View, 72 Headingley Lane,
Leeds LS6 2DJ, and mark it for the attention of Alison Parker
or pay direct into the Guide Dogs for the Blind Association's account:
Sort Code: 40-47-02   Account No: 11087231
and mark it with the reference: 4577194 (G. Cope)

Acknowledgements

Most of the photographs in this book are from Geoff Cope's personal collection, but some appear by kind permission as follows:

Getty Images for those on pages 137, 164, 215, 217 and 237; PA Photos, page 153; Simon Wilkinson, page 229; the Bradford Telegraph and Argus, page 188; Mick Pope, pages 62 and 109; Ron Deaton, pages 68 and 84; Gareth J. Dykes, page 232; Ruby Pothecary Photography, page 243 (bottom); Missy Moo Photography, page 245 and the modern pictures of Geoff on the front and back cover.

Much of this book is shaped by Geoff Cope's own testimony but, in researching and writing it, use has been made of the following books:

Bill Foord: *Cricket Rhymeniscing* (Farthings Publishing, 2010)
John Hampshire: *Family Argument* (George Allen & Unwin, 1983)
Alan Hill: *Johnny Wardle – Cricket Conjuror* (David & Charles, 1988)
Ray Illingworth: *The Tempestuous Years* (Sidgwick & Jackson, 1987)
Ray Illingworth: *Yorkshire And Back* (Queen Anne Press, 1980)
Pat Pocock: *Percy* (Clifford Frost Publications, 1987)
David Warner: *The Sweetest Rose* (Great Northern Books, 2012)
Wisden Cricketers' Almanack
Yorkshire County Cricket Club Yearbooks

A number of newspapers have been quoted:
The Times, Guardian, Yorkshire Post, Bradford Telegraph and Argus and various others, local and national, that appear in Geoff Cope's scrapbooks.

Statistics have been taken from the CricketArchive website.

INDEX